John Russell Brown

Theatre Language

A STUDY OF ARDEN,
OSBORNE, PINTER AND
WESKER

TAPLINGER PUBLISHING COMPANY
NEW YORK

First published in the United States in 1972 by
TAPLINGER PUBLISHING CO., INC.
New York, New York

Library of Congress Catalog Card Number: 72–442
ISBN 0–8008–7629–6

TO REG FOAKES AND
ERNST HONIGMANN
1951–72

Contents

Acknowledgements

The publishers wish to express their grateful thanks to the following for permission to reprint material: Jonathan Cape Ltd for extracts from *The Kitchen, Chips with Everything, Chicken Soup with Barley, Roots* and *The Friends* by Arnold Wesker; Faber & Faber Ltd for extracts from *Waiting for Godot* by Samuel Beckett, *Burnt Norton* and *East Coker* by T. S. Eliot and *Look Back in Anger* by John Osborne; David Higham Associates Ltd for extracts from *The Entertainer, Luther, Time Present, Tom Jones* and *Inadmissible Evidence* by John Osborne, published by Faber & Faber Ltd; Macdonald & Evans Ltd for extracts from *The Mastery of Movement* by Rudolf Laban; Methuen & Co. Ltd for extracts from *Serjeant Musgrave's Dance, The Workhouse Donkey* and *The Hero Rises Up* by John Arden and from *The Birthday Party, The Collection, The Caretaker, The Lover, Night, A Night Out, The Tea Party, The Homecoming, The Dwarfs, The Examination* and *Landscape* by Harold Pinter; the *Observer* for extracts from 'Taking Pains with Pinter' by John Gale, 20 June 1962; Penguin Books Ltd for extracts from *Live Like Pigs* by John Arden, published in *New English Dramatists 3*, ed. Tom Maschler; Mr Harold Pinter for extracts from 'Between the Lines', *Sunday Times*, 4 March 1962; *Sight and Sound*, XXXV, 1966, British Film Institute, for extracts from an interview with John Russell Taylor.

Introduction

If I were given a million pounds to invest in the Arts, to encourage creativity and provide entertainment for the public, the most difficult and dangerous decision would be to try to spend it on the theatre. Here is no certain return for money. New theatres work when they are founded on established procedures and established reputations, as at Minnesota, or Chichester and the National Theatre. Yet traditional ways of setting plays are cumbersome and increasingly expensive, as every individually styled and manufactured article must be. Besides, there is little professional agreement about what kind of theatre to build, what shape, size or location. The St Lawrence Centre, Toronto, and Lincoln Center, New York, had splendid hopes but opened with inadequate productions, and are left with buildings that please very few of the artists likely to work there. Actor-training is frankly experimental. Advertisement, as it becomes more and more the prerogative of television, is prohibitively expensive for a commodity that at best can satisfy only a few thousand persons a week, most of whom will have booked weeks or months in advance of the time of consumption. Not the least of the problems is the loss of a theatre-going habit for more than a very small section of the public: how can a fixed time and place for performance be chosen to satisfy the routines of a young family living miles away and provided nightly with home-entertainment, and home-activity? (The advent of cassette television with choice of programme, time and level of involvement, will still further accentuate the independence of the home-unit.) The handling of an audience when it has

9

arrived presents still further problems, for front-of-house staff is numerous and fully employed for only a few scattered hours of a day. The provision of car parks and eating places make large demands on environmental facilities that do not often suit location, staffing or timing.

Nowhere are the difficulties of theatre as a contemporary art more apparent than in the choice of play for performance. The most assured formula is to find a vehicle for an established star-performer, or a number of television favourites. But crashes are at least as frequent as triumphs in following this policy, and it is no radical solution to choose a play because of its ability to satisfy a limited acting talent. Another solution is to use a dramatic or other text as a starting-point, and to develop with a group of actors working under a director some unique entertainment as much suited to the accidental talents of the actors as to their environment and habits of work. The result will often be exciting, as any practised and whole-hearted group response might be, and also exotic, tied to local enthusiasms and defiantly self-concerned. The third recipe is to revive the classics, and to try to extend the range of acceptable playwrights from the past in order to be able to offer something new.

There are strong arguments for pronouncing the theatre a dead or dying art, and to cut back on all new investment. But this ignores the hardy dinosaurs: the long-running successes and the actors who have 'house full' notices wherever they perform; and Shakespeare who is still an international success and to whom the imaginations of readers and audiences still respond with ever-new, 'contemporary' liveliness. More significantly, it ignores the interest in theatre among young people that seems to grow stronger as commercial and subsidized theatres become increasingly debilitated. Drama as an educational means and

stimulus – and even as an end in itself – is found everywhere
in schools, colleges and universities. At one university a
thousand applicants jostle for twenty-five places each academic year. Teachers put themselves to school in elementary
movement classes so that they may follow their students'
discoveries in physical expressiveness. If drama is not
accepted within the curriculum, it establishes itself in after-
hours and vacations. Among young people the problem is
containment, not resuscitation or injection of new blood.

Theatre is indeed a perennial art, and no one working in
it can doubt this. However depressed about employment
conditions or lack of investment an actor, director, designer,
manager or dramatist may be, when he is engaged on
a production all doubts vanish and he counts himself the
luckiest of people. Between the devoted practitioners, the
eager young audiences and the experimenters, the theatre
has eloquent defenders. Moral and imaginative support is
not lacking: the need is for a careful reassessment of how
best the theatre can function in what is virtually a new
situation.

As a complex organization, theatre is resistant to change.
By nature it is conservative because it inherits old buildings,
old texts and old habits of work. Every element must be
viewed afresh and with careful detail, so that change may
come and theatre re-establish itself at the centre of cultural
life.

*

This general predicament of the theatre provides one of my
twin reasons for writing *Theatre Language*. The other is to
extend appreciation for some remarkable dramatists whose
work has reflected and illuminated life as I recognize it
within and without myself.

I have chosen to study four English dramatists who,
since the Second World War, have written plays that have

attracted the widest attention: Harold Pinter, John Osborne, Arnold Wesker and John Arden. All except Arden have enjoyed West End and Broadway success and, more importantly, all have written a series of plays over at least ten years, in which they have developed individual styles and persisted in experimentation. All were born around the year 1930,* and all have worked primarily in England and so have responded to one particular social, political and historical context.

My task has not been to describe their individual careers or the contents of all their plays. I have tried, rather, to examine how they have made the theatre speak. I have asked: 'How does the theatre work for them, how have they controlled theatrical reality in words, actions and time, so that the plays say what the authors want to say now, to present audiences and in present theatrical conditions?' For each dramatist I have concentrated attention on a few plays, those I consider their most lasting and revealing achievements.

Theatre Language is therefore no 'Guide' or 'Survey' to new English theatre. It looks closely, and as carefully as I am able, at important contemporary plays by authors who have sustained a writing career for more than ten years in a changing world.

Much that is new in the theatre will escape my attention. There are playwrights – like Ann Jellicoe, Edward Bond, Henry Livings, Charles Wood and others – whose promise and achievements are considerable, but who lack either the sustained involvement in their art or the popularly acknowledged theatrical success which would make them suitable for my purposes.

I have also omitted a direct study of the plays of Samuel Beckett, although he is his own translator from the original

* Osborne, 1929; Arden and Pinter, 1930; and Wesker, 1932.

French and some plays were written first in English. My
plan to compare dramatists who have responded to the same
theatrical possibilities is my chief reason for this omission.
Beckett is over twenty years older than any of the four I have
considered, and he was brought up in Ireland and has
worked almost wholly in France. Moreover, his plays are
only a part of his writing and any study of them should also
consider his novels, verse and criticism as well. I have
limited myself to some account of his influence, chiefly in the
concluding chapter.

I do not study any artists other than dramatists, although
I recognize that the theatre must rely for adaptation to new
conditions as much on its managers, actors, designers and
directors as on its writers. Indeed, the role of the writer may
be due for a large shift of emphasis, if the theatre has to
become smaller, more topical and more local in order to
survive. But however that may be – and I think that the
opposite notion, that theatre must become larger, more
expensive, more broadly based, ceremonial and celebratory,
has at least equal weight of argument on its side – whatever
the future of theatre, it will have to use words and actions,
sounds, gestures, patterns, movements, time, space and
performance, and all these elements have been controlled to
good purpose by the dramatists we shall be considering.

Perhaps a production by Peter Brook or a performance
by Paul Scofield holds as much hope for the future of
theatre as any play newly written for our stage; but the production and the performance changed each night, and in no
form do they remain for our examination. By studying the
play-texts of four dramatists we shall be looking at precise
evidence that can be related to as full a theatrical experience
as we are capable of holding in our mind's eye and other
senses.

While basing this whole book on the writing of dramatists,

I have tried to imagine the plays as in performance and to consider wherever necessary the complex problems of staging. In the same way, I do not wish my title, *Theatre Language*, to imply an interest in words alone, but to claim for my subject every means of expression that the theatre possesses and that can be controlled. An alternative title might be 'The Use of Theatre'. Or to rephrase this as a double question, I would ask: 'What can the theatre do now, what has it done already?'

*

An obvious disproportion will be found in my consideration of the individual dramatists: three chapters for Pinter, and one for each of the others. About this I make no apology, although it was by no means a part of my original plan. I found as I proceeded that an interest in what is radical in theatre practice was fed more by Pinter than by any of his fellows. His work encourages the closest attention and therefore he stands first in the volume and has the largest share. His relative importance is another question, and one that should become clearer during the course of my book. Because this is not an inclusive guide or a search for the very latest experiments, I have been able to consider authors and plays for their own sakes, to use the manner that seems most suitable for each individual achievement, whether that is apparent in single plays or throughout careers.

New writers provide images for what their contemporaries, like themselves, are only beginning to recognize and understand. I hope that something of the adventure of trying to respond to these images will be found in my book, and also of my growing conviction that these men had to write for the theatre, that only its complex functioning and its for ever changing illusion of reality could mirror both what they have experienced and what they hope for.

I

HAROLD PINTER

Words and Silence

The Birthday Party and Other Plays

At the centre of Pinter's plays is a scepticism about language of unusual tenacity. Can anything ever be stated correctly in words? Can anything ever be said to be 'stated'? We play with words, and words play with us. We can neither say what we know, nor know what we say. When we stop to think, we do not trust words.

Philosophers have often warned us. In *Adventures in Ideas* (1933), Alfred North Whitehead insisted on the daring delicacy of his task:

In the study of ideas it is necessary to remember that insistence on hard-headed clarity issues from sentimental feeling, as it were a mist, cloaking the perplexities of fact. Insistence on clarity at all costs is based on sheer superstition as to the mode in which human intelligence functions. Our reasonings grasp at straws for premises and float on gossamers for deductions.

This is very like the stance that Pinter took, when, early in his career, he was persuaded to talk for an hour about his work. He spoke with precise and well-timed emphasis, aware that his audience sought to pin him down:

I'm not a theorist. I'm not an authoritative or reliable commentator on the dramatic scene, the social scene, any scene. I write plays, when I can manage it, and that's all. That's the sum of it. So I'm speaking with some reluctance, knowing that there are at least twenty-four possible aspects of any single statement, depending on where you're standing at the time or on what the weather's like. A categorical statement, I find, will never stay where it is and be finite. It will immediately be subject to modification by the other twenty-three possibilities of it. No statement I make, therefore, should be interpreted as final and definitive. One or two of them may sound final and definitive; they may even be *almost* final and definitive; but I won't regard them as such tomorrow and I wouldn't like you to do so today.*

Awareness of the inadequacy of language can infect all social consciousness. In a book recording his conversations, the philosopher Whitehead is shown to be soberly aware of the inadequacy and comedy of talk:

The notion that thought can be perfectly or even adequately expressed in verbal symbols is idiotic. . . . Take the simplest statement of a fact: that we three are sitting in this room. Nearly everything of importance is left out. 'This room' presupposes a building, Cambridge, the university, the world around us of which we are a part, stellar systems of which our world is a part, the infinite past from which we have come, and the endless future which is streaming through us and out ahead of us. It presupposes our separate individualities, each quite different, and all that we know, we are, or have ever done. That verbalization of our sitting here means next to nothing; yet, in much more serious subjects and on a far more ambitious scale, we are constantly accepting statements of historic fact, and philosophical speculations which are much more lacking in accuracy or in any relationship with exact truth. When such over-simplified ideas are addressed to persons who cannot supply the omitted presuppositions, they mean nothing, are not comprehended, are not even taken in. . . .†

* 'Between the Lines', an account of a speech to the Seventh National Student Drama Festival in Bristol, published in the *Sunday Times*, 4 March 1962.

† *Dialogues of Alfred North Whitehead*, recorded by Lucien Price (Little, Brown & Co., 1954; 1956 edn), pp. 264–5.

As a dramatist Pinter explores such inadequacies of words, the presuppositions of speech and the barriers to comprehension. But he is not a destructive investigator; he also delights in words, teases them, appears to wait for them, and purposely avoids them. Interplay between confidence in words and fear of them, and between what is meant and what is betrayed, is a constant source of excitement in Pinter's stage dialogue, as if it were the life-blood and the nerves of all his writing. His audiences are invited to listen with precise attention and to recognize in the words – and all 'around' them – a reflection of their own attempts to make statements and communicate.

Pinter had the wit to see that difficulties in the use of words are potential dramatic capital. He has so constantly exploited what words do *not* clearly define, that he seems to have set out consciously to use the very imprecision of speech in an art that was, traditionally, all precision, composed of speeches each as fine and directly meaningful as could be. Pinter had written unpublished novels, stories and poems before turning to drama, but he found, one day, that drama was the form in which he could explore, control and share what he already had begun to sense happening within himself, and in the world which he inhabited.

His perception of the varying effectiveness of words is particularly dramatic. He is interested in speech as barriers and as bridges between people, as elements in a social combat. In the lecture already quoted, Pinter chose several metaphors from warfare – confront, hilt, overcome, smokescreen, stratagem, rearguard; others are from sickness, physical pressure, commerce, nakedness:

I have mixed feelings about words myself. Moving among them, sorting them out, watching them appear on the page, from this I derive a considerable pleasure. But at the same time I have another strong feeling about words which amounts to nothing less than nausea. Such a weight of words confronts us, day in day out, words spoken in a context such as this, words written by me and by others, the bulk of it a stale dead terminology; ideas endlessly repeated and permutated, become platitudinous, trite, meaningless. Given this nausea, it's very easy to be overcome by it and step back into paralysis. I imagine most writers know something of this kind of paralysis. But *if it is possible to confront this nausea, to follow it to its hilt and move through it, then it is possible to say that something has occurred, that something has even been achieved.*

Language, under these conditions, is a highly ambiguous commerce. So often, below the words spoken, is the thing known and unspoken. . . . You and I, the characters which grow on a page, most of the time we're inexpressive, giving little away, unreliable, elusive, evasive, obstructive, unwilling. But it's out of these attributes that a language arises. *A language, I repeat, where, under what is said, another thing is being said.* . . .

The italicized passages display the essentially dramatic qualities in Pinter's use of language: expectation of achievement, search, surprise, developing understanding. Language is a weapon that is used for exciting tactics in a series of human encounters. Speech is warfare, fought on behalf of thoughts, feelings and instincts. Speech infects and therefore informs silence, too:

There are two silences. One when no word is spoken. The other when perhaps a torrent of language is being employed. This speech is speaking of a language locked beneath it. That is its continual reference. *The speech we hear is an indication of that we don't hear. It is a necessary avoidance, a violent, sly, anguished or mocking smokescreen which keeps the other in its place.* When true silence falls we are still left with echo but are nearer nakedness.

One way of looking at speech is to say it is a constant stratagem to cover nakedness. . . .

I think that we communicate only too well, in our silence, in what is unsaid, and that what takes place is continual evasion, desperate rearguard attempts to keep ourselves to ourselves. Communication is too alarming. To enter into someone else's life is too frightening. To disclose to others the poverty within us is too fearsome a possibility.*

Four years later, when an interviewer for *Paris Review* asked Pinter the bland question

Why do you think the conversations in your plays are so effective?

he replied briefly, and warily, but in much the same terms as he had used in this early lecture:

I don't know, I think possibly it's because people fall back on anything they can lay their hands on verbally to keep away from the danger of knowing, and of being known.†

Given that the dramatist is concerned with eventual disclosure, here, in describing his character's 'conversations', Pinter touches upon the dangerous, or precarious, nature of his plays and their stunning, appalled and held (or arrested) climaxes. From the first word spoken on stage, the hunt is on. In his lecture, he continued to explain:

I'm not suggesting that no character in a play can ever say what he in fact means. Not at all. I have found that there invariably does come a moment when this happens, where he says something, perhaps, which he has never said before. And where this happens, what he says is irrevocable, and can never be taken back.‡

There are obvious dangers in this approach to play-writing. How can the audience be persuaded to attend closely enough, and to wait for clarification? When can the

* 'Between the Lines', op. cit.; my italics.
† 'Harold Pinter: an interview', *Paris Review*, Vol. 39 (1966), p. 27.
‡ 'Between the Lines', op. cit.

smokescreen be permitted to cover the battle totally, how soon, and for how long? When is the time for revelation? Should it come in silence or in words? Pinter's solutions are very varied and meticulous, and reflect a penetrating understanding of how we live.

*

The opening of his first full-length play, *The Birthday Party* (1958), illustrates some of his simpler strategies:

ACT ONE

The living-room of a house in a seaside town. A door leading to the hall down left. Back door and small window up left. Kitchen hatch, centre back. Kitchen door, up right. Table and chairs, centre.

PETEY enters from the door on the left with a paper and sits at the table. He begins to read. MEG's voice comes through the kitchen hatch.

MEG: Is that you, Petey?

[*Pause.*]

Petey, is that you?

[*Pause.*]

Petey?

PETEY: What?

MEG: Is that you?

PETEY: Yes, it's me.

MEG: What? [*Her face appears at the hatch.*] Are you back?

PETEY: Yes.

MEG: I've got your cornflakes ready. [*She disappears and reappears.*] Here's your cornflakes.

[*He rises and takes the plate from her, sits at the table, props up the paper and begins to eat. MEG enters by the kitchen door.*]

Are they nice?

PETEY: Very nice.

MEG: I thought they'd be nice. [*She sits at the table.*] You got your paper?

PETEY: Yes.

MEG: Is it good?

PETEY: Not bad.

MEG: What does it say?

PETEY: Nothing much.

MEG: You read me out some nice bits yesterday.

PETEY: Yes, well, I haven't finished this one yet.

MEG: Will you tell me when you come to something good?

PETEY: Yes.

   [*Pause.*]

MEG: Have you been working hard this morning?

PETEY: No. Just stacked a few of the old chairs. Cleaned up a
   bit.

MEG: Is it nice out?

PETEY: Very nice.

   [*Pause.*]

MEG: Is Stanley up yet?

PETEY: I don't know. Is he?

MEG: I don't know. I haven't seen him down yet.

PETEY: Well then, he can't be up.

MEG: Haven't you seen him down?

PETEY: I've only just come in.

MEG: He must be still asleep.

   [*She looks round the room, stands, goes to the sideboard and takes a
   pair of socks from a drawer, collects wool and a needle and goes
   back to the table.*]

   What time did you go out this morning, Petey?

PETEY: Same time as usual.

MEG: Was it dark?

PETEY: No, it was light.

MEG [*beginning to darn*]: But sometimes you go out in the morning
   and it's dark.

PETEY: That's in the winter.

MEG: Oh, in winter.

PETEY: Yes, it gets light later in winter.

MEG: Oh.

   [*Pause.*]

   What are you reading? . . .

21

The play starts with silence; if this is held for a moment, the audience will wait for Petey to speak. But Pinter breaks the silence with words from an unseen source, so gathering a further curiosity. After 'Is that you, Petey?', a pause repeats the exploitation of theatrical vacuum and still further develops the audience's desire for it to be filled. Pinter does not let go of this tension until line 6, with Petey's 'Yes, it's me', and then Meg appears on stage.

He is not merely withholding information, for the repetitions of words have been carefully judged. This is, indeed, a basic device in all the plays. Meg's first three questions seem at first to repeat the same inquiry, but the slight changes in the use of words reveal progressively that the questions she asks are not truly questions at all, but a challenge. 'Petey' is placed first at the end of the sentence, then more commandingly at the beginning, and then becomes the single questioning word. Moreover, when Petey's voice gives sufficient answer, three more questions follow at once, repeating the ostensible inquiry. Meg is not satisfied until she *sees* Petey, and then she herself responds with an assertion that she has done a job for him. At this point she breaks contact to bring the cornflakes to the kitchen hatch, and this action will make him rise from the table, go to her, and take them from her. Her questions, statements and action all establish that she is calling the tune; she wishes to make him acknowledge her presence and his dependence.

Other repetitions in this passage still further suggest the drama underneath the seemingly inconsequential exchanges. Petey starts by evading any statement – 'What?' – but his second speech begins with 'Yes', as if he were intent on cutting off the exchange. He continues, however, with 'it's me', a repetition of the information given in 'Yes' that is unnecessary and therefore seems insistent or, more likely, irritated or mocking. Petey's third speech defines more closely his desire to disengage by repeating for the third time the essential message with a second 'Yes', which now, in contrast with his previous speech, sounds brief, uninviting and yet, possibly, submissive.

Meg's first entrance on to the stage itself and the preceding pause will gain the audience's attention for her 'Are they nice?'. If the audience has begun to question the validity of speech, it may consider that cornflakes are not likely to vary in themselves and therefore her question may sound like a challenge, asking for attention or praise, rather than a genuine inquiry. The repetition of 'nice' in her next response – 'I thought they'd be nice' – shows that this interpretation is correct, and because this speech adds nothing substantial to the exposition the audience is more likely to become at least partly aware of her pursuit of gratification.

During these speeches Petey is hidden behind the '*propped up*' newspaper, but now Meg challenges this protection with a further question which is now – and the contrast with earlier exchanges will make this point more clearly – overtly a challenge: 'You got your paper?' Then the attack implicit in 'Are they nice?' is repeated in her 'Is it good?'; and the similarity again helps to define the point. A '*Pause*' is now repeated, followed by a new question, this time more apparently concerned for Petey, as if she were recognizing – without ever saying so – that he has not been satisfying the needs which have launched her upon the whole conversation and make her, instinctively, prolong it: 'Have you been working hard this morning?' But as soon as he answers with rather more detail than he has given in earlier exchanges, she accepts the small victory, and now the repetition of 'nice' signals a reversion to her basic, selfish concerns. After the next '*Pause*', these particular repetitions momentarily cease; this in itself suggests a shift of engagement

and throws the new questions about Stanley into relief.
But then there follows another '*pause*' in which Meg looks
and moves around the room and gets some darning to do;
settled again, she tries another inquiry – 'What time did you
go out this morning, Petey?' This reverts to the more
personal challenge of Petey and leads to another question
which in form is like 'Is it nice?' or 'Is it good?'; but this
time, there is an unexpected 'Was it dark?' This could be a
far-reaching modification, expressing fear and apprehension; and it stands out as the first directly affecting word
in the play. Now, for the first time, she seems to question his
response, and she then repeats *his* words – 'Oh, in winter' –
and then she repeats merely her own ejaculation of acceptance or reassurance: 'Oh.' Satisfaction is restored in the
pause, for she returns to the earlier, challenging question
in a less avoidable form, not 'What does it say?' but 'What
are you reading?'

Petey's speeches are as full of repetitions as Meg's. 'Yes'
is common, and it is noticeable that when it comes for the
last time, in 'Yes, it gets light later in winter', it comes
without prompting from a question. At this point it is an
attack rather than an evasion. Three times he simply
repeats Meg's words or phrasing:

> Is that you? . . . Yes, it's me.
> Are they nice? . . . Very nice.
> Is it nice out? . . . Very nice.

And with as little disturbance of the phrasing, he parries or
contradicts her:

> Is it good? . . . Not bad.
> Was it dark? . . . No, it was light.

Petey is disclosing as little as possible, protecting himself,
holding himself still; yet he is rather furtively ready to take
small advantages.

The passage about Stanley is different from the other exchanges. To Meg's first question, 'Is Stanley up yet?', Petey answers briefly – 'I don't know' – but he adds a question: 'Is he?' Other than his first defensive 'What?', this is his only question in the episode, and it provokes Meg to a repetition of his words, and then a statement of her own knowledge which sounds like an excuse: 'I don't know. I haven't seen him down yet.' Now Petey takes advantage and almost attacks – 'Well then, he can't be up.' Now Meg asks an obvious question and gets the obvious answer; and then she concludes with a further obvious statement or excuse. Here the repetitions show questions unnecessarily asked and statements unnecessarily made: Meg goes on, it must seem, because of the subject and because she is apologetic, not because she cannot work matters out for herself.

The repetitions, the disproportions, the easy use of 'nice', 'good' and 'bad', are all occasions for comedy. So are the movements underneath the dialogue as shown by these devices. But, more than this, the two characters are at work with sly, mocking, perhaps anguished, smokescreens. There is 'continual evasion'; even in attack, as little as possible is given away.

The device of repetition, so prevalent here, is not, of course, Pinter's own discovery. It is the stock-in-trade of oratory, comedy and drama, and of all speech. But Pinter uses it with astonishing persistence, repeating the simplest phrases until they yield the secret of their character's hidden activity.

Two analogies offer themselves. First Shakespeare's comic usage, as in Sir Andrew Aguecheek's first entry in *Twelfth Night*, when the foolish knight is forced to repeat his opening greetings to Sir Toby and Maria who are there to mock him. Even his first line, 'Sir Toby Belch! How now, Sir Toby Belch?' is capable of being delivered with a marked

change in the repeated words which could serve an experienced comic actor to establish Sir Andrew's motives and
expectations as clearly as many complicated words. In the
soliloquies of Benedick or Falstaff, small repetitions, often
of apparently simple words such as 'I am well' and 'I'll
never', or 'Honour' and 'a word', mark the climaxes and
changing intentions of the speakers. Such repetitions are all
the more effective in terms of character presentation and
involvement because they involve words that sound at
first unremarkable or casual. The dramatist, through repetition, has flogged life into a dead horse.

Secondly, Eugene O'Neill's use of repetition in his last
plays, especially in *Long Day's Journey into Night*. The repeated phrase of Tyrone, 'I'm as hungry as a hunter',
shows how tired metaphors and mere commonplaces can
become at last alive with personal and precise meaning.
The phrases become a kind of pillory or cross on which the
characters have unwittingly impaled their inward selves.
Meg's use of 'nice' and 'good', and later of 'lovely', are
phrases that catch their user in this way.

The dramatic tactic of repetition is a surprisingly neat
mechanism. By placing a short series of similar verbal
utterances side by side, the audience's attention is drawn
to the dissimilarities. By breaking the series, a change of
direction will register more surely. Obviously this tactic
needs tact in application: too long a series will weary the
audience; variations must be clearly placed, as at the
beginning or end of a speech; and they must be marked by
a changed rhythm. Timing must be slow if the effect is to
be subtle, or there must be motionless pauses in which the
changes can be noticed. (In a slow-motion film or still
photograph, an athlete can discover errors which he
cannot know from a film at normal speed.) Activity on
stage or excitement of plot must not be allowed to distract

attention from simple-seeming words. (O'Neill's plays are very long and their plots slow; Shakespeare's comic scenes are often soliloquies with little obligatory stage-business, and they often fail to forward the plot at all.) Above all, the dialogue must 'ring true' to character and situation. (The hardest test for an impostor is a slow, intimate, undeflecting scrutiny.) *

Pinter's strong ally in all this is the actor. Increasingly since the Second World War, actors have been trained to distinguish 'text' from 'subtext', to appreciate a language 'where, under what is said, another thing is being said'. The ultimate masters are Chekhov for practice and Stanislavski for training and precept. In *Building a Character* (translated 1949), the teacher explains that each actor must create a subtextual life for his part:

This inner stream of images, fed by all sorts of fictional inventions, given circumstances, puts life into a role, it gives a basis for everything the character does, his ambitions, thoughts, feelings . . .

It is the subtext that makes us say the words we do in a play . . .

The spoken word, the text of a play is not valuable in and of itself, but is made so by the inner content of the subtext and what is contained in it. . . . Without it the words have no excuse for being presented on the stage.*

Pinter has said that he learnt little at the acting schools he attended before becoming an actor, but, even if this were wholly true, he could scarcely have worked in the English theatre for the last twenty years without becoming aware of the notion of 'subtext'.

* *Building a Character*, trans. Elizabeth R. Hapgood (Reinhardt & Evans, 1949), pp. 124, 113 and 114–15.

Two exercises described by Stanislavski, and recommended by his followers, show how actors are trained to search below their lines and build their performances on secure subtextual foundations:

If I ask you a perfectly simple question now, 'Is it cold out today?' before you answer, even with a 'yes', or 'it's not cold', or 'I didn't notice', you should, in your imagination, go back on to the street and remember how you walked or rode. You should test your sensations by remembering how the people you met were wrapped up, how they turned up their collars, how the snow crunched underfoot, and only then can you answer my question.*

After this silent preparation, an answer to the question will express the whole wintry experience, even in a simple 'yes'; not explicitly of course, but implicitly. The inner response, being precise and detailed, will control the volume, speed, pitch and tone of the monosyllable. The actor needs to make such a preparation at the beginning of *The Birthday Party* when, as Petey, he has to answer questions about the weather or about his cornflakes.

A more purposeful subtextual life is suggested by an exploratory exercise described in *Building a Character*:

'Now make this test. What response do you give to the words in your ears, "Let's go to the station!"?'
I saw myself leaving the house, taking a cab, driving through certain streets, crossing avenues and soon found myself inside the railway station. Leo thought of himself as pacing up and down a platform, whereas Sonya's thoughts had already allowed her to flit off to southern climes and visit several resorts.
After each one of us had described his mental pictures to Tortsov his comment was:
'Evidently the two or three words were scarcely out of my

* *An Actor Prepares*, trans. Elizabeth R. Hapgood (Bles, 1937), p. 71.

mouth before you mentally carried out the suggestion contained in them! How painstakingly you have told to me all the things my little phrase evoked. . . . If you would always go through that normal process on the stage and pronounce your words with such affection and such penetration into their essential meaning you would soon become great actors.'*

The point of this exercise is threefold: that each student responded according to his own cast of thought and feeling, although the teacher's words and their pronunciation were identical; that an actor must be able to create a lively imaginative consciousness to support whatever he says in a play, be that complicated or simple; that simple words can evoke extensive reactions, based on past experience and future intentions, underneath their simplest meaning.

So, in a Pinter play, two characters may use the same words for totally different purposes, as in Meg and Petey's 'Is Stanley up yet? . . . I don't know. Is he? . . . I don't know.' Behind the two 'I don't knows' are particular and general reactions which are defined, like the students' reactions to 'Let's go to the station!', by two different experiences and two contrasted sets of expectation, desire and fear.

In *The Collection* (1961), Stella and James talk about olives, each taking words from the other to question and assert according to their independent interests:

JAMES: I'd like an olive.
STELLA: Olive? We haven't got any.
JAMES: How do you know?
STELLA: I know.
JAMES: Have you looked?
STELLA: I don't need to look, do I? I know what I've got.
JAMES: You know what you've got?
   [*Pause.*]
Why haven't we got any olives?   (p. 27)

* op. cit., p. 116.

A journalist's account of Pinter taking rehearsals for a
production of this particular play shows him determined
to get the actors to know, precisely, the subtextual import of
each word they use, the hidden motives for choice:

'I'm probably complicating things,' he said to John Ronane,
a young actor, 'but it's worth complicating. We haven't really
ever quite examined this speech, have we? Until we find out
what it means to you, there can't be any real . . . You know?'
Pinter coughed and took off his glasses. 'We have to find . . .
Don't be worried.'

'I'm not worried,' said Ronane. 'I'm just completely – lost.'

'I'm not really getting the way you were committed to yourself,' said Pinter, 'and to what you were committed. I feel
you must be committed to a possibility, d'you know what I
mean?'

With reference to the text, Pinter notes moments for
changing the hidden intention, for marking uncertainties
under seemingly strong statements; and he weighs how
much of the inner concerns can be expressed in intonation
or stress at particular points:

'The early phase, you know, might be too ambiguous. But
just the initial impression. It's a matter of balance. But it's a fact
that this rocks you.'

'I should think that *olives* is *the* word. Whereas, as the change
of concentration is very clear. Your, slight, thing . . . It's a
change at the silence, the change is there.'

Tall, was he?
That's what he was.

'I find this a little too . . .' 'Open?' 'Yes, yes, yes. It could be a
very nasty . . . Well, yes, I think it needs a split second. Well,
yes. Mm. But I think it can take that.'

I don't think mirrors are deceptive.

'Look, you must remember one thing, John. Nothing would

titillate him more. He knows he's pretty good from the back as well. Let him look at you. Yes. I think we should take this again from the beginning.'

Oh, what a beautiful lamp!
(Pinter now speaks to Michael Hordern who played Harry.)
    'Michael, you see, it's not your taste at all. The whole thing's horrid.'

In this last direction Pinter makes explicit what is never stated in words in the text of the play: that Harry is lying when he praises the furniture in Stella's 'contemporary style' flat. This is implicit in Harry's own choice of antiques and Chinese porcelain displayed on the stage-set of his flat. It could also be deduced from his use of 'beautiful' as he enters Stella's flat; this is the opening gambit of a man on strange ground, a man who is fastidious, critical and ironic, and who elsewhere uses conventional words of praise as weapons of attack or self-protection. 'The thing is,' said one of the actors in this rehearsal, 'Harold's plays take such bloody concentration.'*

Certainly Pinter's plays need good actors. If they have not realized that his words are often smokescreens and so have not created a subtextual reality to support them, his dialogue will fall flat, his plays seem idle, trivial and often banal. Without the actors' subtextual realization of their parts, the words, as Stanislavski said, 'have no excuse for being presented on the stage'. And the right 'inner content' must be found that is both consistent throughout the play and capable of supporting every turn of the dialogue. Pinter has not freed his actors to bring their own notions and virtuosity to their parts; as he said in an interview, 'There are certain limits on the actors set by what I write:

* John Gale, 'Taking Pains with Pinter', *Observer*, 20 June 1962.

they can enjoy themselves, but not in the way that Wolfit or McMaster enjoyed enjoying themselves.'*

Since Pinter's plays in performance require good actors who have rehearsed with concentration and consistency, it would seem to follow that they will also need perceptive readers who are equally aware of the words as part of a number of carefully wrought and interrelated performances. But for audiences and readers, he holds much slacker reins. Close and theatrically aware reading is very rewarding, but the plays can be approached at any level of understanding. Sixteen million people watched one of his plays on television in a single night, with all the various distractions to which television is subject. Undoubtedly part of the attraction of the plays to readers and audiences is that each individual is left to catch the inner reality as and when he is able or willing. It is possible to lose patience with the dialogue, thinking it baffling, uneconomic, inapposite, obvious, self-important. But there are many devices to engage attention, and very few will hear or see the plays without catching intimations of the inner drama for at least some strange and disconnected moments. On re-reading or re-seeing, the warfare behind the words will register with growing consistency and clarity.

Talking of his characters and their speech, Pinter uses words like 'true', 'necessary', 'firmly based'; he asks 'Would this be said? Is this possible?':

You create characters, which is a bit of a liberty anyway, then you give them words to speak and you give them a situation to play. And I find you've got to be very careful.†

* 'In an Empty Bandstand: Harold Pinter in conversation with Joan Bakewell', *Listener*, 6 November 1969, p. 30; he refers to Sir Donald Wolfit and Anew McMaster in whose touring companies presenting Shakespeare and other classics he had worked as an actor.

† *Listener*, 6 November 1969, p. 31.

If the subtextual reality of each character has been imagined with fullness and accuracy, and if the actors have given a precise, solid and detailed actuality to it in their perform- ance, then reader and audience may fitfully, progressively and perhaps, at last, with a kind of certainty, come to recognize it, each for themselves and in their own measure and time. The repetitions in the first episode of *The Birthday Party* can all be explained on slow analysis, but in perform- ance the conflict between Petey and Meg is not put into irrevocable words at this stage of the play and therefore it is there only to be 'sensed' by the audience. Pinter's plays are realistic in one important and unusual way: audience and readers do not know everything, and what certainty there is comes very late in the play. The plays offer an oppor- tunity for understanding very like those fleeting and un- certain opportunities that are offered by life.

In effect, Pinter seems to play a game with his audience, giving only a few signposts on the way, a few landmarks or buoys to distinguish the hidden rock and sand. Like his characters, he seems to evade, to obscure intentionally, to blaze false trails. But his concentration on the truth of the dramatic fiction is such that we come to realize that he plays these games of necessity, without setting out to do so. His view of his own characters and the situations in which they are placed makes his task a wary one. He plays hide- and-seek with his audience because he is deeply involved in this very game himself. This is how he sees and hears the world around him and within him.

When Pinter is fully engaged as dramatist, he is fully caught. He knows more than his audience and he knows the direction in which the play will go; but his involvement is to watch, wait and explore, and then to stretch out carefully in order to touch something which is not wholly expected, not wholly prepared for. The plays, written in this way, offer a sequence of partial discoveries, which the audience seem to make for themselves and out of which a sense of overall coherence and meaning seems to be born in each attentive consciousness. Pinter offers his own experience of discovery, and in the same mode of perception.

*

No detail of Pinter's writing can be adequately considered outside the context of the complete drama in which it must play its part. But by examining some short passages, his continuous control may be seen at work, and his awareness of the part words play in dramatic confrontations of considerable complexity but little explicit verbal statement. The more recurrent devices of language illustrate the nature of his perception and the means whereby he ensures that that perception is communicated in his writing.

The most difficult to describe is Pinter's manipulation of rhythms. Speeches run in one kind of phrasing, until some subtextual pressure lengthens, shortens or quickens the utterance and so, by sound alone, betrays the change of engagement. The last episode of *The Birthday Party* illustrates this:

> [MEG *comes past the window and enters by the back door.* PETEY *studies the front page of the paper.*]
>
> MEG [*coming downstage*]: The car's gone.
> PETEY: Yes.
> MEG: Have they gone?
> PETEY: Yes.
> MEG: Won't they be in for lunch?
> PETEY: No.
> MEG: Oh, what a shame. [*She puts her bag on the table.*] It's hot out. [*She hangs her coat on a hook.*] What are you doing?
> PETEY: Reading.
> MEG: Is it good?
> PETEY: All right.
> [*She sits by the table.*]

MEG: Where's Stan?

    [*Pause.*]

  Is Stan down yet, Petey?

PETEY: No . . . he's . . .

MEG: Is he still in bed?

PETEY: Yes, he's . . . still asleep.

MEG: Still? He'll be late for his breakfast.

PETEY: Let him . . . sleep.

    [*Pause.*]

MEG: Wasn't it a lovely party last night?

PETEY: I wasn't there.

MEG: Weren't you?

PETEY: I came in afterwards.

MEG: Oh.

    [*Pause.*]

  It was a lovely party. I haven't laughed so much for years. We had dancing and singing. And games. You should have been there.

PETEY: It was good, eh?

    [*Pause.*]

MEG: I was the belle of the ball.

PETEY: Were you?

MEG: Oh yes. They all said I was.

PETEY: I bet you were, too.

MEG: Oh, it's true. I was.

    [*Pause.*]

  I know I was.

CURTAIN

Meg's first three speeches have two main stresses each, the third containing a greater number of unstressed syllables; then, as she registers Petey's 'No', the rhythm changes, starting with a single syllable 'Oh', and then after a comma three more, the middle one being unstressed: 'Oh, what a shame.' She then moves about the room and begins speech again in much the same rhythms as at first. But when Petey replies this time, the phrasing grows shorter: 'Is it good?' and then, having sat down, a simple two-stressed, two-syllabled 'Where's Stan?'. At this point there is a *'Pause'* during which her energy changes rhythm, for there now comes a slightly longer question, less emphatic, and 'Petey' at the end following a comma's pause: 'Is Stan down yet, Petey?' When Petey answers with broken phrasing and hesitation 'No . . . he's . . . ', she first gains speed – 'Is he still in bed?' – with light front vowels and no more than two stresses. But she then seems to halt with a mono-syllabic question (that repeats 'still' for the second time), but soon runs on with her observation, 'He'll be late for his breakfast'. This assumption of knowledge seems to allow her to change the whole mood of her thoughts, for a pause is now of her making; and when she speaks again, the rhythm is almost lilting, as if she were happily lost in idle thoughts: 'Wasn't it a lovely party last night?' Petey's disclaimer breaks the mood momentarily, but after another pause, again of her own making, she picks up with a longer speech that has varied rhythms within it. The rhythmical jingle of '. . . dancing and singing' is followed by the shorter and slightly disturbing rhythm of a short, verbless sentence 'And games'; this alludes to the frightening part of the evening. But then, as she remembers Petey was not there, the tension is again relaxed. Meg's final speeches begin again with a dreamy ease: 'I was the belle of the ball'; but Petey's question and then his support tighten the rhythms. Her reply to the question starts with a two-syllable assertion, 'Oh yes', and then a rather longer agreement, 'They all said I was'. Her reply to his token of support is short but with two pauses, the first slight and the second more emphatic: 'Oh, it's true. I was.' A *'Pause'* follows and then her last speech with two very short elements and a repeated 'I', in its single phrase: 'I know I was.' The rhythm of this last utterance is short, contained and simple; and, since 'know' carries more stress than 'was', it has a slight falling-off. This tightening of the rhythms of speech is all the more effective for contrast with the lighter rhythms and longer reach of her preceding speeches.

Petey's rhythms start with stark monosyllables: 'Yes . . . Yes . . . No.' When Meg returns to the attack, they are less firm with two-syllables: 'Reading . . . All right', the second giving an abrupt sound in comparison with the light ending of the first. When he is questioned about Stanley, his rhythms are broken, finding their firmest point on the concluding monosyllable, 'sleep'. Petey's next replies seem light, unstressed and smooth in comparison, as if yielding even as he contradicts Meg. When she enters her reverie, he seems to give light compliance with 'It was good, eh?' and 'I bet you were, too', each with a single syllable after a brief pause at the end of the line. The strongest contrast here is in the two-syllabled 'Were you?' that could be delivered slowly or a little weighted.

The two characters have their own rhythms that are shown off by varied contrasts throughout the episode. But there is one point where they seem to speak almost in the same 'breath', with a similar shortness of phrase, though with varying emphasis. This is when Petey's answers grow to 'Reading' and 'All right', and Meg shortens her questions to 'Is it good?' and then 'Where's Stan?' This rhythmic 'meeting' may represent an unspoken acknowledgement of the one urgent matter they must both learn to face and live with. It lasts for only a moment that continues into the pause; then Meg's uncertainty forces the pace again.

If only the sounds of the words were heard, or if the dialogue was followed by someone not knowing a word of English, much of the pressures, tactics and moments of decision in this episode would be communicated. Such response might be more valid and exciting than if a reader registered the words without recreating their sound in his mind as well as registering their implications. Sound and the interplay of rhythms are constant factors in the effectiveness of Pinter's dialogue.

The same passage illustrates further devices of more occasional value. Most notable is barefaced, inescapable falsehood: the apparently simple statement of facts that the audience knows to be wrong. Here Petey fumbles towards his lie, but when it comes it is sharp enough to alert the audience: 'Yes' – Stanley is still in bed. (The audience has just seen Petey watch Stanley march out of the room between Goldberg and McCann, despite his own protest.) The effect is not complete when Petey has given the simple lie, for so briefly is it effected that the elaboration which follows after another hesitation will also be listened to sharply for verification: 'Yes, he's . . . still asleep.' The audience now hears Petey as a man managing his wife and also his own unspoken thoughts. Meg's obvious lie – that 'We had dancing' when, in fact, she had been unable to find a partner – is less crucially managed. It follows the more general deception of 'It was a lovely party' and 'They all said' she was 'the belle of the ball'. Here the comparatively small factual error is sufficient to alert attention and so give a momentary awareness of how far Meg is indulging her own fantasy of rosy success.

Falsehoods are important for Pinter's dialogue, not least when they can be detected only by careful reference from one scene to another – like Harry's pronouncement, in *The Collection*, that Stella's lamp is 'beautiful'. These provide clear clues for the actors, showing the nature of their varying commitment to speech and hence the varying pressure and tone of their utterance. But even the most obscure falsehoods also serve to create a more general sense of suspicion in the audience, as each individual member catches, or thinks he catches, the character out.

Some of the more blatant lies are so casually delivered that the audience is encouraged to look for more than is going to be disclosed. This is a part of Pinter's two-pronged tactic of awakening the audience's desire for verification and repeatedly disappointing this desire. In *The Birthday Party* and *The Caretaker*, he may be said to create mystification by contrary statements and by the absence of verification for what can only be assumed. Where do the characters come from? (Answers are sometimes suggested, but never substantiated.) Is Goldberg's name Nat or Simey, or Benny? (Each name is used.) Was his son called Manney (Emanuel) or Timmy? (Again, each name is used.) Was Stanley married or not? (He is said to have a wife and also not to be married.) Why does Mick, in *The Caretaker*, invent such unlikely and impossible exploits for his uncle's brother who 'married a Chinaman and went to Jamaica'? Why does Aston say Davies snores when on all but one, late, occasion he does not? The effect of such falsehoods, half-truths and contradictions is to raise suspicion about statements that could possibly be true, and which if true, might be significant. So the audience doubts and questions the characters' progress through the play, the clues they seem to drop, the assurance they seem to possess. Their words are undermined, their credit short.

A notable example is Aston's speech at the end of Act Two of *The Caretaker* which follows his strange stories about victimization. Here he tells of a mental hospital more in terms of primitive nightmare than medical practice. Yet there are details that could be true, like needing a guardian's permission for treatment and, more potentially reassuring for an audience, the credibility of its tone as a crazed man's account of actuality.

A fact which the audience has no cause to doubt is sometimes presented so that it awakens the possibility of relevance to some other statement of fact. For instance, is it significant that Stanley, in *The Birthday Party*, speaks of living in Basingstoke (p. 45), when Goldberg has said his Uncle Barney had had a home just outside this town (p. 29)? Uncle Barney, the audience is told later, is the one whom Goldberg's father had said on his death-bed would always 'see him in the clear' (p. 81). Coincidences like these tend to draw attention to each other. Why does Stanley say he connects McCann with a Fuller's teashop, a Boots Library and the High Street at Maidenhead (p. 42), when, later in the same Act, Goldberg, who did not hear this conversation, imagines his own life with some precisely similar detail: 'Not size but quality. A little Austin, tea in Fullers, a library book from Boots, and I'm satisfied' (p. 59)? Has McCann reported back, or are Goldberg and Stanley connected in some previous activity? How does Goldberg know, or why does he say he knows, the date of Stanley's birthday? Or is that invention? Is there a connection between Goldberg talking of his surviving son (the other two sons were 'lost – in an accident') and his pursuit of Stanley? (He says he 'often' wonders what that son is doing now.) Or are McCann's two references to 'the organization', while joining Goldberg in interrogating Stanley, a more reliable clue to the unknown past? Many of the accusations hurled at Stanley are absurd or impossible, so is any one of them 'true'? Goldberg says, at length, that Stanley is being taken to Monty; but why does he merely hint that Monty is a doctor?

In a programme note for *The Caretaker*, Pinter claimed uncertainty as a key dramatic device:

Given a man in a room, he will sooner or later receive a visitor . . .

There is no guarantee, however, that he will possess a visiting card, with detailed information as to his last place of residence, last job, next job, number of dependents, etc. Nor, for the comfort of all, an identity card, nor a label on his chest. The desire for verification is understandable but cannot always be satisfied. There are no hard distinctions between what is real and what is unreal, nor between what is true and what is false. The thing is not necessarily either true or false; it can be both true and false. The assumption that to verify what has happened and what is happening presents few problems I take to be inaccurate. A character on the stage who can present no convincing argument or information as to his past experience, his present behaviour or his aspirations, nor give a comprehensive analysis of his motives is as legitimate and as worthy of attention as one who, alarmingly, can do all these things. The more acute the experience the less articulate its expression.*

So presented, Pinter sounds as if he is making paradoxical play with words; and this is suitable. A more direct statement came in a letter to the *New York Times* in 1967, when *The Birthday Party* was presented on Broadway. A theatregoer had written to say that Mr Pinter was shirking his job and should tell her who the two visitors were, where Stanley came from and whether they were 'all supposed to be normal'. Pinter replied that he couldn't understand her letter, and therefore couldn't reply until she had answered *his* questions: who was she, where did she come from, and was she 'supposed to be normal'? Pinter, in fact, is exploring Whitehead's dilemma, the inability of anyone to describe the fact that he exists and that he is attempting to communicate with others. The philosopher's questions have yielded the dramatic device of blatant falsehood and continuous mystification and suspicion. Used with exaggeration and meticulous control, the device sharpens the

* Programme, Arts Theatre (1960).

audience's awareness of an uneasiness latent in all human encounters.

Of course, the lies Pinter introduces are not any lies. Often the clearest falsehoods introduce, or are accompanied by, the most potent words, words which are found to reveal several levels of meaning or suggest a large wake of association. Petey's

> Yes, he's . . . still asleep.
> Let him . . . sleep.

says more than that Stanley, according to him, is in bed (which was the wording offered by Meg). As Petey had watched Stanley being escorted to the waiting black car, dressed in black, almost blind without his spectacles and quite silent, he could have seen him as if he were going to his own funeral. Moreover, the audience has witnessed Stanley reduced to child-like cries, and then drawing '*a long breath which shudders down his body*'. Just before Petey's entry he had crouched on a chair, shuddered, relaxed, dropped his head and become '*still again, stooped*'. After his 'Birthday', Stanley has regressed as if into the womb, in a foetal position, but quiet and still as if dead. Is Stanley indeed being 'put to sleep'? Or is Petey expressing his own fearful response in trying to let the sleeping lie? After this falsehood, Petey is, certainly, silent, as Stanley was and, probably, still is: is Petey 'sleeping' too, intentionally?

Equally, Meg's 'We had dancing and singing. And games. You should have been there', may be both, 'true and false'. Blind-man's-buff was not the only 'game' played; Lulu had had hers, Goldberg and McCann theirs; Stanley had been about to '*strangle*' her (p. 66). Petey's absence at his 'game' of chess had affected the course of the Birthday Party.

Pinter has an acute ear for those words which carry

suggestions or traces of secondary implications. He places them carefully, often with a lie, as a stepping-off point for a long speech, or as a suddenly satisfactory conclusion to one, or as a conversation-stopper. They are often placed in unremarkable verbal surroundings, or seem to be uttered without reflection and then seized upon, as if a secret source of appropriateness has been unwittingly discovered.

*

That the human mind works in this way had fascinated Freud, who emphasized how often such single, half-involuntary words are accompanied with laughter as a sign of the release of conscious inhibition. In *The Psychopathology of Everyday Life*, he had quoted a Dr Dattner of Vienna:

I was lunching in a restaurant with my colleague H., a doctor of philosophy. He spoke of the hardships of probationary students, and mentioned incidentally that before he had finished his studies he was given the post of secretary to the ambassador, or, more precisely, the minister plenipotentiary and extraordinary, of Chile. 'But then (he said) the minister was transferred and I did not present myself to his successor.' While he was uttering the last sentence he raised a piece of cake to his mouth, but let it drop from the knife in apparent clumsiness. I immediately grasped the hidden meaning of this symptomatic act, and, as it were casually, interjected to my colleague, who was unfamiliar with psycho-analysis: 'You certainly allowed a tasty morsel to slip from you there'. He . . . repeated my exact words with a peculiarly charming and surprising liveliness just as if my remark had taken the words out of his mouth . . . and went on to unburden himself by means of a detailed description of the clumsiness which had lost him this well-paid position.*

If this conversation had been heard by an audience, H.'s sudden energy in speaking of his early struggles might seem

* *Complete Works*, Vol. VI, trans. J. Strachey (1960), p. 201.

surprising. But the words 'tasty morsel', repeated with different intonation, had touched the spring for releasing the speaker's own interests and sense of wrong that had underlain his preceding talk about probationary students. Here are Pinter's dramatic devices of surprise, suggestion and repetition, his interest in the involvement that underlies speech.

In *The Caretaker* there is a run of puns which, under a surface concern for incidental difficulties, expresses a constant fear of being killed or mutilated. The very title of the play is a pun: taking care of the house, and also, taking care of an unwanted enemy; protection *and* liquidation. A further meaning might also be that of taking someone else's cares on one's shoulders. A pun similar to the title-pun occurs early in the play in Davies's:

I had a tin, only . . . only a while ago. But it was knocked off. It was knocked off on the Great West Road.   (p. 8)

The repetition of 'knocked off' shows Davies's attraction for these particular words, that here mean 'stolen', but in a different context could mean 'killed' in much the same way as Freud's Mr H. had said 'tasty' and had meant 'edible', but, in the hidden context, had implied 'financial benefit'. Davies is speaking soon after having been almost 'done in' himself, and his mind immediately reverts to that. He speaks of his health: 'I haven't been so well lately. I've had a few attacks' (p. 9), where 'attacks' also carries a suggestion of physical violence. After a pause his next words, 'Did you see what happened with that one?', is about the physical attack in the fight from which Aston rescued him. Talking of the bed Aston offers him, he speaks first of a 'draught' but then of 'wind', and finally it is Aston who, after a pause and before a pause, seems to speak of 'getting the wind up' in the sense of being afraid:

44

DAVIES: Yes, well, you'd be well out of the draught there.
ASTON: You don't get much wind.
DAVIES: You'd be well out of it. It's different when you're kipping out.
ASTON: Would be.
DAVIES: Nothing but wind then.
  [*Pause.*]
ASTON: Yes, when the wind gets up it . , .
  [*Pause.*]
DAVIES: Yes . . .
ASTON: Mmnn . . . (p. 11)

The silence and imperfect responses that follow 'the wind' getting up suggest that both minds are held by some unspoken thoughts, almost in agreement. A little later, Aston and Davies seem to agree in using 'fixed up' and 'sorted out' in a double sense, but here Aston alone could press the aggressive meaning:

ASTON [*attending to the toaster*]: Would . . . would you like to sleep here?
DAVIES: Here?
ASTON: You can sleep here if you like.
DAVIES: Here? Oh, I don't know about that.
  [*Pause.*]
  How long for?
ASTON: Till you . . . get yourself fixed up.
DAVIES [*sitting*]: Ay well, that . . .
ASTON: Get yourself sorted out . . .
DAVIES: Oh, I'll be fixed up . . . pretty soon now . . .
  [*Pause.*]
  Where would I sleep? (p. 16)

Pinter has said that when he started to write *The Caretaker*:

I thought originally that the play must end with the violent death of one at the hands of the other. But then I realized, when

45

I got to the point, that the characters as they had grown could never act in this way.*

So, early in the play, to 'fix' or 'sort out' may carry suggestions of 'kill, violently and secretly'; and this may well be why the two characters hesitate, or pick over, these words.

Davies suspects that the disconnected gas-stove in Aston's room may be a menace, and tries unsuccessfully to move it; then he accepts the offered bed and the first movement of the play ends with the lights artificially fading to darkness after the following exchange, in which 'fix' and 'glaring' may carry hints of aggression, and the casual but repeated 'worry' may betray an incipient fear:

> Not bad. Not bad. A fair bed. I think I'll sleep in this.
> ASTON: I'll have to fix a proper shade on that bulb. The light's a bit glaring.
> DAVIES: Don't you worry about that, mister, don't you worry about that. [*He turns and puts the cover up.*]
> [ASTON *sits, poking his* [*electric*] *plug* [*that he has been 'worrying' about since early in the scene*]. *The* LIGHTS FADE OUT. *Darkness.*] (p. 21

The Lover (1963) shows a more conscious and jesting use of puns, betraying a satisfied or anticipatory relish, and, possibly at another level, a sense of frustration. Richard returning to his wife, with whom he has spent the afternoon as her lover – this is the basic situation of the play which the audience has not yet been told – speaks of his journey as if he were speaking of their earlier meeting. He invents a reference to the City which allows more general and precise references to their encounter to be accommodated too:

* 'Harold Pinter Replies' (an interview with Harry Thompson), *New Theatre Magazine*, Vol. II, no. 2 (1961), p.10.

RICHARD: Very sunny on the road. Of course, by the time I got on to it the sun was beginning to sink. But I imagine it was quite warm here this afternoon. It was warm in the City.

Sarah, the wife and mistress, invites more talk and they play together with innuendoes:

SARAH: Was it?
RICHARD: Pretty stifling. I imagine it was quite warm everywhere.
SARAH: Quite a high temperature, I believe.
RICHARD: Did it say so on the wireless?
SARAH: I think it did, yes. (pp. 52–3)

A relish for the 'heat' of passion is thus shared between them. Later, Richard speaks blandly of his wife's social graces and culminates his description with a surprise introduction of 'foul' and the following 'confounding', 'source' and 'profound'; so, beneath an account of normal respectability, a more physical appraisal becomes apparent:

Yes. To feel the envy of others, their attempts to gain favour with you, by fair means or foul, your austere grace confounding them. And to know you are my wife. It's a source of profound satisfaction to me. (p. 77)

By this time the audience is aware of Richard in the double role of husband and lover, so 'know you are my wife' has a clear duplicity. Perhaps 'austere' also helps to set off the effect of 'foul' and 'confounding'.

Sometimes a character draws attention to a pun, and then, by making the veiled reference explicit, uses it as an overt challenge. This happens towards the end of *The Lover*, when Richard is trying to assert himself against his wife:

SARAH: I have something cold in the fridge.
RICHARD: Too cold, I'm sure. The fact is this is my house . . .

47

Sarah is evading, being vaguely helpful and rebuking; Richard turns this to a coarse and open jest, and so attacks.

A single word is sufficient for a conversation to turn upon its hidden axis. So Stanley, in *The Birthday Party*, counters Meg's question with ironic impatience, and Meg greedily devours the attack for the satisfaction of her own fantasy:

Was it nice?
STANLEY: What?
MEG: The fried bread.
STANLEY: Succulent.
MEG: You shouldn't say that word.
STANLEY: What word?
MEG: That word you said.
STANLEY: What, succulent –?
MEG: Don't say it!
STANLEY: What's the matter with it?
MEG: You shouldn't say that word to a married woman.

(pp. 17–18)

Later she returns to the word in a different way, gently and inviting:

MEG: Stan?
STANLEY: What?
MEG [*shyly*]: Am I really succulent?
STANLEY: Oh, you are. I'd rather have you than a cold in the nose any day.
MEG: You're just saying that. (p. 19)

Meg hears what she wants to hear. Double meanings, allusions, tones of voice, gratification and fear are continuously changing, even with the speaking of a single word. By making this verbal encounter turn on 'succulent', Pinter reveals the inner drama, making the normally hidden intention almost explicit for the moment.

The time comes in Pinter's plays when a word or phrase

48

that has been used before, without particularly noticeable effect, is thrown down like a trump, a revelation and judgement. A small-scale example is in the playlet *Night* (1969), where after talk of meeting, looking, caring, wondering, smiling, touching, feeling, the duologue between husband and wife in which they recall their first meeting introduces the word 'adore': '. . . you would adore me always'. They continue to reminisce about children and talk, and various forms of contact; but quickly the play concludes. The verbal action has come to rest, their silent and slow passage through time-past has found its effective keel, not with adoration, but with the saying of that word:

WOMAN: And they said I will adore you always.
MAN: Saying I will adore you always. (p. 61)

In this process, the word has changed its force. Both associate 'adore' with 'always'; she with 'men', he with himself. 'Adore' is no longer romantic: it is a mental attitude, receptive and calming, holding every thought still. In a subtle way it is a pun: the audience's understanding of it has changed, even if the conscious understanding of the two characters shows no outward sign of being disturbed by the unconscious revaluation.

Perhaps the most basic strategy in Pinter's use of words is a movement towards a verbal statement that 'is irrevocable, and can never be taken back'.* The course of a conversation or soliloquy can be deflected by another more powerful need, triggered off by a seemingly chance choice of word, or by a lack of response, or a physical action. So the verbal expression is, at least momentarily, 'truer', more instinctive, more necessary, less calculated or less able to deceive. Stanley's fantasy about playing in a concert reveals his desire to be accepted, his concern for his

* 'Between the Lines', *Sunday Times*, op. cit.

father, fear of persecution, desire to be tough and, then, his aggression towards Meg and his desire to fix her in his mind and in his world. Here are many words, written with relish and precision. The rhythms of speech alternate between those of fear and confidence. Underneath there is loneliness and panic, and the dead weight of custom and lethargy. The phrase, 'old piece of rock cake', comes unexpectedly, blatantly and with revealing coarseness and weariness. Perhaps the most 'irrevocable' statement, where words carry most solid and exact meaning, is the final demanding question, 'That's what you are, aren't you?':

STANLEY: Played the piano? I've played the piano all over the world. All over the country. [*Pause.*] I once gave a concert.

MEG: A concert?

STANLEY [*reflectively*]: Yes. It was a good one, too. They were all there that night. Every single one of them. It was a great success. Yes. A concert. At Lower Edmonton.

MEG: What did you wear?

STANLEY [*to himself*]: I had a unique touch. Absolutely unique. They came up to me. They came up to me and said they were grateful. Champagne we had that night, the lot. [*Pause.*] My father nearly came down to hear me. Well, I dropped him a card anyway. But I don't think he could make it. No, I – I lost the address, that was it. [*Pause.*] Yes. Lower Edmonton. Then after that, you know what they did? They carved me up. Carved me up. It was all arranged, it was all worked out. My next concert. Somewhere else it was. In winter. I went down there to play. Then, when I got there, the hall was closed, the place was shuttered up, not even a caretaker. They'd locked it up. [*Takes off his glasses and wipes them on his pyjama jacket.*] A fast one. They pulled a fast one. I'd like to know who was responsible for that. [*Bitterly.*] All right, Jack, I can take a tip. They want me to crawl down on my bended knees. Well I can take a tip . . . any day of the week. [*He replaces his glasses, then looks at* MEG.] Look at her. You're just an old piece of rock

cake, aren't you? [*He rises and leans across the table to her.*]
That's what you are, aren't you?   (pp. 23–4)

*

Pinter not only uses words meticulously and with constant
awareness of the 'other language' that can be locked underneath the spoken words, but he is an essentially dramatic
writer in that he knows how to acknowledge the effects of
time. His writing has tension and climax, and is continually
dynamic. Words run ahead or lag behind the thoughts
of his characters; they surprise, digress, tantalize and,
occasionally, seem to clinch the dramatic conflict.

Pinter has spoken of the nausea which he sometimes
feels for words, and describes his encounters with words as
if he had had to penetrate and master them. This, too, as
well as the perplexity and delight of words, he communicates
to his audience. At a performance one can be lost – like an
actor in early rehearsals – bewildered, amazed, infuriated,
bored, and then find that some precarious statement seems
to clarify, to be held for attention, understanding and
wonder. Even when the discovery is of a simple or dogged
reaction, the experience of so recognizing it gives an
essential dramatic excitement to the statement.

In his plays Pinter has faced his distrust of words and
explored the means whereby the theatre can express in
lively form his perceptions and discoveries. Not only has he
increased the language of the theatre – its ability to speak –
but he has done so in a manner that makes it difficult for his
audiences and readers to forget what they have found;
he has given them an experience in which they have discovered for themselves.

Two comparisons may help to mark the particular
quality of Pinter's use of words. First, T. S. Eliot, who in
the *Four Quartets* is much concerned with a struggle for
verbal expression: for him words are hard, difficult, almost

51

tangible, brittle, elusive. Words have to be chosen, taken hold of, arranged:

> Words strain,
> Crack and sometimes break, under the burden,
> Under the tension, slip, slide, perish,
> Decay with imprecision, will not stay in place,
> Will not stay still. (*Burnt Norton, V*)

> . . . having had twenty years . . .
> Trying to learn to use words, and every attempt
> Is a wholly new start, and a different kind of failure
> Because one has only learnt to get the better of words
> For the thing one no longer has to say, or the way in which
> One is no longer disposed to say it. (*East Coker, V*)

Pinter also observes the decay of words, but with a difference. He explores the decay for its own sake; he is interested in the actual moment of slip and movement. He seems to allow words to 'get the better of him', for he controls them by allowing them to show their mastery over a speaker's intentions.

In a newspaper report, Pinter defines his wrestling with words in gentler, more accepting terms than Eliot:

My plays are getting shorter . . . words are so tender. One-act plays are all I seem to be able to write at the moment. I doubt if I will ever write something mammoth.*

If he has to work slowly in order to use words in their own way, he will accept this. If he tries to make words 'stay still' or respond to his 'way', he finds that he has destroyed the dramatic power of the words. He does not attempt, like Eliot, 'to get the better of words', but accepts their limitations in return for what they give in dramatic interplay.

The other comparison is with Samuel Beckett. His novels

* 'Shorter Pinter', *The Times*, 11 April 1969.

explore the progressive difficulty of speech and writing for the author who wishes to be sure that his utterance and himself are at one. In *The Unnamable*, this issue is crucial:

> this voice that speaks, knowing that it lies, indifferent to what it says . . . it issues from me, it fills me, it clamours against my walls, it is not mine, I can't stop it . . . it is not mine, I have none, I have no voice and I must speak, that's all I know.

Pinter ended the lecture which has already been quoted here, with a passage from this novel:

> The fact would seem to be, if in my situation one may speak of facts, not only that I shall have to speak of things of which I cannot speak, but also, which is even more interesting, but also that I, which is if possible even more interesting, that I shall have to, I forget, no matter.

The narrator of *The Unnamable* is pursued and taunted by the characters he has created, 'all these Murphys, Molloys and Malones' who seem intent on fooling him. It is here that Pinter's position is clearly distinct from Beckett's. He is an actor as well as a dramatist, and therefore partly detached from the characters he has created. No actor can work well without some detachment; otherwise he will be prey to changing moods and run the risk of losing himself in merely dramatic realities. An actor gives the characters he plays a run for their dramatic life: he can entertain the possibility of their existence, pamper them, be moved with them; but he also watches, quite coldly and silently, in order to remain outside them and control them.

Beckett and Pinter both reach moments of ultimate silence, when words have been stripped away; and Pinter is then ready and able to consider another role, mask or impersonation. He capitalizes himself a part at a time, sufficient for each character; and each character takes his knowledge further, of himself and the world around him, as well as of his art and his invented *personae*.

Pinter's scepticism about language is expressed through the dramatic form, and it grows and exists by and in the ever-changing realities of that form.

HAROLD PINTER

Gestures, Spectacle and Performance
The Caretaker, The Dwarfs and Other Plays

An actor must be able to move efficiently so that he does not tire easily in a long and strenuous role. His movements must be meaningful and good to watch, and he must be able to discover the characteristic posture and physical actions for any character he has to portray, young or old, well-balanced in personality or maimed and neurotic. To these ends, acting schools have a 'Teacher of Movement', a specialist who usually takes no other part in the task of training. In England many of these teachers have a diploma showing that they have studied with Rudolf Laban or his pupil, Sigurd Leeder. While exercising no direct influence on theatre management, playwriting or production methods, these men have had a pervasive influence on the English theatre; and this has worked all the more powerfully in that its wider manifestations have been largely unrecognized. The word 'Laban' is customarily associated with exercises for physical training and with a technical language for describing movement. But in providing for these basic needs of working actors, Laban's method has been as influential as the much more notorious 'Method' of Stanislavski.

Through Laban, actors have learnt to look intently and precisely at the physical engagement of individual figures in a group or situation, and to seize upon the essential physical characteristics of each one. Using Laban's technical language, they can describe the effectiveness of a particular silent entry on to the stage. They are able to create and control patterns in space and time using the living elements of their own bodies; they can vary rhythms and place accents. They have become aware of a play as a continuously 'speaking' picture. In short, Laban and his followers have systematized an appreciation of visual and temporal composition for the stage, an art that previously had been instinctive or borrowed piecemeal from a study of painting, sculpture, music, dance, acting and physical education. Through putting this knowledge and expertise into practice, actors have caused Laban's influence to spread to all their associates in the working theatre.

Harold Pinter has not explicitly acknowledged a debt to Laban, but in the demands he makes on actors and the essential use he makes of gesture, posture and movement, he shows an awareness of the possibilities of simple physical statement that would have been very rare thirty or forty years ago, and is rare still among playwrights not practised as actors on the stage. Pinter has said that his plays often begin in his perception of two people in a particular physical relationship to each other and to the room that contains and so helps to define them:

I went into a room one day and saw a couple of people in it. This stuck with me for some time afterwards, and I felt that the only way I could give it expression and get it off my mind was dramatically. I started off with this picture of the two people and let them carry on from there.*

Several plays later, he still talked in the same terms:

* 'Writing for Myself' (an interview with Richard Findlater), *Twentieth Century*, Vol. CLXIX (1961), 1008, p.172.

I find myself stuck with these characters who are either sitting or standing, and they've either got to walk out of a door, or come in through a door, and that's about all they can do.*

For Pinter, position, gesture and movement is rich in statement. By these essential means his characters can 'speak' without knowing it themselves. As an·actor, Pinter knows how such statements are varied and controlled, and he has an 'eye' trained to observe the smallest changes and potentialities.

In his book, *The Mastery of Movement on the Stage* (1950),† Laban compares a crowded city street with an ant hill, and points out how much more readily individuals can be distinguished in the street: they are all marked by unique 'personal effort characteristics'. The street crowd is more like a gathering of animals of all kinds than a swarm of ants or any other single species. Each human figure has an individual shape of a constitutional nature – a 'natural effort disposition' – and his moment-by-moment life is revealed by his movements, 'especially those which might be called shadow movements':

These are tiny muscular movements such as the raising of the brow, the jerking of the hand or the tapping of the foot, which have none other than expressive value. They are usually done unconsciously and often accompany movements of purposeful action like a shadow . . .‡

At any moment, then, a human being, in his body alone, expresses a basic or continuous engagement, a purposive

* 'Harold Pinter: an interview', *Paris Review*, Vol. 39 (1966), p. 20.
† Revised to incorporate improvements Laban had projected and some rewriting and additions by Lisa Ullman in 1960, under the shorter title *The Mastery of Movement* (Macdonald & Evans); quotation here is from this revised edition.
‡ Ibid., p. 12.

activity and, thirdly, an unconscious reaction or accompaniment to his conscious purpose. This is why one person entering a door can hold fascination for Pinter and, in his carefully contrived dramas, for his audiences as well.

Laban taught how to analyse every movement in terms of Weight, Space, Time and Flow. A simple and elementary exercise can give a notion of the most basic elements of this physical .vocabulary, if the reader will actually follow the instructions for himself.

As an experiment, the reader might try to pronounce the word 'no' to express different shades of meaning, and he will then easily recognize that he can say 'no' with the following actions, each producing a different sound quality and expression:
'No' with Pressing Action – firm, sustained, direct.
'No' with Flicking – gentle, sudden, flexible.
'No' with Wringing – firm, sustained, flexible.
'No' with Dabbing – gentle, sudden, direct.
'No' with Punching – firm, sudden, direct.
'No' with Floating – gentle, sustained, flexible.
'No' with Slashing – firm, sudden, flexible.
'No' with Gliding – gentle, sustained, direct.*

The object of the exercise is to show the connection between audible movements (that is speech) and visible movements. But by reversing the process, and starting with the action and then adding a vocalized 'no' in keeping with the action, the sound of the word so produced will help to define the expressive quality of the gesture. Punching, floating, slashing, gliding, etc., provide useful distinguishing marks for gestures and movements that are not purposively created and whose 'message' is not so single-minded nor so strongly expressed.

Once an actor is practically introduced to this vocabulary he may use it in the creation of characters:

* op. cit., p. 100.

The best way to acquire and develop the capacity of using movement as a means of expression on the stage is to perform simple movement scenes. First the student should become fully conscious of the character of the person to be represented, the kind of values after which he or she strives, and the circumstances in which the striving occurs. Then, as a part of his creative function as a performing artist, he must select the movements appropriate to the character, the values, and the particular situation. This selection involves intensive work. Improvisation of the acted scene, however brilliant, is not enough, nor is it sufficient to memorize a seemingly effective movement combination. What is necessary is that the student should, so to speak, get under the skin of the character to be portrayed, should penetrate the various possibilities of rendering the scene, and should *analyse everything in terms of movement.**

Such a silent exercise prepares an actor for presenting the play itself, with its added complication of speech. At no time in an acted scene should movement, the physical statement of the drama, be unmeaningful, whether directly or, through 'shadow movement', indirectly.

Laban claimed that a trained actor must be truthful and penetrating, qualities that are close to Pinter's aims as a dramatist. But the various interplays of drama are very seldom simple: perfectly co-ordinated strength, or an entire committal to one impulse, is a rare and climactic occurrence:

The shapes and rhythms of our movements are powers by which practical actions can be performed, but they also contain strong generating energies which give rise to reactions that carry beneficent or disastrous consequences. For example, charity can become egoism, if the pleasure of giving in friendship, love or sacrifice exceeds the pleasure of making other people happy. Inner impulses wishing to disguise egoism become visible in shadow

* op cit., p. 127; my italics.

moves. The warmth of a gesture may be contradicted by the cold stare of the eyes, or the twitching movements of the face muscles. One part of our body may assent, another part deny. We may breathe heavily or excitedly while otherwise displaying an external calm. The struggle of effort impulses within ourselves is part of the drama. Almost all our decisions are the result of an inner struggle which can become visible even in an entirely motionless body carriage. It is astonishing that inner struggle can be transmitted to the spectator without perceptible movement or sound. Effort analysis can explain this with great exactitude.*

To the knowledge of movement and the ability to control it, an actor needs to pursue accuracy and exactitude, and be able to resolve complications when necessary and appropriate. Here is a programme of actor-training suitable for the recreation of a 'picture' of two people in a room, such as the source of Pinter's writing for his first play.

Pinter knows the effects of Laban's training – he has experienced them at first hand in his actor's exploratory and creative physical work – and in his plays he has contrived the means to make an audience 'see' this physical language for themselves. He uses posture and movement with unavoidable directness, with inventiveness, controlled complexity and, where necessary, with ambiguity. He is often content to conclude his plays with a silent, held tableau. 'I always write,' he has said, 'in direct relation to the visual image of people walking about and standing on the stage.'†

*

The beginning of *The Caretaker* is defined wholly by movement; not a word is spoken in the first episode:

* op. cit., p. 115.
† 'Harold Pinter Replies' (an interview with Harry Thompson), *New Theatre Magazine*, Vol. II, no. 2 (1961), p. 10.

MICK *is alone in the room, sitting on the bed. He wears a leather jacket. Silence.*

He slowly looks about the room looking at each object in turn. He looks up at the ceiling, and stares at the bucket. Ceasing, he sits quite still, expressionless, looking out front.

Silence for thirty seconds.

The best way to appreciate what Pinter is requiring from his actor is for the reader to perform the actions for himself. Look at many individual objects '*in turn*'. Do this at first with ordinary speed, and then fulfil the direction to do it 'slowly'. Remember that the process is completed by looking up – at the bucket that '*hangs from the ceiling*'. This conclusion of motion results in silence during which the actor must be '*quite still, expressionless, looking out front*'. Small, purposive gestures, taken 'in turn' as if in accordance with a specific order or routine, lead to less, not greater, physical statement. If the reader gives sufficient time to this enactment, he will realize the actor's necessity of discovering *how* to cease movement so completely: it is a silent change of engagement, requiring a change of purpose and of consciousness. Is Mick satisfied with what he sees, and therefore has nothing to do but wait for something of greater importance? But if so, why is he '*expressionless*'? Is he uninterested in the outcome, or unable to imagine it? Is he consciously choosing to be inexpressive, as a trick or game, or as a training exercise? Does it imply strength or weakness?

Thirty seconds is an appreciable time for the silence to be held, so that when the drama takes a new turn from a direction outside Mick's gaze, it will sharpen attention in the audience:

Silence for thirty seconds.

A door bangs. Muffled voices are heard.

MICK *turns his head. He stands, moves silently to the door, goes out, and closes the door quietly.*

Silence.
Voices are heard again. They draw nearer, and stop. The door opens.
ASTON *and* DAVIES *enter,* ASTON *first,* DAVIES *following, shambling, breathing heavily.*

Mick's privacy is disturbed, but he acknowledges this only by moving his head: he displays almost the smallest possible reaction. In contrast to the door banging outside, he moves '*silently*' and closes the door after him '*quietly*'. In effect, this is an answer to a challenge coming from outside the room. But the audience having followed the sequence of Mick's behaviour, will still wait for a confrontation as he goes out the door. Pinter has prepared this expectation, but he thwarts it, for the stage-direction calls for another '*Silence*', not a greeting. At this point '*Voices are heard again*', coming nearer and then stopping. All eyes will be on the door as it opens: but two entirely new figures now enter. They are physically contrasted, for the second is '*shambling, breathing heavily*'. Neither betrays any sign that they have met the man who has just left.

Perhaps the audience will not consciously ask where Mick has gone, and why, nor who he was, for now their attention is held by the new contrasting pair. The one in the lead is silent like Mick, but showing purposive action as he '*puts the key in his pocket and closes the door*'. The other is not silent, but '*breathing heavily*': he will therefore draw more attention and will be seen to do what Mick had done for the direction concludes: '*DAVIES looks about the room*'. The repetition is with a difference, for he does *not* look at individual objects '*in turn*'.

By refusing all clearly audible words, by arranging repetitions and contrasts, by encouraging expectation of a meeting and then disappointing it, and, in the figure of Mick who has now left the stage, by requiring unexpected actions, each less expressive or less dynamic than normal,

Pinter has forced the audience to look closely. He has repaid them with a questioning involvement that will be the greater and more unsettling with every point they catch.

Having gained visual attention, Pinter now sustains it by words in support. The two figures are heard (as they have been seen) in relationship to the room and to each other:

ASTON: Sit down.

DAVIES: Thanks. [*Looking about.*] Uuh . . .

ASTON: Just a minute.

> [ASTON *looks around for a chair, sees one lying on its side by the rolled carpet at the fireplace, and starts to get it out.*]

DAVIES: Sit down? Huh . . . I haven't had a good sit down . . . I haven't had a proper sit down . . . well, I couldn't tell you . . .

ASTON [*placing the chair*]: Here you are.

DAVIES: Ten minutes off for a tea-break in the middle of the night in that place and I couldn't find a seat, not one. All them Greeks had it, Poles, Greeks, Blacks, the lot of them, all them aliens had it. And they had me working there . . . they had me working . . .

> [ASTON *sits on the bed, takes out a tobacco tin and papers, and begins to roll himself a cigarette.* DAVIES *watches him.*]

All them Blacks had it, Blacks, Greeks, Poles, the lot of them, that's what, doing me out of a seat, treating me like dirt. When he come at me tonight I told him.

> [*Pause.*]

ASTON: Take a seat.

DAVIES: Yes, but what I got to do first, you see, what I got to do, I got to loosen myself up, you see what I mean? I could have got done in down there.

The suggestion that Davies should 'Sit down' provokes 'Thanks', but also a repetition of his '*Looking about*' together with an inarticulate 'Uuh . . .'. Aston interprets this as looking for a chair and – looking '*around*' with simple purpose – he gets a chair from the various piles of possessions that fill the room. He places it, with 'Here you are', but Davies does not sit down; he talks of the need for a 'sit down', but he does not make the expected movement. Instead, he changes the subject of talk which makes the physical refusal still more noticeable. Aston sits on a bed, making no difficulty of being seated, and at once is silent, concentrating his attention on rolling a cigarette, a physical activity that is small in scale and has a very narrow focus of attention. In effect, Aston cuts himself off from Davies, but now 'DAVIES *watches him*' and still does not sit, even on the quite specific 'Take a seat'.

Until this moment, Pinter has held attention on Davies's refusal to accept the offered (and desired) comfort, on his unease, and lack of physical purpose beyond suspicion of the room and then of Aston, but he now gives him a decisive physical action, accompanied by a loud but incoherent cry:

> [DAVIES *exclaims loudly, punches downward with closed fist, turns his back to* ASTON *and stares at the wall. Pause.* ASTON *lights a cigarette.*]
>
> ASTON: You want to roll yourself one of these?
> DAVIES [*turning*]: What? No, no, I never smoke a cigarette. [*Pause. He comes forward.*] I'll tell you what, though. I'll have a bit of that tobacco there for my pipe, if you like.

Within Davies there was, from the beginning of the scene, some kind of aggressive energy which is expressed only in his talk (with short, piled-up rhythm) and in small physical reactions of fear and suspicion. When an inescapable offer of comfort is made, he resists until the last possible moment; but then he recalls the fight that has just taken place, and the need for self-defence, and the violence comes to the surface in the punch and cry, and the turn away from Aston.

Aston's response to the sudden activity is almost as

unexpected. He must have been concentrating on rolling his cigarette with such intensive purpose that Davies's violence does not distract him. (Later in the play he repeatedly takes pride in being good 'with his hands'.) He proceeds to light his cigarette and follows his earlier purpose by making another offer to his visitor. Davies now turns and, after a refusal and a pause, '*comes forward*' with a counter-suggestion and an acceptance.

An actor who needs to give coherence and believability to his part will have prepared for Davies's violent outburst or Aston's concentration on his cigarette. All the earlier movements and gestures will have been made in an incomplete or unbalanced way, so that these developments were implicit in them, through tensions or 'shadow movements' too small to be noticed by any but the most observant and trained in the audience. When the strong gestures come at last, they will thus be credible and inevitable, made with the authority that springs from the expression of a hitherto suppressed truth. This delayed assurance is a part of the performances that will be responded to by the audience, even if they do not consciously notice or identify it.

After the acceptance of the tobacco, Davies and Aston talk more extensively. At one point, Davies '*shambles across the room*'; but even when he comes '*face to face*' with the Buddha sitting incongruously, and thus questioningly, on the gas-stove, he simply '*looks at it and turns*'. Soon he is '*Coming closer*' to Aston again, now in a boasting vein. When he finishes his speech, which seems to demand some sort of response in acknowledgement of Davies's rights, Aston simply says, 'Uh', and then '*crosses down right, to get the electric toaster*' (p. 9). Nothing in the dialogue explains, or even refers to this action; nor to the unscrewing of the plug, the fetching of another, and the refixing that follows. Aston continues '*poking*' into the plug, through various

65

diversions, until the end of the first episode of the play. When Davies goes to bed and the '*Lights fade out*', Aston is still sitting with the plug and screwdriver in his hand (p. 21). His only verbal acknowledgement of all this activity is just before the end, when, in answer to Davies's inquiry whether he is getting in bed, he says 'I'm mending this plug' and Davies '*looks at him and then at the gas stove*'.* The activity with the toaster is thus given great prominence: the audience is forced to notice it and to observe its import- ance to Aston. The actor must enact it so that it is a re- curring, continuous and, often, overriding concern. The particular posture, the small, 'probing' gestures, and the intensely focused concentration of Aston's attention, will make their verbally unheralded effect. When verbal explanation does come, it will seem insufficient: there is still no answer to why he is mending the plug at this time, with this persistence.

Two kinds of statement are being made here through gesture and movement. One concerns an individual's motivation, the other the relationship between two figures and between them and the room. The statements are co- existent, but not even the individual statements can be fully appreciated from this extract alone. Davies's violence is a preparation for the two occasions when he draws a knife, once in self-defence and once in aggression, both much later in the play. Together these gestures sustain the underlying danger of his apparently pliant and shifty nature. Aston's cigarette-rolling and lighting prepares for his attention to the toaster and its plugs, and together these all look forward to his talk about an electric fire

* In the first version of the play (1960), Aston also explained that the plug 'doesn't work' and that he had a 'suspicion' of the 'root of the trouble'; in the second version (1962), five speeches are cut, and Aston's business with the plug is left more vague.

and to his repeated returns to the toaster. This involvement is never wholly explained, but it is significant that it stops once he has rejected Davies from his room the second time and is determined to get 'busy' with the shed in the garden (p. 76); then he turns his back on both Davies and the toaster in order to look out of the window to the garden where the shed will be built. In some way, the toaster seems to be connected with Aston's interest in Davies, a defence against him and, possibly, consciously or unconsciously, an attack.

In a long speech at the end of Act Two, noticeably without action or gesture, Aston speaks of being forced to have shock treatment in a mental hospital. He says that he had had to be quiet for a time after his escape, talking to no one so that he could lay everything 'out in order'. In hospital, he says, they had brought some electrical appliances round to him:

they looked like big pincers, with wires on, the wires were attached to a little machine. It was electric. They used to hold the man down, and this chief . . . the chief doctor, used to fit the pincers, something like earphones, he used to fit them on either side of the man's skull . . .   (p. 56)

In short, when he was being cared for in hospital, he was treated as he now treats his toaster.

In some way Aston associates his electrical appliance with revenge – 'I've often thought of going back and trying to find the man who did that to me' (p. 57) – and with 'taking care' of Davies. This, perhaps, is why he broke his self-confessed rules, did not 'steer clear of places like that café', and did talk to a stranger, one who was already being attacked. Behind the apparently trivial gestures of the first episode of the play, a conscious or subconscious intention to murder seems to be implied in the small tensions and half-hidden impulses created by the actor to account for his strange actions and to give cohesion to his role. There are other correspondences between this hospital speech and unexplained activity that Aston makes in the presence of Davies: why did he have a sheet and pillow ready for his visitor's bed? Why make him don a white coat as caretaker, one that hung ready by his bed? Why have a glaring light over Davies's bed? Why wake him up and examine his face? All these actions are paralleled by what Aston says, or infers, had happened in the hospital. Through the emphasis of oddity and repetition, and through surprising interplay with words, Aston's silent activity will catch the audience's attention, perhaps without them being able to pinpoint or name them as the source of their apprehension for the safety of Davies and of Aston.

In shorter compass, Mick also has gestures in this first episode that must be given precise meaning by an actor. Only a sense of committal to some unspoken purpose will explain his stealthy exit, his lack of surprise, his stillness. Does he expect Aston to find a victim? Does he 'take care' of his brother, by allowing him to 'take care' of himself by finding an unknown victim? An actor will need to know, for it is far harder, if not impossible, to act such details without some sustaining 'through line' of intention and some cohesive purpose and 'natural effort disposition'. Again, the 'meaning' of these gestures depends on Mick's role as a whole. In his last appearance in the play, when he has smashed his brother's Buddha, crying 'THAT'S WHAT I WANT!', and has passionately asserted that he has his other worries, he denies interest in the house and Aston:

I'm not worried about this house. I'm not interested. My brother can worry about it. . . . I'm not bothered. I thought I was

68

doing him a favour, letting him live here. He's got his own ideas.
Let him have them. I'm going to chuck it in.   (p. 74)

Again '*A door bangs*' and in the ensuing silence neither Mick
nor Davies moves:

[ASTON *comes in. He closes the door, moves into the room and faces*
MICK. *They look at each other. Both are smiling, faintly.*]

Here is the confrontation missing in the first episode, and
together they silently express complicity and satisfaction.
Mick is about to speak, but leaves instead; and then:

[ASTON *leaves the door open, crosses behind* DAVIES, *sees the broken
Buddha, and looks at the pieces for a moment. He then goes to his bed,
takes off his overcoat, sits, takes the screwdriver and plug and pokes the
plug.*]

Significant changes are that Aston leaves the door open,
that he ignores the Buddha, which he had been pleased to
get 'hold of' (p. 18), moves straight to the plug, and does
not bother to speak to either Davies or Mick. The relationships between the brothers are clearly revalued by this
resumption of silence and this assumption of independence.
Within Mick's first, unsmiling silence there must have
been the possibility of this other relationship. If the last
one is to be true, some tensions must have been contained
in the first, waiting to be resolved; or else tensions must
develop, so that, even after his '*passionate*' outburst, Mick is
under some constraint as he leaves Aston in possession.

Pinter is aware that physical performance expresses
inner conflicts and resolutions. He insists that the verbal
drama yield at times to silent passages where the audience
is forced to look, and so to perceive impulses and reactions
that would be altered out of all recognition or just proportion had they been expressed in words. If this physical
language is seldom precise, that is one of its strengths, for

many of the deepest and most irresistible human impulses
are not easily limited or defined: it is these motivations that
Pinter wishes to explore and show in his plays. The interplay between physical and verbal drama, whether by
contrast or correspondence, strengthens expressions of the
indefinable, gives it associations and enforces attention.

*

Pinter's use of movement and gesture has been influenced
and developed through his writing for television. In 1961 he
acknowledged that the cutting from scene to scene that is a
characteristic of that medium had led him to see his work
'more and more in terms of pictures'.* The television play,
A Night Out (1960), though written first for radio, depends
for a major development in the plot on a visual effect:

[*The camera closes on* MR RYAN's *hand, resting comfortably on his knee,
and then to his face which, smiling vaguely, is inclined to the ceiling. It
must be quite clear from the expression that it was his hand which
strayed.*]   (p. 67)

This is the only '*clear*' indication that the impropriety for
which Albert, the central character, is being blamed, is
not his responsibility. In this play, one scene is entirely
visual:

The kitchen. The MOTHER *is putting* ALBERT's *dinner into the oven.
She takes the alarm clock from the mantelpiece and puts it on the table.
She takes out a pack of cards, sits at the table and begins to lay out a game
of patience. Close up of her, broodingly setting out the cards. Close up of
the clock. It is seven forty-five.*   (p. 57)

Such a direction is comfortably within the usual range of
domestic television drama, but at the end of the play,
where the Mother talks purposefully and, then, with

* 'Writing for Myself', *Twentieth Century*, Vol. CLXIX (1961), 1008,
p. 174.

growing intimacy, to the silent figure of her son, Albert, Pinter uses the same technique as at the end of *The Caretaker* where Davies talks and Aston, his back turned on him, is silent. The main difference is that the close-up provided by the television camera has led Pinter to take more time with non-verbal elements and to define more precisely the small gestures and facial expressions appropriate to the developing situation:

> [*He sits heavily, loosely, in a chair, his legs stretched out. Stretching his arms, he yawns luxuriously, scratches his head with both hands and stares ruminatively at the ceiling, a smile on his face. His mother's voice calls his name.*]
>
> MOTHER [*from the stairs*]: Albert!
>
> [*His body freezes. His gaze comes down. His legs slowly come together. He looks in front of him.*]   (p. 86)

In scripts for films, notably *The Servant*, *The Pumpkin Eater* and *Accident*, Pinter has controlled far larger 'pictures', relating physical attitudes and small gestures to wide landscapes and crowded interior scenes. Among his other works, this talent can be seen in *The Tea Party* (1965), a television play which was written in a 'cinematic' idiom.* Its climactic scene is a tea party, served buffet-style, by two elderly ladies to assembled friends and families. Disson, the central character, is again silent as the others talk of cakes and children, twins and second helpings. The effect is accentuated by an entirely filmic device that would be impossible in the theatre:

> DISSON's *point of view.*
> *No dialogue is heard in all shots from* DISSON's *point of view.*
> *Silence.*
> *Figures mouthing silently, in conspiratorial postures, seemingly whispering together.*   (p. 49)

* Interview, *Paris Review*, Vol. 39 (1966), p. 20.

But again the play ends with a group of two, the hero silent and his wife, Diana, speaking:

DISSON *in the chair, still, his eyes open.*
DIANA *comes to him.*
  She kneels by him.
DIANA: This is . . . Diana.
  [*Pause.*]
  Can you hear me?   (p. 53)

When she has said all she can, there is a final, still more restricted image:

DISSON's *face in close-up.*
DISSON's *eyes. Open.*

The television play, *The Basement* (1967), is a revision of an original film script which Pinter entitled *The Compartment.* Here the fluidity of film is used to change the setting against which the three characters are seen: it is, successively, summer and winter; seashore, back yard, entrance area and interior. The interior is at first decorated in comfortable and rather heavy style; then the same room is in Scandinavian style, then in Italian Renaissance style and lastly, it is completely bare. The behaviour and relationships of the characters change according to changes in the setting. Moreover, the point of view is continually altered, the camera, for example, juxtaposing shots of the girl preparing coffee and of the two men fighting with broken milk bottles. Yet at the end, after these many filmic devices, Pinter reverts to a more general sustained view, that could easily be achieved in a theatre. One man opens the front door to another and greets him while the visitor laughs. Here the simple action and words are meaningful, not because of a special camera angle, but because they duplicate exactly the words and actions at the beginning of the play, only the visitor of the opening shots is now the host. The freedom of the film has again led Pinter back to a view of characters in action that is similar to his theatrical practice.

Essentially Pinter is concerned with human confrontations, seen intently. He seems to seek the tangibility of the theatre, the restriction to one stage and to life-sized people, to a single viewpoint and to consecutive events. However much he uses the devices of cutting and montage, and however important a facial expression or imaginary sights may be to this subject matter, he works most consistently in theatrical terms where, as he has said, he is 'stuck' with his characters and their continuous physical embodiment:

What *is* so different about the stage is that you're just *there*, stuck – there are your characters stuck on the stage, you've got to live with them and deal with them.*

He has developed his ways of making his audience see those characters with his own patient and never surprised view, whether he uses a wide focus or a narrow, whether he complicates the drama with filmic devices or follows through the actions of two persons in a room or on a stage.

*

In his concern for the physical facts of human encounter and the expressive power of visual images, Pinter shares a common desire to claim for the theatre a language that is more substantial and less intellectually perceived than a wholly literary language. The most extreme prophet of a physical theatre was Antonin Artaud whose essay on 'Metaphysics and the *Mise en scène*' was translated into English in *The Theater and Its Double* (1958):

Dialogue – a thing written and spoken – does not belong specifically to the stage, it belongs to books, as is proved by the fact that

* Interview, *Paris Review*, Vol. 39 (1966), p. 50.

in all handbooks of literary history a place is reserved for the theater as a subordinate branch of the history of the spoken language. I say that the stage is a concrete physical place which asks to be filled, and to be given its own concrete language to speak.

I say that this concrete language, intended for the senses and independent of speech, has first to satisfy the senses, that there is a poetry of the senses as there is a poetry of language, and that this concrete physical language to which I refer is truly theatrical only to the degree that the thoughts it expresses are beyond the reach of the spoken language.*

This physical language goes beyond the expressiveness of human beings in action such as Laban learnt to control. It uses objects and actions that are expressive in themselves, independent of any particular human being or verbal accompaniment. For Artaud, the art of theatre should become more and more like a Balinese Dance in order to rediscover its unique validity. In his projected theatre:

Every spectacle will contain a physical and objective element, perceptible to all. Cries, groans, apparitions, surprises, theatricalities of all kinds, magic beauty of costumes taken from certain ritual models; resplendent lighting, incantational beauty of voices, the charms of harmony, rare notes of music, colors of objects, physical rhythm of movements whose crescendo and decrescendo will accord exactly with the pulsation of movements familiar to everyone, concrete appearances of new and surprising objects, masks, effigies yards high, sudden changes of light, the physical action of light which arouses sensations of heat and cold, etc. . . .†

Pinter has never divorced theatre from the scale of ordinary

* *The Theater and Its Double* (Grove Press, 1958), p. 37.
† 'The Theater of Cruelty (First Manifesto)', *The Theater and Its Double* (Grove Press, 1958), p. 93.

life or the presentation of recognizable images of human beings in action, but he has extended his language by the use he makes of objects and physical activities. As he gives special significance to a single word by careful placing, timing, repetition or supporting gesture, so he makes a physical detail speak with more precise meaning and gain more attention than is usual in stage plays or in life. The rolling of a cigarette and the 'probing' of electrical appliances in *The Caretaker* are expressive not only as a manifestation of Aston's inner involvement, his nervous state of being, but also in their own right, because of their own physical natures. The thin, whiteish paper, the straggling tobacco and the fingers rolling and the tongue licking; the three wires, with bared ends, the identical, brass terminals and the tightly planned plastic container – these small objects are registered by the audience, over against the untidy jumble and shabbiness of the stage-set. These objects, given such prominence, change the audience's manner of looking, and they awaken associations and expectations beyond those of the dramatic situation and dialogue. They speak of careful fuss and of mechanical exactitude and impersonality.

While Pinter does not use the large-scale physical assault advocated by Artaud, he does use carefully selected objects with blatant theatricality. In *The Homecoming* (1965) Ruth is offered a glass of water by Lenny, her brother-in-law whom she has just met for the first time; they are alone in the living-room of her husband's old home. He then pours a glass for himself, and soon he has told her two stories about himself which display a casual brutality. He then offers to 'relieve you of your glass'; she refuses, and the glass, now half-empty, becomes an object for contention:

RUTH: I haven't quite finished.
LENNY: You've consumed quite enough, in my opinion.

RUTH: No, I haven't.

LENNY: Quite sufficient, in my own opinion.

RUTH: Not in mine, Leonard.

[*Pause.*]

LENNY: Don't call me that, please.

RUTH: Why not?

LENNY: That's the name my mother gave me.

[*Pause.*]

Just give me the glass.

RUTH: No.

[*Pause.*]

LENNY: I'll take it then.

RUTH: If you take the glass . . . I'll take you.

[*Pause.*]

LENNY: How about me taking the glass without you taking me?

RUTH: Why don't I just take you?

[*Pause.*]

LENNY. You're joking.

[*Pause.*]

You're in love, anyway, with another man. You've had a secret liaison with another man. His family didn't even know. Then you come here without a word of warning and start to make trouble.

[*She picks up the glass and lifts it towards him.*]

RUTH: Have a sip. Go on. Have a sip from my glass.

[*He is still.*]

Sit on my lap. Take a long cool sip.

[*She pats her lap. Pause.*

She stands, moves to him with the glass.]

Put your head back and open your mouth.

LENNY: Take that glass away from me.

RUTH: Lie on the floor. Go on. I'll pour it down your throat.

LENNY: What are you doing, making me some kind of proposal?

[*She laughs shortly, drains the glass.*]

RUTH: Oh, I was thirsty.

[*She smiles at him, puts the glass down, goes into the hall and up the stairs.*

He follows into the hall and shouts up the stairs.]
LENNY: What was that supposed to be? Some kind of proposal?
[*Silence.*
He comes back into the room, goes to his own glass, drains it.]

(pp. 33–5)

A glass of wine, a cup of coffee, a glass of gin and tonic (or of any other liquid that looked like water), would not have the same effect. The clear water, at the bottom of the clear glass, especially as it tends to sparkle in the stage-lighting, makes its own specific effect as it stands untouched on the table at Ruth's side, associated with her (for she has drunk some), but separate and complete on its own. The digression about Lenny's name serves, in part, to direct attention back to this small object, still unchanged.

When Lenny threatens to 'take' the glass, Ruth, with only a slight hesitation, equates him with the glass, as if both were of identical importance, weight and significance. The glass has become almost a 'joke', but she then picks it up, lifts it towards him and offers 'a sip'. The glass has now become a potential means of contact, suggesting lip contact, and then, coolness. Perhaps Ruth tilts the glass, and certainly the water will move, catching the light, as she moves towards him. She then asks him to put 'your head back and open your mouth'; it now menaces, for it could be poured over him. She then suggests lying on 'the floor' and pouring it down his throat. He is not on the floor, but the glass is in her hand, its water still moving, perhaps very slightly, now that she is still. When Lenny questions, her laugh releases the tension and she '*drains the glass*'; it is empty in a moment and now a matter of inconsequence. Once she is gone, Lenny 'goes' at once to his own glass, identical in all objective respects, and '*drains it*' without hesitation or words.

A glass of water is both a casual household object and, in

77

a desert or battlefield, an image of life-source and life-saving. In a dream it might be sought after or protected. In ordinary life it is a simple necessity, or bare civility. It is normally passed between two people with simple, un-reflecting care as it is offered and accepted; but it is ad-ministered to another only with difficulty – unless the recipient is very willing and accommodating. It could be sipped, or drunk or gulped; spilt or thrown, or ignored. It is colourless yet light-catching. The water is still if the glass is untouched; if the glass is touched, the water is either moving or almost still. Pinter has used all these properties of this object, variously and in meaningful sequence. When, a few moments later, the father says that Lenny is drunk or mad, the son replies by pouring *another glass of water* and the glass, which this time is ignored, will still speak to the audience, invoking expectations and associations beyond those directly indicative of Lenny's state of mind.

The expressive objects in Pinter's plays never lose their relationship to the characters portrayed, but the characters seem to be drawn to objects and activities as if finding in them a satisfaction or reaction stronger than silence or words. Stanley in *The Birthday Party* is given a drum, and the climax to the first Act is his tapping the drum-sticks together and then tapping the drum. Soon he is marching round the room beating the drum *regularly*; the beating becomes *erratic, uncontrolled*, and at the end of the scene he is *banging the drum, his face and the drumbeat now savage and possessed*. This is, specifically, a 'boy's drum', a toy that yields fierce sound only by disproportionate beating. In Act Two, the drum is reintroduced by Meg, who is now dressed in party clothes, and is placed by McCann so that the blindfolded Stanley stumbles into it and catches his foot. Finally it gives a broken but *sustained rat-a-tat* as Stanley strikes it on its side in the dark. In the third Act, the drum lies broken in the fireplace until Meg notices it and strikes it with her hand to make some sort of '*noise*'. It is now a broken, misused toy, of concern only to Meg who had bought it for Stanley. It is dismissed by Petey, with 'You can always get another one, Meg' (p. 70). Many other objects could have been used to provide the savage climax of Act One, but the little garishly painted drum and its various noises offered to Pinter a special sequence of effects. The drum stands out by its incongruity in a childless family; it awakens specific images of 'innocent' infancy and infantry warfare. Like Stanley, it could be broken and emit only broken sounds.

The drum gave such a range of effects because Stanley, Meg and McCann used it and explored it. So, in *The Caretaker*, Mick pursues Davies with the sucking nozzle of an Electrolux vacuum-cleaner. This happens in the dark, before the audience have seen or (in the revised text) heard of this machine. Later Mick says he has been cleaning the room, but the vacuum machine is rather his chosen weapon to frighten Davies with its sound and its half-seen shape. In the half light it suggests a devouring, sinuous, sustained extension of his own predatory suspicion, and of his desire to dominate. The fact that once the light is switched on there is not even a paper dragon but a familiar household object, is a dramatic anti-climax that destroys any threat at once, except that which remains in Mick himself and in his taunting mockery. This object tends to disappear into the rest of the room and not retain significant associations as does Stanley's drum, or the glass of water in *The Homecoming*.

In *The Dwarfs* (stage version, 1963) Len's attention is drawn to a sequence of objects each of which remains obstinately itself and unmoving. Here Pinter is using the inert quality of physical matter to accentuate the changing imaginary world of distrust and fear, the strange and horrible realities that these objects have in the mind of someone who sees them as almost living entities. The objects remain static or are moved with assurance and smoothness, but the perceiver is dynamic and insecure. At first, the objects Len notices are deficient or unaccommodating: his recorder has 'something wrong' with it (p. 91); the milk can't be found, and the gherkins which he discovers are unacceptable; then the milk is solid in the bottle. A curious toasting-fork which Pete sees on the wall and takes up is dismissed lightly by Len, who knows that it is Portuguese, but a little later Len sees Pete's hand '*lying open, palm upward*' as it has been for some time, and that is 'not normal' for him. He takes a look at it, '*gasps through his teeth*', and pronounces Pete a 'homicidal maniac' (p. 95): the unremarkable, unmoving hand has detonated fears of huge significance in Len's mind. In one speech Len directs attention to a table, chair, bowl of fruit, curtains, an absence of wind, the shoes on his feet; for him almost any object can assume frightening proportions or insubstantiality, or mobility. The audience is made to see both the normal, unchanging physical objects and the ever-changing reactions, defined by each other, through contrast and close attention.

*

The Dwarfs was first written as a novel (which remains unpublished), and then as a radio play. Only after its production in sound alone, was it adapted for stage performance, directed by the author himself. A fourth version (1968) represents a further revision for the stage. This history might suggest, for another author's play, that physical objects and physical performance are of secondary importance, but always, even in the radio version, objects and gestures are essential for the action and for the very sense of the play.

At one point, in stage and radio versions, Len sees the toasting-fork again and takes it to Mark, its owner. Now he says it is 'a funny toasting-fork' and asks if Mark ever makes any toast (p. 104). Then he drops the fork on the floor and while Mark makes no response, he speaks, to Mark and then to himself:

Don't touch it! You don't know what will happen if you touch it! You mustn't touch it! You mustn't bend! Wait. [*Pause.*] I'll bend. I'll . . . pick it up. I'm going to touch it. [*Pause . . . softly.*] There. You see? Nothing happens when I touch it. Nothing. Nothing can happen. No one would bother. [*A broken sigh.*]

At first, he is testing Mark, or trying to bring him to share his fears; but the inertness of the fork brings him back to himself and in his failure to cope with Mark he now seems as helpless as the fork itself. Here Pinter uses a single object lying still and one character sitting still, as contrasts for Len's frightening instability.

In the first radio version, this scene is followed by a soliloquy in which Len objectifies himself, so that his actions leave the same kind of impression as Pete's or Mark's:

Pete talks. Mark talks. I talk. We sit. He stands.
The other stands. I stand. (p. 103)

Soon he says he is standing 'on my hands', but this gesture of Len's has little effect on the others, for his next thought is simply, 'They glance. They talk.' A moment or two later Len is saying 'I reply', and his activity grows in violence. The imagined business grows in complexity, but Len still retains the unvaryingly simple means of expression, as if he is determined to control his grasp of events; or, perhaps, as if everything he describes is in his mind only, and incapable of affecting his feelings or perception.

They glance, and smile, and talk, and walk, and talk.
I turn, bump, ricochet, dodge, retreat, pirouette.

Either Len's responses are deadened, or they have never come alive in this soliloquy. By the end, he has become still: all is silent and only Pete and Mark move:

Pete and Mark drink their tea.
We watch.

Len has become the passive observer, cornered or caught by his own untrusting imagination. He cannot communicate the fears which would alone account for the violent activity because they are for ever shut within his own consciousness.

The next scene is back to normal: Mark pours whisky for Pete, who talks. Len is sitting in one of the two armchairs in Mark's room; Mark sits in the other and Pete stands. But now the human beings lack some obvious responses: neither takes '*any notice of Len*'. He is not offered a drink, or spoken to. And he takes no notice of his two friends, neither rising from his seat nor greeting them. Len, however, does speak, but about himself, and an insect and a few inanimate objects:

I squashed a tiny insect on a plate the other day. And I brushed the remains off my finger, with my thumb. Then I saw that the fragments were growing, like fluff. As they were falling, they were becoming larger, like fluff. I had put my hand into the body of a dead bird.

Len's words betray some mental contact between him and the others, for Pete has just spoken about fighting, guttersnipes and the time to act, and he follows Len with talk of a nutcracker cracking nuts as Len's fingers had squashed an insect. But Len's awareness is his own alone. A seemingly stable environment – even Mark and Pete seem fixed in attitudes and behaviour – is perceived by Len as a challenge and attack upon himself.

When Pete and Mark seem most engaged with each other, Len imagines the Dwarfs of the title, active in hostility, self-absorption or observation. These are human and in-human, a mixture of the elements that Len is wrestling with, but they are not real creatures or objects, and their activi-ties are wholly fantastic, not even possible in actuality:

they've got a new game, did I tell you? It's to do with beetles and twigs. There's a rockery of red-hot cinder. I like watching them. Their hairs are curled and oily on their necks. Always squatting and bending, dipping their wicks in the custard. Now and again a lick of flame screws up their noses. Do you know what they do? They run wild . . .   (3rd edn, p. 106)

In a soliloquy in the first and second versions, the Dwarfs appear more physically alive and purposive than any human being:

They eat, too, in a chuckle of fingers. Backchat of bone, crosstalk of bristled skin.   (1st edn, p. 103)

Towards the end of the play, the scene moves to a hospital, and Len is actually caught in a physical apparatus. Pete and Mark are visitors free to come and go, but Len is in a hospital bed, without his usual clothes, surrounded with white sheets and pillows, unmoving, and with wireless earphones attached to his head: 'They can't do enough for me here . . . Because I'm no trouble,' he says. Passive, he now sees himself to be treated 'like a king'; and he now believes Mark, who had always intimidated him, 'looks as though he's caught a crab'. The scene ends with Len objecting to his friends sitting on his bed and they leave him. When Len next enters it is for the last scene in the play: he now hears nothing of the Dwarfs, but imagines them ready for a 'quick get out', and there is 'All about me the change'; everything, except for some sort of garden, is bare and clean. The final images in his mind's eye are not obviously horrible, but Len is alone in the central 'area of isolation' that Pinter asks for in the stage-set (p. 91), and he finds it 'insupportable'.

In this play, in its first version wholly aural in means of communication, the entire action depends on Len's changing consciousness of persons, places and things. It shows his fight with their powers of suggestion, his struggle to 'keep up with it' (p. 112) and with himself. It concludes with his submission to treatment and his remaining fear of almost nothing. *The Dwarfs* is an exploration of a man and his environment. It discovers an infinitely variable world within small compass, where movement and stillness, speech and silence, are alike both frightening and unremarkable. There is dialogue, but words are dependent on a physical reality which is not monstrously constructed like Artaud's imaginary theatrical spectacles, but normal and precisely realized either on stage or else in the physical implications of the words. The dramatic energy springs from Len's perception of the environment and is expressed in his subsequent reactions in words and behaviour. The more sensitive and expressive the actor and the more unremarkable the details of stage-set and properties, the greater the chance of the play gaining full hold over an audience. In this play, Pinter does not express his concern with physical objects and environment in a dominating and surprising 'objective element perceptible to all', but in using his sense of environment as the basis, the material and the contrast for a temperamental, vocal and physical role of unusual range and affecting intensity.

Pinter's theatrical language, even in this radio play, is not simply 'a thing written and spoken', independent of response to objective environment. It makes 'sense' only in production, in a sound recording or in the theatre, where the 'concrete' is realized as an essential and changing part of an individual life. Here is no divorce between sensation and thought, of the kind that Artaud condemned as leading to a merely verbal and literary drama.

*

The Dwarfs is a very special case that demonstrates in unusually explicit verbal terms, as well as in actions, the questioning and mobile nature of Pinter's perception of physical objects. The same quality is apparent in plays where the physical element is less easy to describe, and where reactions depend less on verbal reactions and more on purely physical performance. Often the effect is assured, in these plays, by divergence between the physical reactions of two or more characters. In *The Caretaker*, there is a bucket suspended from the ceiling, which sometimes shows the insecurity the characters feel in the room that shelters them, and sometimes is a matter of indifference, as if it were merely a part of the general lumber that Aston has accumulated. Attention is first drawn to the bucket by Mick in the silent opening of the play: it is the last item in the room he looks at, and he 'stares' at it rather than '*looks*'. Davies is the next to notice, and he does so 'suddenly' (p. 21) when he is questioned about the man he says has his papers at Sidcup. Davies says nothing and Aston changes the subject by inviting him to get into bed when he wants, but the bucket remains in his mind and when he lays aside his coat and trousers he refers to it, 'I see you got a bucket up here'. The answer to this is 'Leak' and that seems to satisfy Davies, but he again '*looks up*' as he proceeds to get into bed. The three characters have each, now, reacted to the bucket, and each reaction is different. Left alone in the room at the end of Act One, Davies grows in confidence:

some paint buckets remind him of the bucket hanging above and he looks up again; this time he '*grimaces*', remarks 'I'll have to find out about that' (p. 28), and gets on with his exploration of the junk in the room. Reactions to a single physical object have shown the bias of each mind, the disposition of character, that is all the clearer because the various responses seem to be no part of their conscious, pre-arranged efforts or speech.

Davies next looks at the bucket at the beginning of Act Two, and he looks with Mick who is beginning to interrogate him. A '*drip*' in the bucket overhead (p. 30) has this time drawn their attention, and the audience's. Neither speaks of it, but '*Mick looks back to Davies*'. The next drip causes only Davies to look up, and again neither speaks. The third drip is when Aston has joined the others and '*They all look up*' (p. 37), and it is this which causes Mick to break the silence with which Aston had been greeted. Now the bucket has given occasion for a challenge:

You still got that leak.
ASTON: Yes.
    [*Pause.*]
It's coming from the roof.
MICK: From the roof, eh?
ASTON: Yes.

They continue to talk, Aston assuring his brother that tarring the roof will do what is needed 'for the time being'. Mick merely replies with 'Uh', but after another pause Davies asks '*abruptly*', 'What do you do?' – '*They both look at him.*' – 'What do you do . . . when that bucket's full?' After a pause Aston says merely, 'Empty it', and, after another pause, Mick seems again to challenge Aston about decorating the flat. So the drips have entered the play to redirect attention to the bucket, which is now, for Davies,

86

a clearer, practical matter, but still a cause of apprehension; for the brothers it awakens challenge and defence. Aston breaks his brother's line of inquiry by speaking to Davies, 'I got your bag'; Mick rises to snatch it from him and a game of grab, snatch and hide follows between the three of them. Only when Aston takes the bag from Davies, gives it to Mick and Mick gives it to Davies, who at first grasps it then drops it and after a pause picks it up again, only then, when the brothers have so agreed that Davies should have it and he has given them a chance to take it back again, do peace and silence return. At this point the drip in the bucket sounds: ' *They all look up* ' (p. 39), and not one of them says anything about it. Aston asks if Davies has done what he said he would that day. When the three have worked out their play for possession of the bag, the bucket cannot disturb them; they simply perceive that a drip of water has fallen.

For the rest of the play, the bucket hangs there, but it means almost nothing to the three characters. Only Davies speaks of it to Mick, rather blandly, at the beginning of Act Three, supposing that the cracks must have been tarred over, for he has heard no more drips. Neither looks up now, only the audience in the theatre. The bucket is still visible: but Mick and Davies are now concerned with Aston, and for the rest of the play there are other matters to take care of: the bed, a clock, Davies's papers at Sidcup, their treatment of each other, Davies's smell, Mick's interests outside the room, Aston's desire to build a shed in the garden and, above all, who is in possession of the room, bucket or no bucket. Reactions to a physical object, placed conspicuously and capable of making a sound of its own accord, has helped to define and expose the course of the action within the minds of the characters, the level at which the prime concerns of the drama are fully operative.

87

In Pinter's short story, *The Examination,* published with *The Lover* and *The Collection* in 1963, the narrator tells how he starts to examine Kullus and is reassured by his own room, the objects he has chosen for it, the intervals in their talk: these elements speak to him of his power over the examinee. But the comparative freedom that the narrator allows to Kullus in the intervals between phases of examination begin to disturb the arrangement. Kullus asserts his preference for moving towards the window. The short-story form allows Pinter to describe, as it were in slow-motion, the changes in the narrator's perception of the room consequent on his visitor's movements:

When the door opened. When Kullus, unattended, entered, and the interim ended. I turned from all light in the window, to pay him due regard and welcome. Whereupon without reserve or hesitation, he moved from the door as from shelter, and stood in the light from the window. So I watched the entrance become vacant, which had been his shelter. And observed the man I had welcomed, he having crossed my border.   (p. 91)

Very little outward sign of these changes would be visible if the episode were acted, yet together such small changes do make a large impact. Kullus begins to alter the environment:

And when he removed the blackboard, I offered no criticism. And when he closed the curtains I did not object.

This is followed only by one line: 'For we were now in Kullus's room', implying a wholesale change of perception rather than the obvious, outward transformation of the room itself.

By repeated references to things and actions, by contrasting reactions, by changing tensions, intentions and awarenesses within his characters, Pinter's plays in performance give the audience an acute and sensitive awareness of activities, objects and environment, and of men and women involved with them and unsettled by them. Given this subject matter it is extraordinary how objective and naturally scaled the stage-spectacle and stage-behaviour remain. The power of the drama depends on sequence and contrast rather than obvious size. The stage-sets and properties are all precisely 'practicable', following the dimensions of ordinary life and looking worn or new strictly according to their relationships to character and situation.

If all the entries of *The Homecoming* are examined on their own, as a repeated stage-device that is sure to catch the audience's attention, Pinter's careful placing of various effects can be observed. The differences between sitting and standing, between standing in the doorway or hall and walking into or around the room, between speaking first, or second, or not for some considerable time, between being greeted or ignored, all these are used to express changes in character involvement. The declensions of entry have been carefully studied and used, to create a precise physical language without resorting, on more than a few occasions, to verbal support.

*

Speaking of his work on the film-script for *Accident*, Pinter discussed the benefits of his kind of objectivity:

. . . suppose a character is walking down a lane, this lane, as we are now. You could easily note down a stream of thought which might be perfectly accurate and believable, and then translate it into a series of images: road, field, hedge, grass, corn, wheat, ear, her ear on the pillow, tumbled hair, love, love years ago . . . But when one's mind wanders and associates things in this way it's perfectly unselfconscious. Do exactly the same thing on film and the result is precious, self-conscious, over-elaborate – you're using absurdly complex means to convey something very simple.

Instead, you should be able to convey the same sort of apprehension not by opening out, proliferating, but by closing in, looking closer and closer, harder and harder at things that are there before you.

For example, it seems to me that *Marienbad* works very well in its own terms, on the level of fantasy. But there is another way of doing it, and one I personally would find more interesting to explore. In a real, recognizable Paris, an ordinary, reasonably attractive woman sits at a café table, wearing what she would be wearing, eating and drinking what she would be eating and drinking. An equally ordinary, everyday sort of man comes up to her. 'Excuse me, but don't you remember, we met last year at Marienbad?' 'Marienbad? Impossible – I was never in Marienbad last year . . .', and she gets up, walks out to an ordinary, believable street and gets into a real taxi . . . And so on. Wouldn't that be just as strange and mysterious and frightening as the way the film does it? Perhaps more so, because of the very ordinariness of the surroundings and apparent normality of the characters.

It's something of that sort of feeling we're trying to get here . . . It's just the same as the way that a novelist may need five or six pages to introduce a character, to tell us what we need to know about his appearance, age, bearing, education, social background and so on. In a film the actor just walks into a room and it's done, it's all there – or should be. So in this film everything is buried, it is implicit. There is really very little dialogue, and that is mostly trivial, meaningless. The drama goes on inside the characters, and by looking hard at the smooth surface we come to see something of what is going on underneath.*

In Pinter's *Landscape* and *Silence*, both first produced on stage in 1969, the range of physical behaviour allowed to the actors is enormously reduced. For *Landscape* there is only one, initial, stage-direction, other than *Pause*, *Silence* or

* Interview with John Russell Taylor, *Sight and Sound*, Vol. XXXV (1966), pp. 183–4.

(once) *Long Silence*. It describes the 'kitchen of a country house' and the position of two seated figures, and then adds a 'NOTE':

DUFF *refers normally to* BETH, *but does not appear to hear her voice.*
BETH *never looks at* DUFF, *and does not appear to hear his voice.*
Both characters are relaxed, in no sense rigid.

They speak of activity and objects; of touch, sight, hearing and taste; of 'stinging', 'wooing', being 'excited' and 'flurried', of being 'naked' and trying to 'listen', of a 'desolate beach' and a house 'running like clockwork'. Their thoughts are full of physical things, but as they sit relaxed and only partly in contact with each other the audience is forced to close in, and look more and more intensely, harder and harder, at things that are there before them: the faces, the relaxed bodies, the intimations of what these two characters know, or sense, of what has happened, or might have happened, to them, between them and individually. Pinter has dared to make a 'smooth surface' that does nothing, itself, to attract attention. He risks this without lessening but, rather, by still further particularizing, his apprehension of their physical beings, surroundings and properties. None of his plays introduces more reference to persons off-stage who are of importance to what is told of the characters; none is so descriptive of objects and movements whether of people, dogs, ducks, children or machines; none has more references to the sea, rain, shadow or sunlight. The activity portrayed through the two enigmatical presences and their voices is highly contrasted: Duff finishes with 'bang' and 'slam – ' as he speaks of assaulting Beth; she finishes by speaking of quiet acceptance. Beth's thoughts are conscious of the silent sky above her and the gentle sound of the tide, and then of herself speaking: 'Oh my true love I said'. The actor's task in giving credibility to the quietness of the setting, the relaxed beings of the two characters and the contrasts and implications of what they say, in the sequence that is directed, will first of all demand a careful and imaginative realization of the physical realities lying behind their words, and then an unforced expressiveness of utterance. The task that the audience will find thrust upon it, is close attention, the need for listening to nuance and looking hard. The experience of the play in performance will seem all the more mysterious, sensitive and frightening by being contained and transmitted by such perilous, 'ordinary' means. For many members of the audience, the effort and precision will be a waste of time; few if any will be sure of what they have heard and seen.

While developing a theatrical language that speaks through appeal to the senses as well as through words, Pinter has not used the pulsating, irresistible force envisioned by Artaud, with its obvious assault on emotions and its reliance on shock and cruelty. He can and has used two or three figures held still, caught, in small areas, vibrating according to their own relaxed, yet insistent wills.

3

Action and Control
The Homecoming and Other Plays

Harold Pinter has explored words and gestures so consciously and meticulously that he may seem more interested
in theatre language than in theatre speech. He treats the
money in his pocket with extraordinary care, but is never
seen to purchase anything with it. He *seems* to be like the vin-
tage car enthusiast who keeps his vehicle in a garage, in per-
fect working order, and never uses it for going on a journey
– only his car is constructed from up-to-the-minute materials,
and he is always making new parts, or rather, new cars.

Such views of Pinter's finesse gather strength because
nowhere do his plays contain argument about the nature of
life, nor do they give explicit expression to policies or
prophecies. On reflection, his scepticism about words is
sufficient cause for this, but it is disconcerting to have
nothing to quote in order to illustrate an author's engagement with the world he lives in. Moreover, the basic
elements of drama, the normal structural foundations,
seem inconsiderable in his plays. The plots are slight, and
can be told in few words. The characters do not explain
where they have come from, or the causes of their attitudes
and actions. Social and political background is sketched
only by passing remarks, hints and ambiguities. There
seems little substance in either narrative or theme, or
social portraiture.

Pinter, himself, has encouraged us to suppose that he writes without any palpable purpose: 'What I write has no obligation to anything other than to itself', he once said.* He has never contrived a play as vehicle or embodiment for 'any kind of abstract idea', and 'I wouldn't know a symbol if I saw one', he has asserted.† He will not pose as reformer or social commentator:

If I were to state any moral precept it might be: Beware of the writer who puts forward his concern for you to embrace, who leaves you in no doubt as to his worthiness, his usefulness, his altruism, who declares that his heart is in the right place, and ensures that it can be seen, in full view, a pulsating mass where his characters ought to be. What is presented so much of the time, as a body of active and positive thought, is in fact a body lost in a prison of empty definition and cliché.‡

But in all this, there is an obvious seriousness that reaches beyond the mechanics of theatre or indulgent self-gratification. When Robert Bolt wrote an article attacking his fellow-dramatists for lack of purpose and staying power, Pinter questioned his basic criteria. Bolt had dismissed Ionesco in one sentence:

Ionesco seems to me to be very private, rather sexual, and obscure, and therefore fundamentally rather frivolous.

'*Why?*' rejoined Pinter:

Private, sexual, obscure, *therefore* frivolous. Even if one were to agree with the postulates, I see nothing axiomatic about the conclusion.§

* 'Between the Lines', op. cit.
† 'Writing for Myself', *Twentieth Century*, Vol. CLXIX (1961), 1008, p. 174.
‡ 'Between the Lines', op. cit.
§ 'Between the Lines', op. cit.

In effect, Pinter has questioned, seriously and continuously, the traditional subject matter and traditional purposes of drama. His meticulous techniques of language and gesture serve a consistent and active dramatic purpose. He dispenses with verbal statement, because he distrusts it; he follows no recognized rules of dramatic structure unless he needs to do so. He hides his hand (and his heart) in order to win at the game in which he finds himself involved.

*

While, like Keats, Pinter rejects writers 'with a palpable design upon us', he still, again like Keats, seeks 'truth' in the whole as in the detail of his work. It is this overall control, expressed in the relationships between the smallest details, that most clearly shows the seriousness and, indeed, the utility of his plays.

His general strategy is progressive discovery, and in our examination of individual words and gestures this mastering plan has already been observed at work. The warfare under smokescreens of speech, the manoeuvres for domination implicit in entries and exits, each partial statement of a character's engagement in the dramatic situation, all lead forward from activity to clarification, from effort to understanding. The conclusion is often marked by violence, a kind of explosion necessary to realign the forces of human mass and movement. Elsewhere, the end brings some quiet recognition of a shift of power that had been working surreptitiously throughout the action, or some new contact between characters or, more frequently, some gesture indicating their necessary isolation.

Nearly always in Pinter's plays, the action seems at the last moment to be held up, arrested: the dramatic situation now becomes static, as if energies have reached a point of balance or exhaustion. Each play, as it is performed, has a moment-by-moment excitement in that, for characters and audience alike, awareness is almost wholly in the active present – talk of past or future is from the point of view of the present moment – but, at the conclusion of each play, time seems to stop: all intimations of what has been or might be, seem now to be satisfied or effectively kept at bay; no one has another step to take. It is not unlike a stalemate at chess, for the final impasse has become progressively necessary through the elimination of other possibilities of manoeuvre; and, when it is at last declared, the minds of the audience are able to 'see' the preceding action, reflected in that static confrontation.

Because Pinter works on his plays as if they were explorations of the potential energies within a small number of characters, he requires almost no story-line. Their action needs, rather, variation and fluidity by means of which the characters can encounter a wide set of stimulants and possibilities. In early plays, like *The Room* or *The Birthday Party*, entries and exits were used to shift the balance of power within a small narrative development. By means of visits and departures, and the ordinary routines of living, together with the theatrical devices of prolonged silence, sustained utterance or exploitation of ignorance, Pinter was able to change the effectiveness of individual characters, and bring a full range of reactions into play. By the time he wrote *The Caretaker*, he was ready to use black-outs (and fade-outs) within an Act to suggest a change of time and so permit instantaneous realignment; and this is developed in *The Lover* and *The Collection*, both first shown on television where this device is a standard means of providing the necessary variety of visual image and speed of exposition. *The Dwarfs* has the greatest fluidity of all, with little reference to a continuous story-line and no continuous sense of time; it moves from situation to situation, and from one theatrical style to another, according to the need to clarify what happens within the mind of Len, the central character. The coherence of this play depends almost wholly on the audience being able to follow Len's shifts of consciousness, his subterfuges and attacks, as they become necessary to him, not as he responds to a sequence of recognizable day-by-day occurrences.

For two television plays, *Night School* (1960) and *A Night Out* (1960), Pinter has provided simple stories, where the sequence of events forces the characters to new knowledge and activity but, because of the nature of this medium, Pinter could keep each episode short and vary the location or point of view very rapidly and so escape from too close a confinement to external cause and effect. In *The Homecoming*, as the title suggests, a number of encounters and adjustments arise naturally from a basic story; but here Pinter has used the various places of entry on his stage-set – from the road, the kitchen, the bedrooms and from Lenny's room – and the ability of characters to come and go, singly and in pairs or groups, so that with only two black-outs and one Act-interval the assembled family are constantly realigned with freedom and energy.

More important than story-line, for Pinter, is scope and occasion for his characters to work through, and work out, the potentialities of their beings and relationships. In *A Slight Ache* (1959–61), Edward and Flora are, for most of the play, simply left alone with the silent matchseller and so initiate every move and each new variation that will lead to their eventual separation and differing enslavements. In *Landscape* and *Silence* (1969), each character speaks his mind freely – as freely as his past, present and future seem to permit – without interruption and without sustained desire for communication. There is no event on stage, no entry or exit, except three small moves in the latter play, each ineffectual in that the positions at the end are

97

identical to those at the beginning. Here, Pinter has found a way of making his characters speak or move only when their inner natures prompt them. His characters now seem to have free scope to express and, thereby, resolve or expend their personal and individual energies.

Clearly the shape of Pinter's plays depends above all on the potential of their characters, and on the dramatist's determination to show *them* determining a new relationship or new knowledge according to their own dynamism. This is how he talks of his task:

I started off with this picture of the two people and let them carry on from there.*

I like a feeling of order in what I write . . . I have a pretty good idea of the course of events and I know whereabouts it must stop, but I very rarely know how it is going to stop. All the preconceived notions I have are invariably wrong, for they are remedied by the characters in the writing . . . Characters always grow out of all proportion to your original conception of them, and if they don't the play is a bad one.†

Such a sense of engagement with their 'material' can be found in many recent painters, such as Jackson Pollock:

When I am *in* my painting, I'm not aware of what I'm doing. It is only after a sort of 'get acquainted' period that I see what I have been about. I have no fears about making changes, destroying the image, etc., because the painting has a life of its own. I try to let it come through. It is only when I lose contact with the painting that the result is a mess. Otherwise there is pure harmony, an easy give and take, and the painting comes out well.‡

* 'Writing for Myself', op. cit., 1008, p. 173.
† 'Harold Pinter Replies', *New Theatre Magazine*, Vol. II, no. 2 (1961), p. 10.
‡ 'My Painting', *Possibilities* Vol. I (1947), p. 79.

This kind of artistic engagement depends on careful handling of detail and continuous awareness of possibility and achievement. But all this would achieve nothing if the original image, the characters and the configuration, was not powerful. It must be capable of leading the artist on to master, with difficulty, some significant experience or response to experience.

For Pinter, the relationship between himself and his dramatic material seems direct:

I am objective in my selection and arrangement, but, as far as I'm concerned, my characters and I inhabit the same world. The only difference between them and me is that they don't arrange and select. I do the donkey work. But they carry the can. I think we're all in the same boat.*

Although he imagines the plays in action before him as he writes, he does not seem to see specific individuals. Rarely do his stage directions (or dialogue) give details of personal appearance, in the way that Bernard Shaw, Osborne or Wesker customarily explain height, weight, colour of hair, or manner of speaking. If Pinter imagines such details, so that he could recognize one of his characters off-stage, he does not consider the likeness important enough to tell his audience. For him, the salient points are sex and age, and that's the only lead he gives the audience. The published list of characters for *The Birthday Party* runs as follows:

PETEY, *a man in his sixties.*
MEG, *a woman in her sixties.*
STANLEY, *a man in his late thirties.*
LULU, *a girl in her twenties.*
GOLDBERG, *a man in his fifties.*
MCCANN, *a man of thirty.*

* 'Harold Pinter Replies', op. cit., p. 9.

The list for *The Homecoming* is similar, not even the relationship of Max to his sons, or to his brother, being mentioned.

Of course, family relationships will become apparent soon enough and they are clearly important bases for the writing of the play. (A page from an early draft of *The Homecoming*, reproduced in *Paris Review*,* shows that Max figured at this stage simply as 'F', for Father, and Lenny as '3', for Third Son.) But it is necessary for Pinter's dramatic strategy that these essentials become apparent only in and through performance. In the same way, clothes, height and other physical characteristics are mentioned in dialogue when this is necessary, but such descriptions are not always accurate or consistent and, in any case, reveal at least as much about the speakers as about the persons described.

Reading Pinter's plays is to enter a curiously faceless world; to see them acted in different productions is to meet a single world that changes in all but certain mysterious aspects, of which modes of awareness and an inherent tendency towards being known more fully seem to be dominant. The 'characters' as Pinter has indicated them in dialogue and stage-directions require substantiation: the actors do their share of this, but characters do not become clear until the audience has also begun to create them for themselves, piecing together hints, details, strangely various moments in which they express the cause of why they are thus and not otherwise.

The settings of the plays vary from fashionable to impoverished, from fanciful to brutally bare. The manners and apparent interests of the characters, the stage-business, the lighting and supposed 'weather' change likewise, often within a single play. But none of these details seems to nail a character down to any precisely confined range of behaviour. Flora, in *A Slight Ache*, can be a retiring wife, a

* op. cit., p. 12.

gracious lady, a mother, a child and a mistress. Davies of *The Caretaker* is a tramp, sometimes speaking cockney and sometimes, possibly, Welsh; but at the end, his speech is simple, supplicatory, all but anonymous in its run on a few words and in its hesitations. There is consistency of rhythm and vocabulary in individual parts, and sometimes the social background seems consistent and solidly imagined; but these are not overriding considerations in the creation of character and action. In *The Homecoming*, when Teddy leaves his wife Ruth, she turns from business-like talk about prostitution to call him by a name not used before, 'Eddie', and then 'Don't become a stranger' – a phrase which seems to express dependence or concern, holds the future open and suggests possibilities about the past and her mode of understanding that are unexpected and out of the 'key' of her role as a whole. She is not to be defined wholly by her obvious talents and her sustained manner of half-mocking speech.

Pinter's characters 'inhabit the same world' as himself so that their reality is imaginary. Their strength and conviction depend on Pinter's sensitivity to the forces moving within them and not on his observation of physical facts or social environment. At the end of the play they are 'finished', except as they go on living in the minds of the writer, the actors and the audience. So they belong in the theatre only, in that exploratory world where they have their only substantial existence. One cannot imagine them in relation to other characters or in other settings; and they have no activity which is not precisely necessary to the drama. They seem confined, even though presented in so many varying combinations and in so many apparently conflicting guises. They never speak to the audience; they often make jokes, but the audience overhears these and is not invited to enjoy them with the comic performer. The characters are there

for our inspection, but, while Pinter has ways of drawing
our precise attention, this is never demanded overtly, nor
is it necessary for the play in performance. We have the
unusual impression that we can come and go; indeed that
some withdrawal is almost expected of us, so wholly private
is the interrelated life of the characters, their activities and
consciousness. His plays show private worlds: self-contained,
obscure, 'rather sexual', instinctive, irrational, frivolous
perhaps – yet moving all the time until they have worked
themselves out, until the subterfuge is expended and the
interplay settled.

On the one hand Pinter has not given us pictures of
'real life' and on the other he has not drawn us into a
theatrical fantasy by splendid performances, challenging
arguments or unavoidable statements. Rather he displays
the reality of stage characters who at first seem alive only
to himself, and who therefore have all the bafflement and
complexity of his own mind – and the energy of that mind,
which reaches forward and seeks to be 'true'. At the end
of a performance, there is, perhaps, a sense of let-down, or
anti-climax; for all the audience is left with is a mode of
perception and a recognition of forces within characters
that are clearly special, insubstantial, almost general. The
great achievement of these plays is when the audience
transfers this mode of perception from theatre to life; to
this transference both the finish of the plays and the nature
of their characters invite, by their own obvious limitations.

*

In Pinter's view, fantasy is at least as powerful in human
motivation as rational thought or objective reality. All the
plays show events, behaviour or settings that are outside
the experience of any actual world. At first this element was
expressed blatantly in stage-action: in *The Room*, Rose
suddenly goes blind; in *The Birthday Party*, there are

nightmare interrogations and Stanley suffers a physical metamorphosis; in *The Dumb Waiter*, fantastic orders are delivered and a cistern flushes as if by magic. In some plays written for television or radio the setting is fantastic, as in the changing furnishings of *The Basement* or the abundant blooms and the path to the monastery of *A Slight Ache*. In the latter play the silent matchseller is a character with almost no plausibility in any 'real' world.

Where setting and events are close to the actual world, fantasy is present in speech and behaviour. In *The Dwarfs*, Len's imaginary, watching and ever-active creatures whom he talks about are obviously a fantasy of his mind and so, sometimes, are his conceptions of his friends, Pete and Mark, of the nurses in the hospital, of objects seen and touched. Pinter has realized the imaginary horrors springing from Len's distrust of activities and speech, and so in this play setting and incident only seldom and slightly depart from ordinary reality. In *The Caretaker*, written just before this, each of the three characters reacts to almost credible events in ways that show the imaginary gloss or distortion with which they view them. But here actions and speech are less directly fantastic, and often sound factual when they are not. (The clearest example is Aston's long speech about his experience in a mental hospital at the end of Act Two.) In *The Lover*, husband and wife actually act out their fantasies of being mistress and lover, dressing up and obviously pretending until, at the end, at least the outward charade is stopped. In *The Collection*, by keeping silent about what actually happened in Leeds, the two people who must know all, and the two who cannot know, with something of the same energy, express their own fantasies of what did happen; and, by the way, they also express their fantasies about themselves and their opposites in the four-sided confrontations.

By 1965, when *The Homecoming* was ready for production, Pinter had written two television plays, *A Night Out* and *Night School*, in which the fantasy was wholly restricted to personal reactions to events, all of which could be taken for actual and real, and are presented as such without ambiguity. The same may be said of the full-length stage-play, but the basic reactions of the characters here have a wholesale quality, a thoroughness of rejection or acceptance, that outstrips ordinary behaviour and so takes the play into fantasy while retaining an apparently unconfusing surface of ordinariness.

In *Landscape* and *Silence*, all speech directly reflects the thoughts of the characters. Events, objects and statements take on size, colour or power according to conscious and subconscious reactions. What is expressed is the interplay of fact and fantasy, the content of daydreams and self-indulgent thought. In *Silence* the setting is almost non-physical, Pinter asking only for ' *Three areas. A chair in each area.* ' This play concentrates with the least conceivable distraction on what three characters, after some contact, can, and must, make of what they have been given by time and each other. The characters are separate and yet linked by what is now outside their control, a sequence of quite credible events. They can talk with each other, and even ask simple questions: but these sound like old interchanges, and in the wider and more sustained speeches each character is alone. At length they must rest in silence, in their unuttered fantasy and memory.*

For Pinter, fantasy and reality are inevitably mixed; this is the nature of the conscious life that theatre can reflect. Even in the earliest plays his handling of seemingly realistic

---

* Shortly before writing *Silence* Pinter acted in a television production of Sartre's *Huis Clos*; it is possible to see *Silence* as his version of death, or of life without the definement and curtailment of shared bodily existence.

details serves this view of life. He selects, emphasizes and controls in order to disclose the forces that exist within his characters, regardless of chance or human contact. For all the minutely defined details of everyday life that the audience perceives as if they were moments of actual human intercourse, the plays express the largest and most general issues of personal existence: fear and hope; defence and aggression; dependence and dominance; trust and withdrawal; helplessness and confidence; the objective, limited facts of living and its subjective, limitless potentialities; the child and the man; the male and female; the family and others; the self in all its various manifestations and in its essential confinement, in its intentions, deceptions and actual achievements as seen by others and as realized, imperfectly, by itself in actual being and in strange and for ever fugitive consciousness.

In *A Slight Ache*, man and wife meet an unknown, human derelict with a tray of damp and useless matches, in the setting of a garden and house on a gloriously fine midsummer's day. Edward has travelled to tropical regions and has speculated 'for years', in his thoughts and writings, on primitive cultures and on space and time. He wakes with a 'slight ache' on this day and meets, or thinks he meets, in the person of the matchseller whom he has observed for some time, a resistance to all easy evasions and polite gestures. So his own mind leads him to hear mockery and challenge, and to think of his own youth and training, of moonlight and the sea. Finally, he makes a desperate effort to understand his encounter and himself in a whispered 'Who are you?', an unavailing move towards knowledge of a human being. The play changes from daily ordinary realism to a struggle with overwhelming fantasies and fears. Flora, the wife, begins irritated but sedate; she is careful of her husband, their house and 'the garden'. But, by the end of her encounter with the match-seller, she is happily careful for the unknown visitor, whom she decisively calls Barnabas. The garden flowers are now 'my japonica, my convolvulus . . .'. The 'whole house' is polished, and she and the visitor walk hand-in-hand to the garden, as if entering a rediscovered innocence. She gives her husband the tray of matches, with 'Here is your tray'; and she assumes command. The play is about abundant nature, possession, loss, service; about what is normally a 'slight ache' in the head, and about a human encounter in a sun-filled garden and a cluttered home.

The Birthday Party intermixes reality and fantasy more thoroughly. For its basic action in three Acts Pinter relies on three main activities: a visit, a party and a departure. Each is calculated to arouse basic reactions from the characters, especially when the events are presented in a purposefully confusing way so that they all question what is happening or conceal their distrust by fantastic evasions. The party is avoided, accepted or elaborated by each character in his own fashion, as if each had a *divertissement* to create in some corporate dance. It is stage-managed by Pinter carefully, and he introduces odd occurrences without apology. So Goldberg and McCann have a game with an electric torch, that involves turning out the lights and shining the torch in the face of the 'birthday boy', Stanley. A game of blind-man's-buff is extemporized at Lulu's suggestion. By these devices, Pinter makes darkness a recurrent element in the party and varies its effects. The light outside the room, and shining in the window when the lights are turned off, is at first '*faint*' (p. 57); then it becomes '*fainter*' (p. 59); but when Stanley is blindfolded, catches Meg and begins to strangle her, there is a sudden '*blackout*' (p. 66) and this time Pinter directs, '*There is now no light at all through the window. The stage is in darkness.*' In this darkness the torch is found and then lost, and then found again. The party is at its end and Stanley is discovered 'spread-eagled' over Lulu on the table. Goldberg and McCann converge on him with the torch and he flattens himself against the wall, giggling furiously, when the curtain falls. This is obvious dramatic artifice – although Pinter does provide an excuse in explaining later that the shilling-in-the-slot electric meter had turned off the light at the crucial point. The fading daylight is controlled to work exactly in time with this. Pinter wants the party to end in darkness and violence, in a kind of death for Stanley, a confrontation with his two visitors in a small circle of light. He has been progressively isolated; his glasses have been removed and then broken, and his intended victims have been released. His reactions start submissively – his only words are near the beginning, asking politely for his glasses – and then the inarticulate responses are progressively wild, dangerous, clumsy, childish and helpless. For Stanley, the Birthday Party is a blind, furtive, dangerous struggle; he is alone and desperate; his response instinctive and final. Pinter uses the dramatist's power to invoke coincidence, to arrange the setting and, as it were, to choose the weapons, so that the guest of honour is down and out, his defences removed and his resources exposed.

When, for his departure in Act Three, Stanley is led silently into the room by McCann, he is dressed as if for a funeral; he is made to sit on a chair and McCann pronounces him 'A new man' (p. 86). As Goldberg and McCann promise to 'save him' and offer him 'proper care and treatment', a free pass, re-orientation, success and many other attentions, Stanley remains quite still. When he is asked for a reply, he lifts his head 'very slowly', clenches and unclenches his eyes, trembles, and finally emits a strange breathing sound. Then

[*They watch him. He draws a long breath which shudders down his body. He concentrates . . .*]

[*They watch. He concentrates. His head lowers, his chin draws into his chest, he crouches.*]   (p. 89)

Stanley is now in the foetal position, as at birth, and his responses are noises: 'Uh-gughh' and 'Caaahhh'. He is twice asked his 'opinion of the prospect', but

[STANLEY'*s body shudders, relaxes, his head drops, he becomes still again, stooped.*]

A few moments later he has to be helped out of his chair and moved towards the door, almost like a corpse, and so taken to Goldberg's waiting black car.

In these ways, Pinter has chosen events for *The Birthday Party* which involve the characters in a watch and a death, as well as in a kind of birth and remembrance. The words spoken support the dramatic metaphor, the associative extension from particular, almost ordinary circumstances and behaviour to a universal and wide arena for human effort. The gestures and stage-business support the metaphor by expressing the characters' physical and instinctive involvement. The final curtain marks the action as complete when the party is over and when the 'party' who has been worked upon is taken away to a new life or death. The characters make their own clearest individual statements as the basic action is finished.

*

The basic action of *The Homecoming*, as for earlier plays, is marked by the ambiguous title: Teddy comes back to home; and leaves for his other home; Ruth comes to a new home; Joey 'comes' (in a sexual sense) for Ruth, in his own home; Sam seems, at the end, to come to his 'last home'. For all the characters truths come home, and in the last silent moments of the play, centred on Ruth, with Max, the father, on his knees before her, a new home-circle is established.

Reality and fantasy are combined in the stage-setting which is, on the one hand, 'An old house in North London', but on the other, a spacious hall or throne room. Pinter effects this double setting by an unusual direction:

A large room, extending the width of the stage.
The back wall, which contained the door, has been removed.
A square arch shape remains. Beyond it, the hall.

It is hard to imagine this structural alteration being made to any large, and already draughty, old house in North London; but for the play's action the effect is important.

It provides an arch, within the proscenium arch of the theatre, 'square' and therefore more vertical in emphasis than the broad rectangular stage-picture. This arch gives room for group entries and emphasizes the isolation of a lone watcher. It accentuates the height of the room and reveals a staircase going up to the bedrooms and a door to the street, and so it realizes the nature of each entry and exit more precisely. Above all, it gives visual emphasis and depth to the centre of the stage. The last static gathering will be backed by this inner arch, as if it were seen in a frame, so that set and actors together provide a last sculptural statement of homecoming.

The furniture is carefully chosen to accentuate this throne-room aspect of the living and entering space. There are 'odd tables, chairs' but also 'two large armchairs'. A large sofa is placed off-centre to the left-hand side and against the right wall is a large sideboard. The dialogue clearly marks one of the chairs as belonging to the father, Max; the other, presumably belonged to the dead mother, Jessie. At the end of the play Max is not in his chair, but Ruth sits in what the stage-directions now call 'her chair' (pp. 81 and 82); this may be Max's or Jessie's, or one of the 'odd chairs', now given a new, central significance.

During the course of the action, events usual in any home are elaborated in a way to command watchful attention, and move from the confinement of reality to the freedom and release of fantasy. In the previous chapter, Lenny's provision of a glass of water for Ruth, and then for himself, has already been examined. These actions are part of a whole series involving preparation and acceptance of food and drink. Lenny's first attempt to question his father, Max, is to ask about the dinner he has cooked, and this leads to general resentment: 'Why don't you buy a dog? You're a dog cook. Honest. You think you're cooking for a lot of dogs' (p. 11). Later Sam helps himself to an apple from the sideboard, with a brief excuse, 'Getting a bit peckish' (p. 16), and Max makes no comment and no effort to provide. Immediately after this, Joey enters and takes his jacket off, and, before he has sat down, proclaims 'Feel a bit hungry' (p. 17); Sam agrees, but now Max responds:

Who do you think I am, your mother? Eh? Honest. They walk in here every time of the day and night like bloody animals. Go and find yourself a mother.

The next provisions of food and drink are the glasses of water and, at the end of the Act in an early-morning episode, the clearing-up of breakfast off-stage by Sam who simply enters '*with a cloth*' and so provokes Max's scorn:

You resent making my breakfast, that's what it is, isn't it? That's why you bang round the kitchen like that . . .   (p. 39)

Sam tries to hand the cloth to Max, but at this point Teddy and Ruth come down the stairs and into the room. By this series of episodes concerned with food and drink, Pinter has drawn attention in the first Act to basic home-

making activities, defining his characters and leading on to
other domestic rituals. No meal is consumed on stage, in
the manner of realistic plays of home life, but this allows a
greater variety of handling and a more constant concern
with these matters. Notably each episode leads to a questioning of family relationships: Max as father and mother;
Ruth as stranger or mistress; Sam as brother.

Act Two begins with an after-lunch ritual:

MAX, TEDDY, LENNY and SAM *are about the stage, lighting cigars.*
JOEY *comes in from* U.L. *with a coffee tray, followed by* RUTH. *He
puts the tray down.* RUTH *hands coffee to all the men. She sits with
her cup.* MAX *smiles at her.*
RUTH: That was a very good lunch.
MAX: I'm glad you liked it. [*To the others.*] Did you hear that?
[*To* RUTH.] Well, I put my heart and soul into it, I can tell
you. [*He sips.*] And this is a lovely cup of coffee.
RUTH: I'm glad.
[*Pause.*]

The silent business with cigars and coffee cups takes little
time to read and to comprehend, but in action on the stage
it is an elaborate and strange piece of business. Joey is not
the most usual attendant, nor cigars their usual pleasure.
Each of the six cups of coffee has to be poured and handed,
and must therefore occupy an appreciable amount of time,
during which no word is spoken. This fantastic dumb-
show of polite acceptance is followed by Max's smile, who
shortly before the end of Act One had greeted Ruth as an
intruding whore. Mutual congratulations follow and Max
is soon expatiating on his pleasure in seeing 'the whole
family' together again and on Jessie's virtues and the way
he had pampered her:

I remember the boys came down, in their pyjamas, all their hair
shining, their faces pink, it was before they started shaving, and

they knelt down at our feet, Jessie's and mine. I tell you, it was like Christmas.

[*Pause.*] (p. 46)

The feast is thus linked with images of a holy family. It looks forward, too, to the end of the play when all the boys except one, and Max himself, gather around the feet of Ruth, the new centre of the family. She has Joey's head in her lap and strokes his head; but there is now no food or drink.

Two more food and drink episodes precede the last tableau. The first is on Ruth's curt, 'I'd like something to eat. [*To* LENNY.] I'd like a drink. Did you get any drink?' (p. 60). Whisky is provided by Lenny under Ruth's criticism, while Joey professes himself incapable of cooking. As the others accept the drinks and Joey '*moves closer to* RUTH', Ruth disturbs the usual patterns by not answering Joey and by walking '*round the room*'. She now seems intent on getting Teddy, her husband, to speak of his 'critical works'. As he does this, he shows that he despises his family and he silently accepts the drink. The second episode follows a blackout as Teddy sits '*in his coat*' ready to go (p. 62). Lenny looks for a cheese-roll he has made for himself; he suspects Sam of taking it but Teddy coolly acknowledges the theft, in words which echo the talk over Ruth's glass of water: 'I took your cheese-roll, Lenny', and later, 'But I took it deliberately, Lenny.' This gives occasion for Lenny to attack his brother, verbally, with memories of the past, scorn for the United States where he and Ruth now live, and apprehension of his father's death. The climax is Lenny's claim that the family, as he lives with it, does 'make up a unit' (p. 66).

The rest of the play is concerned with home-making in more general and more precise ways. Joey rejoins the family after two hours with Ruth in bed. Max asks where 'the whore' is (p. 69) and then proposes that Ruth should stay with them so that there is 'a woman in the house'. Teddy leaves and Ruth stays encouraging the fantasy proposals of the others that she should be set up in luxury as a prostitute near Greek Street. As Teddy is saying that Ruth will 'Keep everyone company', Sam comes forward and announces that 'MacGregor had Jessie in the back of my cab as I drove them along'. Having said this, he collapses (p. 79) and is left on the floor, not directly contradicted but condemned by Max for a 'diseased imagination'. The 'home' seems to be breaking up and Teddy stands to go; with cheerful concern for the journey, brief farewells and Max's donation of a photograph of himself for Ted's boys, he has soon left. Ruth calls him back for a last word and then in silence, like the silence at the beginning of the Act, the characters realign themselves for the last family group around Ruth. She is the new provider who does not move to cook nor bother to respond with words or anything else, other than a mechanical gesture:

> [TEDDY *goes to the front door.*]
> RUTH: Eddie.
>> [TEDDY *turns.*]
>> [*Pause.*]
> Don't become a stranger.
>> [TEDDY *goes, shuts the front door.*
>> *Silence.*
>> *The three men stand.*
>> RUTH *sits relaxed in her chair.*
>> SAM *lies still.*
>> JOEY *walks slowly across the room.*
>> He. *kneels at her chair.*
>> *She touches his head, lightly.*
>> *He puts his head in her lap.*

113

MAX *begins to move above them, backwards and forwards.*
MAX *turns to* LENNY.]

Max is the only one to speak now, and he soon falls to his
knees and sobs like a child. Crawling past Sam's body,
he looks up at Ruth:

[*He raises his face to her.*]
Kiss me.
[*She continues to touch* JOEY's *head, lightly.*
LENNY *stands, watching.*]

CURTAIN

These are family gestures that complete the play, that show
appetite and dependence; contact, withdrawal and submission in power or weakness.

Pinter has elaborated and controlled a sequence of
normal-seeming events that carry a comparatively simple
family story, but at the same time they are used to accentuate basic appetites, provisions and refusals. He starts with
jocularity, petty quarrels and easy submissions, but moves
towards cold confrontations and at last concludes with
mutually sustained silence. The centre of the family in
Max and the absent mother, Jessie, is continually marked
by words; and, by showing the men providing food and
drink for themselves, gestures and stage-business mark
the changing positions and roles of provider and dependant.
The stage-design and furniture accentuate the central
sitting position, and the route of escape to bedroom or
street; together they help to mark what is constant and what
changing in the picture of Homecoming. The play stands
or falls not by a plot or statement, but by the coherence of
the episodes and the revelation of how, in events and
behaviour, very like those ordinarily experienced by the
audience, strong and repetitive forces work among male and
female, within individuals and within a family.

This is the main progress of the play, but with it subsidiary explorations of character and relationships are made. There are self-concerned actions like Lenny's correction of his tie in front of a mirror or Joey's shadow-boxing. Some actions are obviously and blatantly meaningful, such as Lenny and Ruth dancing slowly together, or Joey and Ruth rolling '*off the sofa on to the floor*', as Max explains that he is talking about 'a woman of feeling' (p. 60). But quite as much is expressed by a series of smaller, almost unremarkable activities: various kisses, handshakes, touches; putting on and off of clothes, entrances and exits, movements of sitting and standing, quiet responses of smiling or chuckling.

After watching the play, the audience's attention is attuned. Pinter has said nothing that is explicit and unambiguous about the basis of family life, of a mother's role, a brother's, a wife's, a child's, or about life outside the home affecting the home, but the audience has noticed how these elements of life operate within usual encounters and habits, and betray themselves to our understandings. He has also shown the characters all moving, with final ruthlessness and lack of self-regard, towards greater clarity and a finality of expression. This is, perhaps, the largest difference between the play and daily life; it is also the source of dramatic excitement, as Pinter slowly and stealthily reveals the interplay of his characters, and as he shares his own exploration. While the dramatic events are not progressively exciting, or optimistic, enjoyable, or pitiable, the dramatist's pursuit of an ending that has particular and corporate 'truth' to all his invention does possess all these theatrical qualities, and his play, by the energy, danger and acuteness of its theatrical language, is able to transmit these to his audience.

The characters chosen by Pinter for each play are few in

number and from a limited social range. They live in the present time only, without direct enactment of more than could be effected in an hour or two of real time. But if his dramatic material is thus limited, he presents it with compensating intensity. Everything is kept to a sharp minimum; in revision of his texts the main change is elimination, and in criticizing his early works he speaks of glibness or too many words.* His writing has an astringent athleticism that gives his plays what is, perhaps, their rarest quality, a density and weight achieved without mass effects and without loss of excitement. Pinter's art is explorative and yet intense, restless and yet deliberate, related to ordinary talk and behaviour and yet releasing in powerful form the inner drives of his characters in final exposures that seem timeless and of general relevance.

The end of *The Homecoming* is like a group of statuary that the audience can encounter as it wishes. It is as massive, compulsive and generally eloquent as a silent *coup de théâtre* of Aeschylus, like Clytemnestra standing over the bodies of Agamemnon and Cassandra. The monumentality is achieved without a chorus; that perhaps is the role of the audience, for which Pinter has written no words. It is also found in characters who occupy the same time as the author and his audience, and not in figures from a mythical past.

This achievement seems to have come unsought. Pinter has followed his own sense of involvement in what immediately confronted him in his life and mind. He did not presume to create large figures of timeless relevance; rather his sense of 'truth' in theatrical exploration of immediate experience has led him towards these mammoth and eloquent conclusions. Considering the effect his plays have

* See revisions of *The Dwarfs* (1966 and 1968) and of *The Caretaker* (1962); his self-criticism is in *Paris Review*, Vol. 39 (1966), p. 26 and *Listener*, 6 November 1969.

in performance, I do not know whether to wonder more at Pinter's individual sensitivity and dedication, or at his use of the theatre's power to transform and heighten. My second thought is to remember that his art is precarious, depending wholly on the active involvement of the audience's conscious and subconscious mind: his great figures are seen in a small, precise and sometimes distant mirror.

4

JOHN OSBORNE

Theatrical Belief

Look Back in Anger, The Entertainer, Luther,
Inadmissible Evidence and Other Plays

Ostentatious display and large-scale effects are part of the theatre's inherited language. Plays, in the past, have provided spectacles for whole cities, for princes and for pilgrims. Even today, in Greece, it is not unusual for 20,000 people to view a single performance of ancient tragedy in the open-air at Epidaurus. But audiences, conditions of performance, theatres and societies have all changed, and no dramatist writing today can expect this kind of production. The buildings in which their plays are performed may be called the Globe, the Royal Court, the Hippodrome or the Everyman, but audiences are comparatively small and represent only a small section of the populace. Certainly no general holiday is proclaimed so that all may crowd to see a dramatic performance lasting most of the daylight hours and performed in the centre of a town or at a place of national worship. But the ability to amaze and enthral, and to enlarge the views of an audience, remains a potential of the theatre, and for some dramatists it is a perpetual challenge and inspiration.

John Osborne has said:

I'd love to write something for a circus, something enormous and immense, so that you might get a really big enlargement of life

118

and people. What's so boring about television is that it *reduces* life and the human spirit. Enlarging it is something that the theatre can do best of all.*

In the same interview, Osborne explained that he did not worry 'as a dramatist' about reaching a mass audience. He wants to write for a circus in order to realize, control and use what the theatre can do supremely well, to create an image of life on the stage that can dominate and excite.

After the success of two plays in the West End of London, Osborne wrote (and directed) a large-scale musical, *The World of Paul Slickey*, but this proved a false direction. His work, as a rule, does not demand large casts or elaborate showmanship. Each of his two plays that were first performed in 1968, requires a single and simple stage-setting, no elaborate lighting effect, and no song or dance; their casts number eight and nine. Here the size comes from what Osborne has called 'arias',† elaborate, unashamedly sustained vocal solos, written to be performed by a star actor. They are calculated so that they may be shown off and, equally, so that they will show off the actor. Somewhere, in each of Osborne's plays, often in several ways and in numerous places, the theatre displays the pull and power of its circus affiliations. Perhaps this is the reason why Osborne has had more West End successes than any other dramatist who is at all close to him in experiment and innovation.

*

Read in sequence, a dozen or so of his plays give a dominating impression of Osborne's zestful invention. He is a Picasso of the theatre, confident that he can handle his material, employ strong colour and, where he wishes, reduce

* 'That Awful Museum' (a conversation with Richard Findlater), *Twentieth Century*, Vol. CLXIX (1961), 1008, p. 216.

† 'John Osborne talks to Kenneth Tynan', *Observer*, 30 June 1968, p. 21.

all to a single fluent line. He knows he is in charge and so he directly draws attention. He changes settings and themes from play to play; he writes about people like himself or about the current British monarchy (*The Blood of the Bambergs*); or he falls in with a suggestion that he should adapt a sensational Lope de Vega play about a crucifixion and a nameless shepherd (*A Bond Honoured*). On the other hand, Osborne does not meticulously revise his own work; nor does he make a point of avoiding repetition of character, sentiment or action. He is free of that sort of calculation, but is inventive in his artifice, zestful in playing the game of playwriting. He takes a powerful grip of his subjects and enjoys the strenuous effort which subdues, enlarges and displays. If he cannot write like an eagle, either seriously or playfully, then he will brood and be silent.

His first play was produced when he was seventeen,* but *Look Back in Anger* (1957) was the first to reach London and, after the initial puzzled and defensive reactions, it was hailed as a new beginning for the English theatre. For example, Arnold Wesker has said: 'When I saw it, I just recognized that things *could* be done in the theatre'; at that moment Wesker turned his attention from film to theatre.† This play gave a title to the first and still most comprehensive 'Guide' to post-war English theatre, John Russell Taylor's *Anger and After* (1962). However, *Look Back in Anger* 'embarrasses' Osborne today; he sees it as 'a formal, rather old-fashioned play . . . [that] broke out by its use of language'.‡ This perhaps will be the more lasting judgement, for confrontation and talk are indeed the meat and the bones of the play. It displays five people who in their struggles,

* See *Declarations*, ed. T. Maschler (1957), p. 62.
† 'His Very Own and Golden City' (an interview with Simon Trussler), *Tulane Drama Review*, Vol. XI (1966), p. 194.
‡ 'That Awful Museum', op cit., p. 214.

together and apart, release feelings that are recognizable as immediate and mutually responsive. These stage-characters were greeted as the first to reflect the world of Osborne's contemporaries, but they would never have been seen on the London stage were it not for the spirit and resource of the writing.

The actors and director responsible for preparing the first performance may well have been puzzled and uncertain. On the one hand, their lines, and their implications in terms of individual performances, obviously worked, and they could catch the appropriate physical gestures and tones of voice. But their characters achieved so little. The play is in three Acts, and has a beginning, middle and end. Nothing is very mysterious and actions have consequences that are explicable in terms of ordinary behaviour. This was as they expected. But what happens in the first Act? Some exposition is provided about the household of Jimmy, Alison and Cliff, but almost nothing is said to explain the marriage of Jimmy and Alison that has taken place before the play opens. During the Act, the characters do not go for a drink, do not go to the cinema, and do not get a meal cooked or a second pot of tea brewed. Alison does get the ironing done, and she and Cliff smoke cigarettes; and Jimmy talks and moves about the room. There is a fight in which Jimmy throws Cliff against Alison causing her to burn her arm with the iron. This is the first 'movement' of the Act and the second has scarcely more action in the conventional sense of the word. It starts with a duologue between Alison and Cliff in which she says she is expecting Jimmy's baby. A reconciliation follows for husband and wife, but then a friend of Alison telephones and the Act ends with another, fiercer fight, Jimmy touching his wife only with words. She does not tell him about the baby.

A lengthy stage-direction shows that Osborne consciously

matched his characters against each other. As the curtain rises, two men are reading newspapers and a woman stands ironing:

JIMMY *and* CLIFF *are seated in the two armchairs* R. *and* L., *respectively. All that we can see of either of them is two pairs of legs . . . When we do eventually see them, we find that* JIMMY *is a tall, thin young man about twenty-five, wearing a very worn tweed jacket and flannels. Clouds of smoke fill the room from the pipe he is smoking. He is a disconcerting mixture of sincerity and cheerful malice, of tenderness and freebooting cruelty; restless, importunate, full of pride, a combination which alienates the sensitive and insensitive alike. Blistering honesty, or apparent honesty, like his, makes few friends. To many he may seem sensitive to the point of vulgarity. To others, he is simply a loudmouth. To be as vehement as he is is to be almost non-committal.* CLIFF *is the same age, short, dark, big boned, wearing a pullover and grey, new, but very creased trousers. He is easy and relaxed, almost to lethargy, with the rather sad, natural intelligence of the self-taught. If* JIMMY *alienates love,* CLIFF *seems to exact it – demonstrations of it, at least, even from the cautious. He is a soothing natural counterpoint to* JIMMY.*

Standing L. *below the food cupboard, is* ALISON. *She is leaning over an ironing board. Beside her is a pile of clothes. Hers is the most elusive personality to catch in the uneasy polyphony of these three people. She is tuned in a different key, a key of well-bred malaise that is often drowned in the robust orchestration of the other two. Hanging over the grubby, but expensive, skirt she is wearing is a cherry red shirt of* JIMMY's, *but she manages somehow to look quite elegant in it. She is roughly the same age as the men. Somehow, their combined physical oddity makes her beauty more striking than it really is. She is tall, slim, dark. The bones of her face are long and delicate. There is a surprising reservation about her eyes, which are so large and deep they should make equivocation impossible.*

(pp. 9–10)

This could serve as a textbook example for dramatic construction. The characters are alike in some points, contrasted in others. Two of them contain opposing forces within their own make-up. Osborne describes the effect as an 'uneasy polyphony', a term that shows he is aware of the almost musical possibilities of arrangement and rearrangement, of progress and return, repetition and variation. What is more extraordinary in the playwriting is the almost total reliance on these variations for dramatic interest throughout the first Act.

The main gain is 'enlargement' and display of temperament. The attic room is a circus ring, alive with tripartite combat. If the characters' reactions, in themselves, are readily acceptable, their fire, attack, strength are pitched above anything that was familiar at that time to audiences of English plays with contemporary, domestic settings. From bright-eyed love-games and a silent, happy embrace, Jimmy and Alison are divided by the telephone call and on her return to the room he is *unable to sustain his anger* while she speaks *quietly* with cold precision. Then she is *vehement* and withdrawn, and he finds his voice to attack with renewed eloquence. All this variation of behaviour and mood occurs within four pages of text.

The fighting is all the more exciting in that Osborne gives as much attention to defence as attack, to weakness as to strength. When Jimmy has assaulted Alison with a mercilessly satirical picture of her brother, Nigel, there is a stage-direction:

[*There is no sound, only the plod of* ALISON's *iron. Her eyes are fixed on what she is doing.* CLIFF *stares at the floor. His cheerfulness has deserted him for the moment.* JIMMY *is rather shakily triumphant. He cannot allow himself to look at either of them to catch their response to his rhetoric, so he moves across to the window, to recover himself, and look out.*] (p. 21)

The power of Jimmy's invective first holds attention, but then a neat silence registers Alison's resistance and Cliff's unease. The next development is a move for Jimmy that draws attention to his insecurity and need for reassurance. This use of physical gesture rather than words is a change of weapon, for the dramatist and for his characters. It does not revalue what has been said or make the audience unsure of what is happening, as in Pinter's plays, but, rather, it varies the 'play', gives a further variation of the fight. The silent stage business leads to renewed verbal attack, that is now in a *conversationally* sarcastic manner. It also allows Osborne to keep all three characters in the audience's attention and so maintain a wide view of the stage and indicate further possibilities of manoeuvre.

With these tactics, even the slender exposition serves to heighten excitement. Because there is no direct information on how these characters came to be living together, the audience has little clear idea of what holds them together. Osborne makes the audience wait for explanations, and in the meantime uses dialogue to prompt all the obvious questions. 'Why' is used repeatedly. The first words of the play are Jimmy's 'Why do I do this every Sunday?', and there is no answer. His questions continue: 'Why do you bother? . . . Why don't we have a little game?' A simple, answering 'Why?' from Alison is followed shortly by his, 'Why not?' (pp. 23–4). When she says she'll go out of her mind, he asks, 'Why don't you?' (p.22). Most of Cliff's questions are variants of, 'Oh, why doesn't he shut up?' (p. 16), but later he says more simply, 'Why the hell she married you, I'll never know' (p. 31). When in Act Two, Scene Two, Alison's father arrives, he too brings questions until he draws Alison to protest: 'I've been on trial every day and night of my life for four years' (p. 67).

Among all the unanswered questions in this first Act, the one certain piece of exposition is that Alison is expecting Jimmy's baby, but that is kept from his knowledge, partly to heighten the excitement of the ending of the Act. He tells her that he would like to watch her face 'if you could have a child, and it would die':

I wonder if you might even become a recognizable human being yourself; but I doubt it. (p. 37)

She makes no articulate reply, and by now the audience knows that she could not. This supports the effect of all the unanswered questions and now makes it certain that the characters are seen to be fighting helplessly. This has been the repeated implication of Jimmy's restlessness, Alison's quiet resistance and Cliff's momentary and evasive attempts to intercede. The constant element in all their manoeuvres, attacks and defences is their submission, their inability to find reasons or alternatives: – the unanswered 'whys'. As the conflict in words and actions becomes ever stronger, this sense of helplessness is a counterpoint to verbal precision and limited engagements.

Such dramatic strategies of scale, variation and contrast are dangerous, for they court disbelief. Truly conceived situation and character can seem false and powerless by the use of overwrought theatricality. This is the risk Osborne runs, but he saves his play by his words. They so take possession of the audience that belief is compelled or given.

*

Pinter's dialogue is accepted for its quiet finesse, its careful accuracy and hidden power; Osborne's carries because it reaches out, fills and exhilarates the mind. Confidence alone would not ensure this, though Osborne's delight in words is as marked as Pinter's wariness and occasional desperation. The common excellence of these dramatists is their ability to write firmly muscled dialogue that pays its way, moment by moment. In Osborne's, this hardness and efficiency are combined with fluency and variety. The listener finds his mind overflowing with impressions and sense-reactions.

The characters in *Look Back in Anger* seldom search for words, images, examples or illustrations. Cliff is uneducated and basically slow in mind, but this is expressed more by reticence than long slow speeches. The characters speak up and then shut up. Even Cliff's comparatively long speeches have much to say, as in:

I don't think I'd have the courage to live on my own again – in spite of everything. I'm pretty rough, and pretty ordinary really, and I'd seem worse on my own. And you get fond of people too, worse luck.   (p. 27)

There are at least three major statements here, two in the last short sentence. In rhythm, this speech is characteristic of Osborne's basic style, in its variety – the long first phrase; the second sentence split in three; the shorter units at the end of the first and last sentences, giving concluding sharpness and mobility.

Jimmy's talk makes up most of the dialogue in *Look Back in Anger*, and here Osborne's compelling style is most fully seen. At the beginning of Act Two, Helena provides Jimmy with a new target to attack and he challenges her morality and superior posture after a glancing blow at Cliff:

JIMMY [*to* CLIFF]: I suppose you're going over to that side as well. Well, why don't you? Helena will help to make it pay off for you. She's an expert in the New Economics – the Economics of the Supernatural. It's all a simple matter of payments and penalties. [*Rises.*] She's one of those apocalyptic share pushers who are spreading all those rumours about a transfer of power.
                                                                            (p. 55)

The short second sentence – 'Well, why don't you?' – points attention at Cliff's inability to reply, but, because it is in two phrases, it also sharpens the rhythm and so reveals a quicker attention under Jimmy's opening gambit. Then the phrases lengthen until the unexpected 'New Economics', which is punched home with a rounder, polysyllabic and partly repetitive phrase. The growth of power is further shown by the assurance of the following almost throw-away sentence with neat, running alliteration at the end: – 'It's all a simple matter of payments and penalties.' This relaxed verbal tension is offset by a growing physical exertion as Jimmy '*Rises*', and then the climax of this part of the speech can come freely in its longest sentence and its largest single phrase, 'those apocalyptic share pushers'.

The final 'power' probably needs special stress to make its point fully, and to mark the manner in which Jimmy makes his hearers wait through the intentional mystification of 'all those rumours'. Through varying rhythm, developing metaphor, placing of salient words, through tension and relaxation, Jimmy's speech certainly sounds alive. More than this, the stage-direction, '*Rises*', shows that Osborne creates the words as part of a fully realized performance. By accompanying movement, that is at one with the rhythmic statement of the speech, Jimmy is seen to have instinctive and physical life, as well as mental agility.

A stage-direction now marks what in performance is obvious: '*His imagination is racing, and the words pour out.*' The phrases become shorter, and rhythms quicker with alliteration and doublets, and more emphatic repetitions. When words are at their quickest and the rhythms begin to lengthen again, Jimmy is again directed to move: he '*faces them*' for renewed, less hectic emphasis. Then speed returns and he '*Crosses to above table*', to a dominating yet more open position. Now he is more surely in command, and his periods become rounder. After a brief introductory 'Tell me', he finishes with a resounding rhetorical question, followed hard by two short, repetitive, double-stressed exclamations:

Reason and Progress, the old firm, is selling out! Everyone get out while the going's good. Those forgotten shares you had in the old traditions, the old beliefs are going up – and up and up and up. [*Moves up* L.] There's going to be a changeover. A new Board of Directors, who are going to see that the dividends are always attractive, and that they go to the right people. [*Facing them.*] Sell out everything you've got: all those stocks in the old, free inquiry. [*Crosses to above table.*] The Big Crash is coming, you can't escape it, so get in on the ground floor with Helena and her friends while there's still time. And there isn't much of it left. Tell me, what could be more gilt-edged than the next world! It's a capital gain, and it's all yours.

So far the speech has been heavily sarcastic and before Jimmy drops this tone, he moves round to the side of the stage where he faces Helena. While he still speaks of her in the third person, the rhythms are at first relatively gentle: 'You see, I know Helena and her kind so very well'. After its brief introduction, this sentence almost breaks into three short, light phrases; only the word 'know' has any obvious attack. Then, with a quickening 'In fact', three more emphatic, shorter phrases follow, the last a sentence on its own. Now verbal images become more abundant, and again the phrases lengthen. A metaphor of struggling to move in a crowd is followed by references to romanticism and history, to light and dark, a cosy cottage, ugly problems, isolation, social struggle, comfort. The sequence is forced home with a more sustained double metaphor linking ecstasy with excretion. Calling Helena by her name and shortening the phrasing, Jimmy then develops this further by linking ecstasy and guilt with farting. At this point, with a gesture betraying self-consciousness in attack, Jimmy drops all verbal colour and metaphor to force, in the tersest form of words, a physical confrontation:

You see, I know Helena and her kind so very well. In fact, her kind are everywhere, you can't move for them. They're a romantic lot. They spend their time mostly looking forward to the past. The only place they can see the light is the Dark Ages. She's moved long ago into a lovely little cottage of the soul, cut right off from the ugly problems of the twentieth century altogether. She prefers to be cut off from all the conveniences we've fought to get for centuries. She'd rather go down to the ecstatic little shed at the bottom of the garden to relieve her sense of guilt. Our Helena is full of ecstatic wind – [*he leans across the table at her*] aren't you?

[*He waits for her to reply.*]

The concluding 'wind', or fart, is an example of Osborne's fondness for placing a simple, strong word late and emphatically. These are often verbs, suggesting basic physical activity. In the exchange that follows, Helena illustrates this device with a cool, controlled manner and then Jimmy, with a word that changes the grounds for battle, in deliberate and surprising style:

HELENA [*quite calmly*]: It's a pity you've been so far away all this time. I would probably have *slapped* your face.
   [*They look into each other's eyes across the table. He moves slowly up, above* CLIFF, *until he is beside her.*]
   You've behaved like this ever since I first came.
JIMMY: Helena, have you ever watched somebody *die*?

As Jimmy takes up Helena's challenge by moving close to her, words and stage-movement again make common meaning. Helena's reply is now a single sentence, sounding less calculated and assured than the double statement with which she began. The challenge is more veiled and Jimmy is free to answer, tauntingly, with a question loaded at the end with 'die'. She tries to escape, but is caught. She only repeats more sharply her first challenge:

JIMMY: Helena, have you ever watched somebody die?

    [*She makes a move to rise.*]

    No, don't move away.

    [*She remains seated, and looks up at him.*]

    It doesn't look dignified enough for you.

HELENA [*like ice*]: If you come any nearer, I will slap your face.

    [*He looks down at her, a grin smouldering round his mouth.*]

For all the invention, point and confidence in Osborne's use of words, the audience is made to pay attention to the full stage picture, to the effect of words as well as their impact, to the unheralded and perhaps instinctive reactions that are expressed silently in movement and facial expression, even at those moments when words are most simply alive – indeed, particularly at those moments.

*

Silent physical confrontation is as crucial for Osborne's dramatic strategy as the repeated question 'why?'. As two characters face each other in silence, there is a point of balance, a stillness, from which the fight seems capable of moving in any direction. When a new speech begins, the audience will be drawn by the new activity, with attention the sharper for having to wait for the clarification that comes, here, with a return of words. Besides these general effects, the silent confrontation draws the attention of the audience to what seems to be within the speakers' minds. It will look for signs of unspoken thought and, when words return, it may question them, or at least sense that, although the words are clearer in meaning, they still leave much out.

For all the confidence, momentum and energy of Osborne's words, they are only a partial expression of character in motion. Indeed, the centre of dramatic interest is seldom expressed directly in words or in positive, independent stage-business. These provide the sword-play and defensive shields for a conflict among and within the characters that is far less variable, but which sustains the drama as a whole.

Osborne is not, like Pinter, using words to betray another struggle underneath. His characters use words with belief, committed to their limitations as well as their effectiveness. If they discard words, they seem to choose or acquiesce in the change of expression. Osborne captures and uses theatrical belief for words, gestures *and* silence, according to the requirements of the moment. But it is in the simple silences without movement that the sustaining energy of his characters is most nakedly revealed. Between the various and resourceful engagements of their encounters, there are moments when the characters are not fighting or defending themselves, and then they reveal their basic desires and needs, that are dumb and helpless.

*

With his ability to compel belief, Osborne has a sharp awareness of the difficulty of believing anything, especially in those parts of life that need trust and mutual acceptance between human beings. The passage where Jimmy Porter tells Helena and the others what it was like to see his father die has the customary variation and energy when he speaks of his family, his mother or warfare, or even of his own fears, isolation and bewilderment and the 'sweet, sickly smell of a dying man'; but within this eloquence, there is a repeated return to 'I', and to 'caring', knowing and experience. The climax is not on an up-beat, but as Jimmy '*sits*' and says, with broken rhythms and probably some hesitation, the four words ' – love . . . betrayal . . . and death'. A slight recovery of rhythmic strength comes when he refers outwards from his own feelings to his contact with his listeners:

For twelve months, I watched my father dying – when I was ten years old. He'd come back from the war in Spain, you see. And certain god-fearing gentlemen there had made such a mess of him, he didn't have long left to live. Everyone knew it – even I knew it.

[*He moves* R.]

But, you see, I was the only one who cared. [*Turns to the window.*] His family were embarrassed by the whole business. Embarrassed and irritated. [*Looking out.*] As for my mother, all she could think about was the fact that she had allied herself to a man who seemed to be on the wrong side in all things. My mother was all for being associated with minorities, provided they were the smart, fashionable ones.

[*He moves up* C. *again.*]

We all of us waited for him to die. The family sent him a cheque every month, and hoped he'd get on with it quietly, without too much vulgar fuss. My mother looked after him without complaining, and that was about all. Perhaps she pitied him. I suppose she was capable of that. [*With a kind of appeal in his voice.*] But *I* was the only one who cared!

[*He moves* L., *behind the armchair.*]

Everytime I sat on the edge of his bed, to listen to him talking or reading to me, I had to fight back my tears. At the end of twelve months, I was a veteran.

[*He leans forward on the back of the armchair.*]

All that that feverish failure of man had to listen to him was a small, frightened boy. I spent hour upon hour in that tiny bedroom. He would talk to me for hours, pouring out all that was left of his life to one, lonely, bewildered little boy, who could barely understand half of what he said. All he could feel was the despair and the bitterness, the sweet, sickly smell of a dying man.

[*He moves around the chair.*]

You see, I learnt at an early age what it was to be angry – angry and helpless. And I can never forget it. [*Sits.*] I knew more about – love . . . betrayal . . . and death, when I was ten years old than you will probably ever know all your life.

[*They all sit silently. Presently,* HELENA *rises.*]

HELENA: Time we went. (pp. 57–8)

The stage-direction asking Jimmy to speak with '*a kind of appeal*' and the italicized '*I*' give the necessary information that Jimmy, for the moment, will believe the simplest words. Later, when Alison has written to him saying, 'I shall always have a deep, loving need of you', he tears her words apart with ridicule and scorn:

Oh, how could she be so bloody wet! Deep loving need! That makes me puke! [*Crossing to* R.] She couldn't say 'You rotten bastard! I hate your guts, I'm clearing out, and I hope you rot!' No, she has to make a polite, emotional mess out of it! . . . Deep, loving need! I never thought she was capable of being as phoney as that! (pp. 72–3)

In the earlier scene, when Jimmy has spoken of angry helplessness, Alison says – '*softly*' – 'All I want is a little peace', and this is sufficient to make Jimmy cry out, as if in pain:

Peace! God! She wants peace! [*Hardly able to get his words out.*] My heart is so full, I feel ill – and she wants peace! (p. 59)

To Jimmy she is a 'Judas', 'feeble' and 'phoney', yet she has used large and demanding words no more directly than he has just done. The conflict is not over words, but over belief in them and the need to have that belief shared.

Notably in *Look Back in Anger* several of the more significant changes of relationships and steps forward in the narrative depend upon non-verbal recognitions. Immediately before the fight in the first Act, when Alison gets hurt with the iron, the church bells start ringing and it is this, not anything the others say or do, which takes Jimmy the last step in verbal anger before action takes over (p. 25).

When they are reconciled, soon after this, Jimmy must simply see the burn on Alison's arm, for he then '*takes hold of her bandaged arm*' before asking her 'How's it feeling?' and saying he's 'sorry'. The moment of recognition itself has no direct means of expression, but provides the impetus for a new development between the warring characters. At the end of Act Two, Jimmy is telling Helena: 'Now leave me alone, and *get out*, you evil-minded little virgin', but, when she '*slaps his face savagely*', his belief, or part of it, has to change:

[*She slaps his face savagely. An expression of horror and disbelief floods his face. But it drains away, and all that is left is pain. His hand goes up to his head, and a muffled cry of despair escapes him.* HELENA *tears his hand away, and kisses him passionately, drawing him down beside her.*] (p. 74)

The crucial element here is Jimmy's change of mind, shown only in his facial expression. In the third Act, Alison's reappearance, having lost her baby, is what causes Helena to relinquish her hold on Jimmy. Its effect is described some time after it has happened, when Helena says: 'When you came in at that door, ill and tired and hurt, it was all over for me' (p. 91). Here Helena explicitly describes a private, and at first inarticulate, reaction. The stage direction at the actual moment asked only for '*a stunned pause*'; after this only Alison and Jimmy had spoken or moved, and '*the two women are left looking at each other*' (p. 87). Here words and gesture clearly follow, and are dependent on, the intimate centre of the drama.

When Osborne said that he would like to write for a circus, he also acknowledged that his ideal theatre was only part circus, having as well the 'intimacy'* of the conventional, small playhouse designed for 'naturalistic' performances. He writes, in fact, for a theatre that couldn't actually exist, but the idea of such a theatre encourages him to polarize enlarged human behaviour and instinctive sentiment, to capitalize on two basic resources of theatre language. Besides showing characters who believe in the words

* 'That Awful Museum', op. cit., pp. 214–15.

and actions, and while filling the stage with active and varied performances, he also shows their disbelief in still, intense moments of dramatic balance.

*

I suspect that Osborne's dramas draw, in this respect, upon his own experience as an actor. In performance he can commit himself to the demands of his roles and yet experience moments of disbelief. It is said that the 'mask drops', but that phrase suggests an occasional lapse from fictitious existence. The kind of actor's experience I have in mind is a continuous half-conscious awareness of the limitations of dramatic identification with words and physical performance that takes whole possession of the mind when, for brief moments, performance becomes consciously inadequate.

In *Look Back in Anger*, Helena Charles is an actress and, at one point, Jimmy suggests that she has been giving Alison words to say 'from one of those plays you've been in' (p. 73). Jimmy himself is often shown to be consciously acting: he speaks to Cliff, knowing that Alison or Helena is listening; he assumes '*a reverent, Stuart Hibberd voice*' (p. 21) when, in fact, he feels cheated and destructive; he draws Cliff and Helena into the surface gaiety of a music-hall act, when truly he is in despair.

For many of the leading characters in his plays, Osborne has chosen people with something of the actor in their characters or professions. Archie Rice, the hero of *The Entertainer* (1957), is a music-hall artist, coming from a music-hall family. *The World of Paul Slickey* (1959) is about a journalist whose words intentionally deceive and who, at the conclusion of the play, masquerades as a woman while his wife, a pop-star impresario, has turned into a man. The heroes of *Luther* (1961) and *Inadmissible Evidence* (1964) are respectively preacher and solicitor, who must both marshall their words to express ideas not wholly their own and to impress their listeners. The short *Plays for England* (1962) shows a photographer who poses as royalty and a man and wife who enact various charades for their own sexual satisfaction. *A Patriot for Me* (1965) is about a homosexual spy, who has to pretend to patriotism and heterosexuality; there is a large, central scene at a transvestite ball. Two plays, first performed in 1968, are about 'show business' people, an actress being the central character of *Time Present* and a film scriptwriter of the *Hotel In Amsterdam*. When Osborne was challenged by the question: 'Isn't it limiting to concentrate on show business people as much as you do?' he replied:

Not at all, because nowadays almost everyone is tainted with show business. Dockers are interviewed in the streets, and writing a play about show-biz people isn't the kind of 'in' experience that it used to be. . . . It isn't a closed metaphor any more.*

But this wasn't a new predilection for Osborne: performers are in all his plays, in one guise or another. The new point is that in public life the element of 'show' is more fully recognized now that television has brought the basically false statement into almost every home on every evening. This is not to say that 'real life' people on television intentionally deceive or misrepresent; but they do speak *for* television and in a framed situation and this is not the same as speaking for oneself, or to oneself.

Psychologists, from the Renaissance onwards, have recognized that to consider human behaviour as 'performance' is a useful way of describing levels of consciousness and varying intention. 'There be some,' wrote Bacon, 'whose lives are as if they perpetually played upon a stage, disguised to all others, open only to themselves.'† In 1959,

* 'John Osborne talks to Kenneth Tynan', op. cit., p. 21.
† 'Of Friendship', *Essays* (1612).

Erving Goffman published a study of *The Presentation of Self in Everyday Life**, based on an analysis of assumed roles and various kinds of performances. Goffman and others have taken theatrical terminology as a means of describing both the motives of false assumptions in personal activity and the varying success of them.

In *Look Back in Anger*, pretence, or play-acting, penetrates the most private elements of behaviour. There are two episodes when Jimmy and Alison pretend to be a bear and a squirrel, like the soft and battered toys that sit together on the chest of drawers at the beginning of the play. In the first Act, this impersonation alone makes close and mutual intimacy possible between them. Jimmy gives the cue, after seeing, quite suddenly, how alarmed Alison is, how open to attack:

ALISON [*alarmed at this threat of a different mood*]: Jimmy – please no!

JIMMY [*staring at her anxious face*]: You're very beautiful. A beautiful, great-eyed squirrel.

[*She nods brightly, relieved.*]

Hoarding, nut-munching squirrel. [*She mimes this delightedly.*] (p. 34)

In this game, nothing is mentioned of the antagonisms and suspicions that keep them estranged through most of the play. For Jimmy, conventional words are now loaded with some kind of meaning, and for Alison noises (like 'Oooooooh!' and 'Wheeeeeeeeee!') and animal gestures predominate; both at last embrace simply. The episode is finished and mutual acceptance disturbed, when Jimmy questions her belief: 'What makes you think you're happy?' It seems a poor pretence, a performance strictly limited, without an audience and with small vocabulary. But the play ends with a

* Allen Lane the Penguin Press, 1969.

reenactment. The difference here is a gain in self-conscious-ness: Jimmy describes the bear's cave and squirrel's drey before they enter it; Alison mocks her own acceptance of the invitation before giving him added affection, pity and contact:

JIMMY: . . . There are cruel steel traps lying about everywhere, just waiting for rather mad, slightly satanic, and very timid little animals. Right?
  [*Alison nods.*]
  [*Pathetically*] Poor squirrels!
ALISON [*with the same comic emphasis*]: Poor bears! [*She laughs a little. Then looks at him very tenderly, and adds very, very softly.*] Oh, poor, poor bears!
  [*Slides her arms around him.*]

CURTAIN

In many ways this is a conventional, sentimentally in-dulgent ending to the sex-tangle and the wider references of this play to class, politics, education and social injustice. It is a quiet, tender assumption of togetherness and it implies that the now-chastened man and wife will make the best of bad things. But *Look Back in Anger* is not such a petty play: it boldly runs the risk of being one, so that it can show that even its conclusion is a contrivance, an acceptance of each other that acknowledges an obligatory pretence. Even in 'love', there is 'betrayal' and 'death', in belief, disbelief.

*

The presentation of a man acting a role, or failing to act a role, is one of the most constant elements of theatre langu-age. Hamlet's first long speech to his mother is about 'actions that a man might play', and about something, undefined, that is within him that 'passes show'. Shakes-peare's Coriolanus is required to act a 'part' of a 'mild' politician that he can never perform 'to the life' (III ii

105–6). In tragedy, the hero may strive to 'end his part in peace' on a 'great stage', where all is 'true', and in comedy there is often a sense that the whole illusion of reality is like a play, and that within the artifice is another, simpler, purer world capable of being born. On the one hand a character may discover, with Kierkegaardian faith, that there is a 'midnight hour when all men must unmask', and on the other may come to realize, with Valentine in Congreve's *Love for Love* that 'the comedy draws towards an end, and let us think of leaving acting and be ourselves . . .' (IV 614–15).

In his use of this perennial resource of theatre language, Osborne reveals many of his distinctive achievements. For him to write is to project performances, to give to his chosen characters the opportunity to put themselves over:

Of course [he has said], when I'm writing I see all the parts being played beautifully by me, to perfection.*

The word 'parts' in this quotation is significant, for Osborne's view of character is essentially theatrical: they are made so that they 'work' in terms of performance, and their motivations, utterances and situations are all seen as occasions for performances. In *Look Back in Anger*, the dramatic structure depends on the assertion of roles and the discarding of them. The most vital and believable speeches are offset by moments of non-acting, of 'disbelief', 'defeat', or direct 'appeal', as the stage-directions variously call them.

The effects of this attitude to playwriting are far-reaching. Most noticeably it gives a persistent contentiousness to the plays. The characters commit themselves to opinions on a wide range of social, political, religious, psychological and moral issues, and do so with such dramatic point that they

* 'That Awful Museum', op. cit., p. 216.

are often taken by journalists and others as their author's mouthpieces and quoted out of context. Jimmy Porter's 'There aren't any good, brave causes left', that expresses his frustrated and resentful need for self-justification in a particular context, was pinned as a considered opinion upon Osborne himself, despite his protests:

Immediately they heard this, all the shallow heads with their savage thirst for trimmed-off explanations got to work on it, and they had enough new symbols to play about with happily and fill their columns for half a year. They believed him, just as some believed Archie Rice when he said: 'I don't feel a thing' or 'I may be an old pouf, but I'm not right-wing'. They were incapable of recognizing the texture of ordinary despair, the way it expresses itself in rhetoric and gestures that may perhaps look shabby, but are seldom simple. It is too simple to say that Jimmy Porter himself believed that there were no good, brave causes left, any more than Archie didn't feel a thing.*

Years after these early complaints, it is easier to see that the plays feed minds that seek quick explanations because of the belief-in-the-moment that energizes the writing. But equally, it can be seen that Osborne's plays feed upon reactions such as these. The audience is excited by the words and plausible half-truths: it expects answering opinions and seeks for general implications. If the plays do not satisfy all the intellectual questions raised, they do gain attention, and so Osborne can follow his own purposes: to lead the audience to understand 'ordinary despair', and the level of living beneath, or beyond, that of 'rhetoric' – a level at which these characters exist with their most convincing performances taken away.

The theatrical basis of Osborne's plays is clearest in *The Entertainer*. Its hero, Archie Rice, is a man whose inherited

* *Declarations*, op. cit., p. 69.

profession of comedian is to make people happy and who needs acceptance; but his private life seems to be compounded of evasion and despair. He is shown as his career ends in bankruptcy. The other characters are all performers too, who are put to some test of credibility. Billy Rice, Archie's father, is a retired music-hall comedian; he lives now in memories of his successes and of the more gracious world that he believes he once inhabited. He dies during the play when he tries to recoup Archie's fortunes by making a professional return to the stage.

Phoebe, Archie's wife, had been a plain girl without much sense, who had determined to 'make something' of herself (p. 55). She had made Archie 'want' her, but now that performance is over and his inmost feeling for her is pity. In the play, Phoebe desperately tries to patch together an appearance of dignity, feeling and good sense.

Jean, Archie's daughter by an earlier marriage, has been working in London and trying to find a way of living that she can respect. But she finds that Graham, her fiancé, is held in fixed social attitudes and that to marry him would be to forget her family and imprison whatever it is within herself that she wishes to satisfy. She knows by the end of the play that she cannot move to another world or find a new role: 'We've only got ourselves. Somehow, we've just got to make a go of it' (p. 85). This is a phrase repeated in Archie's comedian's patter:

But I have a go, lady, don't I, I 'ave a go. I do.

(pp. 59, 73 and 88)

Archie has two sons by Phoebe who are clearly contrasted. The younger, Mick, does not appear in the play, although his story affects all the other characters. He has been conscripted into the Army and so, off-stage, he does what he is told to do and performs as a soldier; he is captured in

war and then killed. The elder son, Frank, is a conscientious
objector and now stokes boilers in a hospital. His job is
quite unsuitable for him because he has a weak chest, but
at home he has developed a comedian's routine, as explained in a stage-direction:

[*He has allowed himself to slip into the role of* ARCHIE's '*feed*' *because
this seems to be a warm, reasonable relationship substitute that suits them
both. He is impulsive, full of affection that spills over easily. He is
young, and will probably remain so.*]   (p. 51)

Besides Graham, who makes a brief, stiff appearance
near the end, the only other speaking character is Archie's
brother, William, a highly successful lawyer. He speaks with
care and offers unsympathetic kindness. In trying to help,
but not to meet with, his poor relations, he is a bad actor,
stiff and uncommunicative for all his self-assurance.

The cast is completed by a silent nude who poses in
Archie's show as Britannia, complete with helmet, bulldog
and trident. In the general plan of the characterization of
this play, she is not only the vulgar centre of Archie's
appeal to his public but also the one composed, enigmatic
performer among the cast. She also represents 'God and
Country', the final appeal of several of Archie and Frank's
songs, as of Billy's reminiscences and Jean's scorn; she is a
living equivalent of the Union Jack that drapes Billy's
coffin when the whole family attend his funeral. In this
composed, nude and static performer, Osborne embodies
the ideals of the British Empire.

The theatricality of *The Entertainer* goes beyond characterization, statement and plot, to a style of presentation that
ensures changing modes of perception. Osborne divides the
play, like a music-hall programme, into 'numbers', preceded by an Overture and divided by two Intermissions.
He directs that:

[*The lighting is the kind you expect to see in the local Empire – everything bang-on, bright and hard, or a simple follow-spot. The scenes and interludes must, in fact, be lit as if they were simply turns on the bill. Furniture and props are as basic as they would be for a short sketch.*]   (p. 12)

Some scenes with Archie Rice appearing 'solo' with an orchestra, against a backdrop or nude tableau, are clearly music-hall.

The play starts by alternating domestic and music-hall scenes, but their two realities are directly connected in the words of Archie's songs:

> Why should I care . . .
> What's the use of despair . . .   (pp. 24–5)

and

> We are all out for good old number one,
> Number one's the only one for me!   (pp. 32–3)

In 'Number Five', Archie returns to his home 'making an entry' with the energy, patter and joke-telling of his theatrical performances. He forces the pitch of the general talk until Phoebe cries out at the uncertainty of their lives ('Oh, Christ, I wish I knew what was going to happen to us!'), and is persuaded to go to bed. From Billy, Archie gets a final song which, by the old man's choice, is 'Onward Christian Soldiers'. Archie and Jean are then alone, and he reveals that he has been covering up his knowledge that Mick has been taken prisoner of war. At the end of this 'Number' and of the first Act, Archie falters while telling a story about two nuns:

[*He trails off, looking very tired and old. He looks across at* JEAN *and pushes the bottle at her.*]
ARCHIE: Talk to me.

CURTAIN

In Act Two, there are only three numbers, the first and last together showing a prolonged family party, celebrating Mick's safety and the promise of his safe return. Phoebe starts '*flushed with drink*', speaking with stronger confidence and stronger desperation. Archie enters '*prepared to be gay*', but he '*is tired and has begun to give up the situation*'. He makes a theatrically rhetorical attack on their pretensions and 'kills' Phoebe's 'story' by means of which she had tried to face the economic facts of their life. Soon he is calling for everyone to 'pull themselves together', singing:

Let's pull ourselves together, together, together. Let's pull ourselves together, and the happier we'll be!   (p. 58)

He tries to get Phoebe to dance and Frank to sing, and for everyone to 'whoop it up'. But at this point item 'Number Seven' in the programme intervenes. Now Archie is seen alone facing an audience supported by music, but:

[*Just now and then, for a second or two, he gives the tiniest indication that he is almost surprised to find himself where he is.*]   (p. 59)

He speaks as his father – 'You should have heard what James Agate said about *me*!' – and then comes '*Back again*' with 'But I have a go, Lady, don't I?'. He '*stumbles*' in his performance with:

Look at me – it's all real, you know. Me – all real, nothing shoddy. You don't think I'm real, do you? Well, I'm not. (p. 59)

and then retrieves the half-real performance with a song:

> Now I'm just an ordinary bloke . . .
> Thank God I'm normal,
> I'm just like the rest of you chaps.

As the orchestra plays 'Land of Hope and Glory', he turns the song into a parade of patriotism:

It's chaps like us – yes you and me,
Who'll march again to victory.
Some people say we're finished,
Some people say we're done.
But if we all stand
[*Spotlight behind gauze reveals a nude in Britannia's helmet and holding a bulldog and trident.*]
By this dear old land,
The battle will be won.

Mick's fighting and capture, Billy's sentimental regard for the past, the notion of greatness inborn and victorious, is celebrated theatrically over against the shiftless and apparent defeat of Archie's life and art.

After this half-real, stumbling performance, the scene shifts back to the party. Archie is in the middle of a story and soon Frank is singing one of Billy's old songs. Even Phoebe sings, knowing that it sounds 'bloody awful', but as the party begins to break up she holds up the moment to tell Jean of her niece's letter inviting Archie and her to Canada to manage a family hotel. Frank is in favour of accepting this, for he can think of no good reason for staying where he is, but Archie, who is getting really drunk, shows his hostility in every way he can. Again he is left alone with Jean, but this time he talks. He first discloses that her mother had 'caught' him in bed with Phoebe, had immediately left him and shortly afterwards died. Jean hardly responds, and this provokes a last story about being alone in a bar in the States, and an account of a performance that none of theirs matches:

One night I heard some negress singing in a bar. *Now you're going to smile at this*, you're going to smile your educated English head off, because I suppose you've never sat lonely and half slewed in some bar among strangers a thousand miles from anything you think you understand. But if ever I saw any hope or strength in the human race, it was in the face of that old fat negress getting up to sing about Jesus or something like that. She was poor and lonely and oppressed like nobody you've ever known. Or me, for that matter. I never even liked that kind of music, but to see that old black whore singing her heart out to the whole world, you knew somehow in your heart that it didn't matter how much you kick people, the real people, how much you despise them, if they can stand up and make a pure, just natural noise like that, there's nothing wrong with them, only with everybody else. I've never heard anything like that since. I've never heard it here . . . I wish to God I were that old bag. I'd stand up and shake my great bosom up and down, and lift up my head and make the most beautiful fuss in the world. Dear God, I would. But I'll never do it. I don't give a damn about anything, not even women or draught Bass.   (pp. 70–71)

He brings the point home with, 'Do you think that you're going to do it? Well, do you?' Jean gives no answer and Archie goes on in a mixture of confession and boasting.

At this moment, however, Phoebe returns to say there's a policeman downstairs, and Frank follows to announce that Mick has been killed. Only Archie responds as he sings a blues:

Oh, Lord, I don't care where they bury my body. . . .

The whole of Act Two demonstrates that a performance is no defence, unless it is 'whole' and 'natural', and 'good'. The Act finishes with a brief performance from Archie imitating the old fat negress, at least in musical form. This is more than a quick reflection: it draws together all the incidents of the play until this point, all its despair and whatever bravery there is behind the continued attempt to amuse, to cover and to give meaning.

The third Act starts with a blues by Frank at the piano concerning Mick and the 'Britain' he died for, but the style of the other scenes is now less clearly either theatrical or domestic. Number Ten is talk after the funeral, during which Jean attacks her father for thinking he 'can cover' himself (p. 77) and no one wants to listen to her. The scene ends with two developments in the plot: Billy is to return to the stage: he has seen the parents of a young girl Archie has been promising to marry in order to finance his next show, and he has told them that Archie is already married. Billy's determination to prevent deception has made Archie's bankruptcy certain unless he can gain money by making a theatrical 'come-back'. The next number is very short: Archie announcing to some kind of audience that Billy 'will not appear again', and then a tableau of the family gathered around his coffin, supported by '*snatches of old song . . .*'. For Number Twelve there are two dialogues proceeding simultaneously: Jean and her fiancé, and Archie and his brother. The two 'successful' men offer a security that neither Jean nor Archie believes in. Archie will go to prison rather than to Canada; Jean will stay with Phoebe and her family to whom she needs to 'say something'. By juxtaposing the two confrontations, Osborne ensures that the audience compares all four figures, and sees in Jean's rejection of Graham the same stubborn attempt to be 'truthful' – believable to herself – as lies behind Archie's acceptance of defeat.

An intenser focus upon the isolated performer comes in the last scene, Number Thirteen. In front of the nude tableau, Archie Rice performs again, beginning this time with a song: 'We're all out for good old Number One'. He presses on in his familiar manner – 'I'm doing me nut, you know that, don't you?' – but he '*puts in a line*' here and there. Performance becomes a nightmare soliloquy. The two styles of the first Act are now one. Archie is exposed in a spotlight before the real audience. Before he finishes with the questioning song, 'Why should I care?', the theatrical

scenery has all disappeared and the music is 'soft'. Alone
'*in a little round world of light*', Archie swaggers, falters,
stops and '*stares ahead of him*', and then '*picks up*' again.
Again he fails, but this time stares '*up*' before going on;
before he finally stops, Phoebe appears with his coat and
hat. Archie goes to her and she helps him on with his
outdoor coat, but then he hesitates, walks back into the light
and thanks his audience. The curtain does not come down
yet, for Archie has still to turn his back on the audience and
walk upstage with Phoebe, leaving the spotlight hitting the
stage-apron. Then the light '*snaps out*' and the stage is
bare and dark: there is only the music, and then 'Curtain'.

In many ways this conclusion allows Osborne to bring all
his themes together, and to use the '*little world*' of the stage
to present Archie most openly to the audience. The Entertainer knows he is performing, and yet he confesses that the
nude Britannia has 'got more clothes on than I have'
(p. 86). As the performer breaks down, he knows he
'cares', quite hopelessly. As Osborne says in a preparatory
note:

I have not used some of the techniques of the music hall in order
to exploit an effective trick, but because I believe that these can
solve some of the eternal problems of time and space that face
the dramatist, and, also, it has been relevant to the story and
setting. . . . Its contact is immediate, vital and direct.

Osborne's view of men as performers has never been so
directly stated as in this play. There is sentimentality, in
the empty stage, darkness, retiring figures and music,
because he employs hackneyed theatrical trickery and calls
for only generalized and easy responses. But Osborne has
placed the whole characterization and action in theatrical
terms and so this ending may also be received as a conscious
assumption of a merely theatrical comfort that the audience

will necessarily 'see through', and in their rejection be forced to question the whole contrivance of the play. Because Osborne plays with belief, he opens his work to total disbelief. As Archie says, early in the evening, 'We're characters out of something that nobody believes in' (p. 54). By following this play throughout its action and changing stage-realities, we can see that Osborne entertains us knowing that this is all that he does: he calls for belief and disbelief, and at the end of the play both seem to coexist.

*

After *The Entertainer*, changing the styles of presentation within a play becomes a dominant element in Osborne's playwriting. In the 'unsuccessful' *World of Paul Slickey*, the variety is heightened by devices of musical comedy and revue. The mutations here often seem crude, arbitrary and over-obvious, but because of the expense of production on an appropriate scale it is unlikely that the play will have a second chance to justify itself. Financially, at least, Osborne had overplayed his hand.

For *Luther*, the next play, Osborne chose a well-known historical figure who gains belief in his own right. But he is still almost as bold in manipulation of stage illusion, as a note before Act Two shows:

After the intense private interior of Act One, with its outer darkness and rich, personal objects, the physical effect from now on should be more intricate, general, less personal; sweeping, concerned with men in time rather than particular man in the unconscious; caricature not portraiture, like the popular woodcuts of the period, like Dürer.

Already, within the first Act, Osborne has switched styles several times. The formal ritual of the service in which Martin is received into the order of St Augustine is followed by a procession off-stage in which the hero is only one among many identical figures. Then his father, Hans, talks with a companion about the 'impressiveness' of the service and the loss of a son, in a careful, self-conscious expository duologue. By the end of this talk, Hans changes: he '*has ceased to play a role*', as a stage-direction makes clear, and asks bluntly what made Martin do it. The scene then returns to formality, a holy reading while the brothers eat and Martin serves at table, and this changes to a communal confession during which Martin's agonized outcries contrast with concern for petty omissions and requests for forgiveness. When the brothers move to the Choir, Martin is again '*lost to sight in the ranks*', only to break through the singing with violent cries. After a physical struggle and a slowly enunciated 'Not! Me! I am *not*!', he is dragged off-stage and the singing resumes without faltering. From the outset of this play Osborne has used varied theatrical styles to establish belief and disbelief.

In Acts Two and Three, Martin is shown as a solo performer giving two sermons and a statement of self-defence at the Diet of Worms, and finally one nightmare sermon in which he is challenged by the 'Knight' who has fought for the religious and social causes stirred up by Martin's preaching. And again the central character is surrounded by other performers: his father; Tetzel, the Indulgence vendor and ecclesiastical trickster; Cajetan, the Cardinal who offers the Church's love to Martin and then reveals that the price is total submission; Leo, the Pope, who can amuse himself while performing his holy functions. Staupitz, the Vicar General of the Augustine Order, appears with Martin early in Act Two, counselling and encouraging the young man without any sign of disbelief. He questions Martin's obsessions with the Rule of the order, but not the grounds for his belief. In the final scene, however, Osborne brings Staupitz back and shows him after dining with

Martin and the ex-nun the ex-monk has recently married. Staupitz now asks why Martin had delayed at Worms before he had refused the papal demand for recantation. When Martin confesses that he had not heard God's voice in that predicament, only his own, and that he was not 'sure' of his grounds, Staupitz kisses him and says, 'Thank you, my son. May God bless you . . .' With the basis of Martin's performance made thus explicit, the play is all but finished. Martin calls for his baby son, and says that at Worms he was 'almost like' him:

as if I'd learned to play again, to play, to play out in the world, like a naked child.   (p. 102)

Then Martin remembers, hopefully, Christ's promise that He should be revealed.

Osborne's play, *Luther*, moves more quickly and confidently than *The Entertainer* from style to style; it uses a wider variety of 'performance' techniques and attempts to give at the close a more precise and verbally defined notion of the nature of belief. Its last scene is low-toned and reflective, and yet there is still the obvious sentimental appeal of a father holding a baby. Even here Osborne risks sentimentality to make the private centre of the play strong enough for his final curtain, a last crude assumption of theatricality, but one based on the simplest and largest hopes.

Few of the later plays run such risks. In *Time Present* and *Hotel in Amsterdam*, the only shifts of style come in and with the dialogue, although in the former play the performances of Pamela's actor-father, in a grand, 'big', Shakespearian manner, hold some contrasting interest as they are described and viewed in photographs. In these plays the shifts of perspective and of belief are incessant; the performers are quick, accomplished, fashionable and nervously insecure.

Occasionally, especially in *Time Present*, this shifting illusion of reality is explicitly noted:

CONSTANCE: You don't mean that.
PAMELA: But I do, my darling. It's like everyone thinks actors have got no brains and live in some world walled up from the realities everyone else is immersed in. Something . . .
CONSTANCE: Your voice sounds quite different sometimes. I suppose it's when you don't believe in the lines you're reading.
PAMELA: How can I convince you?
CONSTANCE: You have. (p. 35)

In the published script for the film *Tom Jones* (1964), the change of style is clearest as the scene moves to London. A 'Technical Note' explains that Tom now '*sees a world of luxury and vice heightened as it must be in the eyes of a country boy*' and explains that the style consequentially changes, the colour taking on '*a new violence and garishness*' (p. 98). Here is a specific acknowledgement of a shift in the mode of illusion in order to expose a character's behaviour and response.

In *A Patriot for Me* (1965), Osborne uses many characters and an episodic structure, all demanding stylistic changes. His main intention seems to be, not the epic picture of a society, but the building up of a complex view of his central character as a low-born officer performing in an aristocratic army, a homosexual performing, sometimes, as a heterosexual, a man of honour performing as a spy. A transvestite ball, a Freudian lecture and a bedroom provide contrasting realities for the sexual narrative; shift of countries, or from masters to servants, provides for other elements of the story. In his last moments the exposed spy and adventurer is shown talking in terms of national responsibility rather than his own needs. Those motivations have been clearest – least hidden by performance – in free and helpless impulse when he had a boy in his arms.

Inadmissible Evidence (1964) is the only play to develop in the straight line from *Look Back in Anger* and *The Entertainer*. It centres on a dominant performer-character to such an extent that he is on-stage for the whole play. The stylistic changes depend directly and solely on his mode of perception. It starts with a dream and the rest, which is a kind of flash-back from the future predicated by the fantasy, moves from realistic comings-and-goings and interchanges of talk to telephone conversations, interviews and a one-sided, ineffectual conversation with a silent daughter, that are much closer in style to the dream talk at the outset. A note requires that they:

[*should progressively resemble the feeling of dream and unreality of* BILL's *giving 'evidence' at the beginning of Act 1. Some of the time it should all seem actually taking place at the particular moment, naturally, casual, lucid, unclouded. At others the grip of the dream grows tighter; for example, in the call that follows now, the presence of the person on the other end should be made very real indeed, but sometimes it should trail off into a feeling of doubt as to whether there is anyone to speak to at all.*]

(p. 59)

Maitland, the solicitor who specializes in divorce and sexual cases, speaks progressively to himself and for himself: he holds the stage unambiguously, except in his own mind. Here Osborne has developed his basic style and theme further and more boldly than anywhere else.

*

All of Osborne's plays present, in various ways, a story of defeat, and from defeat some personal affirmation develops. Such a basic action serves well for Osborne's twin exploitation of highly theatrical performances and intimate exposures. His climaxes do not reveal new powers or personal alignments as do Pinter's; nor, like those of *A Slight Ache*, *The Caretaker* or *The Homecoming*, do they lead the audience to see the characters of the drama in a wider, more timeless perspective. But at the centre of Osborne's revelations of character-in-defeat is a realization of the need for courage to continue with the most basic elements of life that are, by the last scenes, known only too well.

In most of the plays, the main story is accompanied by one or more accounts of actual death, of defeats from which there is no return. In *Look Back in Anger*, Alison's baby dies and Jimmy's friend Mrs Tanner. Before the action begins, but recollected at an emotional climax, Jimmy's father has died, misunderstood and isolated. In *The Entertainer*, Mick and Billy die off-stage and, before the play begins, Archie's first wife, Jean's mother. In *Luther*, the deaths are multiple, the slaughter of thousands of helpless and frustrated peasants in the wars that broke out after Martin had defied the Pope, and which Martin denounced. The contrasts provided by these off-stage deaths are purposeful, and yet suggest that the dramatist is evading a direct presentation of death itself. Even the deaths of Redl and Leonido, the central characters of *A Patriot for Me* and *A Bond Honoured*, are not shown on stage.

Inadmissible Evidence is the main exception. No actual death is involved, but the central character's defeat is viewed much more relentlessly and, at the end, he has exhausted all his known resources. There is no acceptance of a further life, in the manner in which Archie accepts prison, Martin a child, and Jimmy the bears and squirrels. This 'death' is foretold in the nightmare 'judgement' scene at the beginning of the play and so the audience's attention is directed on how Maitland fails, his pains and fears. At the close he can only cut himself off from everyone and wait for the cruel help of the Law Society, or someone, sometime. It is the slowest and most relentless of the plays, but Osborne's verbal and theatrical command does not appear to falter. While some of the dream-like soliloquies seem to echo Lucky in *Waiting for Godot*, the context for this change of style is quite unlike that of Beckett's play: Maitland has a supposedly helpful judge to set him off and a fully imagined personal story is reflected in the struggling, failing language. Moreover, his urgent attempt to give point to his appeal is at least as like Archie's last performance as it is like Lucky's. His attempt to remain within the ritual of the law courts is like Martin's anguished conformity to the 'rule' of his order, only not so hopefully endured.

Besides directing attention to the manner of Maitland's defeat the dream-opening also gives meaning to the subsidiary characters. Its Judge and Clerk of Court become the managing clerk and assistant in the solicitor's office, and so their continued stage-presence is a reminder of the Society's rebuke and potential opposition. To similar effect, Maitland's clients are played by a single actress and by the actor of Jones, the clerk. As Maitland interrupts Mrs Tonks's evidence with admissions of his own failures, and takes over from Mrs Anderson with his view of his own wife after his death, it is clear that his fear and guilt take over from his professional conduct, so that he sees a continuing personal struggle in the affairs of individual clients. He falls silent as he offers to supply Marples with a missing witness so that client and solicitor 'look at each other' in silence, and then Marples takes control. The continuing presence of the one actress and the merging of Jones with Marples ensure that the audience views the stage with something of Maitland's own obsessions, seeing a continuing confrontation. As Maitland is no longer objective, and can no longer make decisions, so the stage is no longer restricted by what could actually happen. This picture of law-routine is distorted, restricted and extended as in Maitland's mind.

The interview with his daughter still further changes style

and viewpoint. Jane is silent throughout, cool yet distressed and scared. Maitland speaks with longing in response to her unselfconscious confidence. Acknowledging her departure, he must then see Joy, the telephonist with whom he has just had sex. He hears that 'like everyone else' she finds him 'unlikeable'. Next Liz, his mistress, enters and, after subterfuges expressing pleasure and interchanges of criticism and recollection, the last duologue is precise on both sides. They agree to cancel their prospective weekend, an explicit parting which both of them had expected and delayed throughout the encounter. A mutual acknowledgement of pleasure in their love-making is not enough to keep them together. He communicates by words, and she by touch, but they have no means of relating this or their pleasure to a way of life that could reflect their mutual experience, no way of trusting each other. She leaves and he rings Anna, his wife, to say he is not coming home.

Words and actions are now making real the end of his statement to the Judge in the opening dream:

I am not equal to any of it. But I can't escape it, I can't forget it. And I can't begin again. You see?   (p. 20)

The audience does see now, without an easy, generalized ending. Osborne has provided a series of encounters with four clients and the four women currently in Maitland's life that give a remorseless exposure. All his artifice is defeated and all his pretence stripped away. His power to sympathize with others now feeds his self-laceration. Maitland comes to a full stop, dead to the ordinary world, and yet more alive in recognition of his own and other people's needs than in his most confident moments before the routine of his solicitor's life had broken down. His victory is inadmissible.

In this play, Osborne has not evaded death; he has shown

the end of a life among others, and the preservation of the life of heart and mind. Moreover, he has ensured that the audience sees with his victim's eyes and thinks with his mind. Theatrical language, through exploitation of acting possibilities and a changing dramatic illusion, has expressed an individual, inward struggle with love and life, and done so with sensitive particularity and thoroughness.

5

ARNOLD WESKER

Theatrical Demonstration

Roots, The Kitchen and *Chips with Everything*

'I want to teach': Arnold Wesker made this aim clear as early as 1958 when only *Chicken Soup with Barley* had been seen in London. In an article called 'Let the Battle Commence'* he announced his grand purpose of creating a new audience for 'popular' theatre:

I want to write my plays not only for the class of people who acknowledge plays to be a legitimate form of expression, but for those to whom the phrase 'form of expression' may mean nothing whatsoever.

All art for him was 'a tool, equipment for the enjoyment of living, for its better understanding'. As a 'beginning', he acknowledged that 'each work of art is an attempt to convert', by establishing 'values', and his method was to show life on the stage:

I want to write about people in a way that will somehow give them an insight to an aspect of life which they may not have had before; and further, I want to impart to them some of the enthusiasm I have for that life.

Before writing his first play, Wesker had attended the London School of Film Technique and this may have

* *Encore*, Vol. V, no. 4 (1958), pp. 18–24.

suggested the basic realism of his approach. Certainly in *The Kitchen*, written in 1957, he broke most of the rules of dramatic construction by assuming that human activity could be reproduced on the stage in full, with little basic plot and with anonymous as well as named characters. The main interest is held by one or two figures within the bustling context of a kitchen serving a large restaurant, and the focus constantly moves from one group to another. Even when the play was revised for London production in 1961, so that it ran for the customary length of time and was divided into 'Two Parts with an Interlude', it still had thirty named characters and prefatory notes that detailed the complicated work-routines. Wesker wrote in this way for the stage because he wished to show life as he found it outside the theatre: 'The world might have been a stage for Shakespeare,' he said at this time, 'but to me it is a kitchen. . . .'*

When the new dramatist went to see *Look Back in Anger* at the Royal Court Theatre, and saw in action the small cast and tight-knit theatricality of Osborne's play, his response was to write *Chicken Soup with Barley*. Compared with *The Kitchen*, it is conventional, with three Acts, a single line of action and a series of built-up climaxes and curtain-lines. But for Osborne's four characters, Wesker used ten, for his one set and short time-scheme he substituted two sets and changed the time from 1936 to 1946, to 1947, to 1955 and finally, to 1956. The play moves across the years as quickly as the film, and off-stage, outside the set, a complex activity of filmic proportions is always in process: political meetings, mob violence, strikes, trade-union debates, marriage, setting-up home, starting a business, a world war, and life in a kitchen.

Obviously Wesker's world is no smaller than in *The Kitchen*,

* *The Kitchen*, 'Introduction and Notes for the Producer'.

but he is here attempting a more economical, conventional and possibly stronger theatrical style.

Chicken Soup was followed a year later by *Roots* (1959), and the following year by *I'm Talking About Jerusalem* (1960). Together these plays form a trilogy, sometimes repeating characters and alluding to events common to all three. They show Wesker trying to 'teach', exploring conventional and original ways of making the theatre mirror life and assert values.

*

At its simplest, Wesker's plan for the trilogy was to substitute talk for the more complex action. In *Chicken Soup*, four or five characters comment on events that take place off-stage; they debate issues, question motives, consider reactions, and keep the talk going:

SARAH: ... You have to start with love. How can you talk about socialism otherwise?

MONTY: Hear, hear, Comrade Kahn. Come on now, what is this? We've just won one of the biggest fights in working-class history and all we do is quarrel. (pp. 28–9)

The problem talked about could scarcely be larger nor the dialogue more self-consciously sustained. Often two opposed views are each given their run:

ADA: ... When Dave comes back we shall leave London and live in the country. That'll be our socialism. Remember this, Ronnie: the family should be a unit, and your work and your life should be part of one existence, not something hacked about by a bus queue and office hours. A man should see, know, and love his job. Don't you want to feel your life? Savour it gently? In the country we shall be somewhere where the air doesn't smell of bricks and the kids can grow up without seeing grandparents who are continually shouting at each other.

SARAH: Ada, Ada.

RONNIE: And no more political activity?

ADA: No more political activity.

RONNIE: I bet Dave won't agree to that. Dave fought in Spain. He won't desert humanity like that.

ADA: Humanity! Ach!

RONNIE: Listen to her! With a Labour majority in the House? And two of our own Party members? It's only just beginning.

ADA: It's always only just beginning for the Party. Every defeat is victory and every victory is the beginning.

RONNIE: But it is, it is the beginning. Plans for town and country planning. New cities and schools and hospitals. [*Jumping up on chair to* HARRY'*s facetious applause.*] Nationalization! National health! Think of it, the whole country is going to be organized to co-operate instead of tear at each other's throat. That's what I said to them in a public speech at school and all the boys cheered and whistled and stamped their feet – and blew raspberries.

ADA: I do not believe in the right to organize people . . .

(pp. 40–41)

During this argument Wesker keeps a non-theoretical involvement going at the same time: the mother, Sarah, gently reproves by calling Ada by name; Ada echoes 'Humanity' scornfully and exclaims; Ronnie mounts the chair to ironic applause from his father. This more 'human', individual drama often speaks without words, or words are turned against their obvious meaning. It is sometimes a question whether debate is killed by this dramatic device, or drama by the debate: at its best, however, this style allows the one to comment on, or support the other. So at the end of this particular debate, the long speeches stop and personal bickering and old-established antipathies show themselves. Ronnie is then given an answer to both the talk about the welfare state and the evidence of disappointment in marriage. He simply collects the dishes and, '*escaping to the kitchen*', announces, 'I'll wash up' (p. 43). Among all the

talk about mutual help, no one on stage notices his departure; but movement, rhythm and contrast will all draw the
audience's attention to Ronnie, and so his contrasting
'value' will be demonstrated.

Wesker once said that his plays were:

attempts to continue arguments that I have had with friends and
relatives and people that I worked with. Discussion is never
satisfactory – you always go away and remember the thing you
should have said.*

Occasionally he seems to be doing just this, but more often
he is aware of larger dramatic issues: the personal embodiment of ideas, the pull away from theorizing and
argument, the need to sharpen and excite by seeking out
arguments that are unexpected, positions that seem in-
defensible, attempts at persuasion that are misunderstood. In *I'm Talking About Jerusalem*, the chief characters
are Dave and Ada, now married and living in the country,
and Wesker brings on stage to talk with them not only
mother, brother and maiden aunts from the other plays, but
also two uninterested furniture removers, a boy apprentice
and an aggressive-defensive cynic from Dave's earlier life
in the RAF. In *Roots*, he introduces Stan Mann, a neighbour who is old, drunk and content, to talk and be talked
about; he plays no part in the plot, but is there to contrast
the labouring lives and the earnest dissatisfaction of Beatie
Bryant.

But, progressively, Wesker moved away from argument.
Even in *Chicken Soup with Barley*, the climax to each Act was
not a debate-point or affirmation, but the confrontation or
separation of two or more characters. At the end of Act

* 'His Very Own and Golden City' (an interview with Arnold
Wesker by Simon Trussler), *Tulane Drama Review*, Vol. XI, no. 4 (1966),
p. 192.

One, Sarah comforts Ada, while Harry, the father, tells the world in the street that Ada is mad: the curtain falls as Ronnie, then aged five, enters and watches '*bewildered*'. At the end of Act Two, Ronnie tries to prevent his father opening a doctor's letter for the hospital that is about his illness: he asserts his will and his father becomes like a shrieking child; they are both frightened, and they impulsively embrace. Ronnie explains that his father's lies and weakness warn him of what he may become in his turn; and then his father shuffles '*miserably to his room, perceptibly older*', saying:

You can't alter people, Ronnie. You can only give them some love and hope they'll take it. I'm sorry. It's too late now. I can't help you . . . Don't forget to have supper. Good night.   (p. 56)

Ronnie is left alone and in this stage-picture is implicit the themes of the play, the need for love and courage, and the helplessness of life. At the end of Act Three, Ronnie has returned after years abroad, dispirited and disillusioned, and his mother rallies him with argument and the story of Mrs Bernstein's chicken-soup-with-barley that had saved Ada's life when her father had given up caring. Ronnie tries to escape from his mother's eloquence and her embrace, but can only mumble that everything is 'too big to care for'. This time it is Ronnie who leaves and his mother is left shouting after him: 'You'll die . . . if you don't care, you'll die'; and then he '*turns slowly to face her*' (p. 77).

For each of these 'curtains', the climax is inert, narrowly focused and verbally inexpressive, and this seems to have dissatisfied Wesker. Rather than seek for ways of giving precise meaning to such confrontations, he sought out fuller and more sustained activity that could express the involvement of a greater number of characters. The whole of *Roots*, he claimed, is:

163

a theatrical demonstration of a point that is made in the last speech. When I have people coming on with a tin bath and sweeping up and washing up, it's not simply because I want to capture real life; what I'm trying to do is demonstrate all the little things which go to make up a point.*

In a stage-direction near the beginning, Wesker warns the actors and director:

BEATIE *helps collect dishes from table and proceeds to help wash up. This is a silence that needs organizing. Throughout the play there is no sign of intense living from any of the characters –* BEATIE*'s bursts are the exception. They continue in a routine rural manner. The day comes, one sleeps at night, there is always the winter, the spring, the autumn, and the summer – little amazes them. They talk in fits and starts mainly as a sort of gossip, and they talk quickly too, enacting as though for an audience what they say. Their sense of humour is keen and dry. They show no affection for each other – though this does not mean they would not be upset were one of them to die. The silences are important – as important as the way they speak, if we are to know them.* (p. 90)

Silences are not used to sharpen attention on particular words, gestures or hesitations that can reveal individual involvement as in Pinter's plays, nor as the still centres of dramatic conflict as in Osborne's. Here silences are usually corporate, and indications of personal and social limitations rather than clues to hidden power or tension. They are often filled with activity that is, specifically, of a routine nature: they indicate a kind of death rather than a hint of unaccustomed life or half-acknowledged crisis. Wesker is intent on presenting a way of living, shared and, in his view, largely bankrupt.

For Mrs Bryant, Beatie's mother, he has a special stage-direction:

* 'Question and Answer' (interview with Jill Pomerance), *New Theatre Magazine*, Vol. I, no. 3 (1960), p. 6.

[MRS BRYANT *is a short, stout woman of fifty. She spends most of the day on her own, and consequently when she has a chance to speak to anybody she says as much as she can as fast as she can. The only people she sees are the tradesmen, her husband, the family when they pop in occasionally. She speaks very loudly all the time so that her friendliest tone sounds aggressive, and she manages to dramatize the smallest piece of gossip into something significant. Each piece of gossip is a little act done with little looking at the person to whom it is addressed.* ...] (p. 105)

Wesker's concern is to show how she fits in, and how she is isolated. What interests him about her speech is chiefly how it contributes to his view of rural life and of a society with little enjoyment and mutual activity. For the curtain of Act Two, Mrs Bryant is given a precise action that is very different from her usual behaviour and implies contact and agreement with her daughter. She had turned off Mendelssohn's Fourth Symphony that Beatie had just found on the radio, and Beatie attacked her saying that her country life had 'no majesty', no experience comparable to the music. They argue about the worth of culture, and of talking and reading, and so Beatie chooses a record for her mother to listen to. She ignores interruptions to explain how two simple tunes interact and knit together; she dances; she says it makes her 'feel light and confident and happy'. The music is now faster, and she cries to her mother:

God, Mother, we could all be so much more happy and alive. Wheeeee . . .
    [BEATIE *claps her hands and dances on and her Mother smiles and claps her hands and* –] (p. 130)
        THE CURTAIN FALLS

To close this Act Wesker has found an affirmative action that gains in power by contrast with the slow and dispersed rhythms, the lack of contact and inadequacies of the preceding action. The music is Bizet's *L'Arlésienne* Suite and a stage-direction explains that the dance is outlandish, '*a mixture of a cossack dance and a sailor's hornpipe*'. This Act-ending climax is a clownish kind of resolution, a temporary escape with implications of a potential 'majesty'.

For the end of this play, Wesker devised a large-scale, spectacular episode, where two contrary ways of living are visibly manifested. Beatie's fiancé, Ronnie, is expected from London, and the whole family, or those who can bear to be in the same room as each other, are gathered for a high tea of welcome; and he fails to turn up. As Beatie weeps, her father asks, 'Well, what do we do now?' and her mother answers, 'We sit down and we eat, that's what we do now'. Beatie cries that she hates her mother and she is slapped on her face for her words. There is a despairing and frightening row between the two women, until Beatie is asked to explain what she means by saying they have no roots. Then, instead of quoting Ronnie all the time, she finds words of her own. She decries Ronnie's view of the good rural life and blames herself and her family for being content with the third rate. She stops, pauses and with an '*ecstatic smile on her face*' recognizes that she is speaking for herself at last, staking her claim to be alive and demanding:

I'm not quoting no more . . . Listen to me someone . . . God in heaven, *Ronnie*! It does work, it's happening to me, I can feel it's happened, I'm beginning, on my own two feet – I'm beginning . . .   (p. 150)

She is indeed standing above the family who sit down to eat, with nothing to add or comment. In most productions the girl is standing on a chair, or holding a chair aloft. The stage-direction insists that she is '*alone, articulate at last*', as the curtain falls. The play is about a girl who breaks with her absorbed and absorbing family, and from a tutelage to someone who seems more free and 'majestic' than he is.

She claims independence and seeks for roots that are those of aspiration and responsibility, at least to one's self. At the last moment, this is 'demonstrated' in a significant action that supports the arguments of the play as a whole and moves beyond them with a new 'voice' and self-awareness.

The contribution of the family to the ending of *Roots* is an eloquent demonstration because it is prepared for throughout the play. It is a development of earlier meals, tidyings-up, washings-up, incomplete family gatherings, a culminating expression of communal life, a recognizable ritual of mindless solidarity. In *I'm Talking About Jerusalem*, Wesker's Act-endings are also climactic, but the one which is most clearly a demonstration in the manner of *Roots* strains towards a more general and ambitious relevance. At the end of Act Two, Dave and Ada play with their child, Danny, using a game called 'Look I'm alive'. Wesker asks for '*the touch of magic and of clowning*', and directs that the light should fade towards evening during the game (p. 201). But even with this help, the audience will experience a jarring switch from immediate narrative interest and argument to the miming of the act of creation and the voice of a child imitating a 'human being'. Elsewhere there is talk of creating a new world and walking into paradise, but only here at the end of Act Two and in brief moments when Dave offers an olive branch in '*homage*' to Ada, or Ronnie impulsively lights a fire or the Kahn family sing a folk-song, does Wesker try to demonstrate in expressive action what this world might be like. Argument, narrative and demonstration do not work continuously and climactically together as in *Roots*: here the dramatist stops the drama for a tendentious symbolic insert.

About this time, Wesker said in an interview that he had developed:

to the stage where I am no longer satisfied if characters in my plays are simply on the stage talking to each other, throwing their emotions all over the place. . . . What I try to have them do is *demonstrate* an idea, live it out, act it out.*

*

After completing the trilogy, Wesker went back to *The Kitchen,* a play based on activity, to revise and lengthen his earlier version. Narrative, argument and character are all subordinate here to spectacle and action, to 'living it out'. When Wesker had said that for him 'the world' was 'a kitchen', he continued to explain that in a kitchen:

people come and go and cannot stay long enough to understand each other, and friendships, loves and enmities are forgotten as quickly as they are made. (p. 93)

This implies an attitude to plot and character that is diametrically opposed to the accepted tenets of play-writing that ask for regular exposition, definition of character, development of emotional climaxes and revelation of hidden motives. But *The Kitchen* stands as an example of a play that deliberately breaks these 'rules' to make its own kind of demonstration.

It is arguable that any dramatist wishing to establish 'values' in day-to-day living should show life without the excitements of narrative, whether these be of wooing, warring or intriguing, and without choosing dominating and exceptional characters. Chairman Mao has spelt out the Marxist view that the essential facts and values of society will be found in corporate daily activity:

A Marxist regards human productive activity as the most fundamental practice determining all other human activities. Cognitively man depends mainly upon his activity in material

* 'Question and Answer' , op. cit., p. 6.

production for a gradual understanding of nature's phenomena, its characteristics, its laws, and its relation to himself; at the same time, through productive activity, man comes to understand gradually and in varying degrees certain human interrelations. None of such knowledge can be obtained apart from productive activity. ... In various kinds of class societies, members of society from all classes come in different ways into certain relations of production with each other and engage in production to solve the same problem. This is the fundamental source of the development of human knowledge.*

Wesker knows from first-hand experience as a pastry cook how a large kitchen works, and he supplies full instructions for the actors. But, carefully, he simplifies and heightens the ordinary events. Starting with the lighting of the ovens, he builds up activity during the first part so that the tempo of language increases with that of the action, and so that the focus shifts with ever-increasing speed from one person or group to another. Beginning with an empty stage and almost casual entrances, the audience observes the growing activity until

> all the waitresses have got into a continuous circle of orders round and round the kitchen, as the volume of the ovens increases and the lights slowly fade to blackout. The calls of orders and for plates and more meat, etc., continue through the blackness until the stage is clear and ready for the interlude. (p. 136)

Because no food is used on stage and because the actors are well-drilled, it is easily possible to build up the 'fast and hectic' pace that Wesker asks for (p. 94) more overwhelmingly – more theatrically – than in any off-stage kitchen. Moreover, in suitable manner, narrative and character

* Mao Tse-tung, 'On Practice'; quoted from *Essential Works of Marxism*, ed. A. P. Mendel (Bantam Books, 1961), p. 499.

also contribute to the overall dramatic effect. While narrative is not the play's backbone, there are many small narratives set afoot briefly. Peter's quarrel with Gaston and his love-affair with Monique are the most strongly developed, but even these occur in four or five non-consecutive episodes. The new cook, Kevin, is introduced to the kitchen in several shorter episodes and one of these serves as a 'guide' to the kitchen: as its working is explained to Kevin, the audience, who must be even more bewildered than the fictional character, will also learn to recognize some elements of the activity. A new waitress, Violet, is also fitted in. Daphne quarrels with her husband, Nicholas. Dimitri delivers a radio set he has made. Waitresses and cooks start to dance until warned of the owner's approach; who then does not appear. Bertha quarrels with Michael about some potatoes. Cynthia flirts. The cooks eat a hurried and interrupted meal. All these narrative developments are inconclusive for, before any are worked out, the personal drama gives way to the corporate preparation for 'service' of lunch. Hans scalds his face and rushes on stage in pain and panic; but even the concern for him is soon forgotten as the second chef says, 'He'll live', and disperses the crowd with, 'All right, it's all over, come on' (p. 120).

This pattern of the personal drama being submerged under the impersonal activity is repeated during the service of 2,000 customers, only now the tempo is heightened so that the personal interruptions seem like mad, disregarded thrusts of dying individuality. Among orders and replies, questions and complaints, there are a few words of endearment, of teasing and of protest. Violet drops plates full of food and three times cries out that she can't work like this: but the china is soon swept up and service continues. Peter helps Kevin until he's called back to his own station, and he is then ready to mock the new cook's difficulties. The last fully articulate speech in this part of the play is Kevin's 'Have you all gone barking-raving-bloody-mad?' (p. 136). Then the routine of inhuman activity wins and buries all that is individual, questioning, affectionate or angry. The first part of Wesker's demonstration is brutally and exhilaratingly complete.

In the second half, evening dinner is being prepared. This does not involve the frantic tempo of lunch service, but enough is repeated for the audience to expect a similar climax. Only this time the human machine is wrecked as it moves into action. Peter is taunted by Monique and is irritated by Michael, who accepts the kitchen's demands, and by those who try to advise him. He takes away the soup that had been given to a beggar, and gives him cutlets instead, against the intentions of the chef. But service is now beginning. Winnie faints and it is subsequently learnt that she has had a miscarriage but, like Hans's burn, her predicament does not stop the machine. Peter reluctantly starts serving, but when he is harried he loses his temper. When Violet calls him a Boche, a 'bloody German bastard', it looks as if he will attack her but instead he knocks plates off a counter, breaks away from those restraining him, takes a chopper and cuts through the gas mains. The sound of the ovens stops for the first time in the play, and there is silence. Uproar follows, but Peter rushes into the dining-room and for a moment there is another silence. He returns having smashed tables full of crockery; his hands are covered with blood and he looks '*terribly exhausted*'. By breaking out he has stopped the inhuman world; but he has also wrecked himself and has to be taken off in an ambulance, helpless.

Wesker's demonstration is complete when Marengo, the owner, comes in uncomprehendingly. For him Peter is a 'Bloody fool' (p. 161). When he asks what more he could have done, he gets no reply. When he has run after Peter, he turns to find his whole staff facing him: they

stand around, almost accusingly, looking at him. And he asks again – What is there more? What is there more? What is there more?

That helpless, mutual silence is the end of the play: an arrested moment, rather than the triumphant, machine-like climax of Part One.

Wesker's basic dramatic strategy had one drawback: the lack of time in the kitchen's routine to establish a normal behaviour for at least some of his many characters. Moreover, a dramatic transition, in longer rhythms and slower tempo, was necessary for contrast between the two main phases of activity. Both problems were solved by introducing an 'Interlude' supposed to be taking place during the afternoon when only a cleaner and the pastry cooks are working. While time is on their hands, Peter asks for the 'dreams' of his fellow-workers: what would they wish for if the kitchen were to disappear? The answers disappoint Peter: sleep, women, money, a workshop and, from Paul, a 'friend'. Clearly Wesker thought it necessary to be explicit, not by argument but by statement. He needed to spell out that the cooks could hardly imagine another way of life. Although Peter can play games by making a triumphal arch through which he goose-steps and although he asks for the dreams to be told, he is incapable of describing any dream of his own, and he escapes for a walk with Monique. The kitchen is not a place for dreams: in the interlude, the characters are set to talk, and they cannot. The unlikely, artificial inquisition that Peter has to set up to fulfil his dramatist's purpose shows that no one, there, has an alternative to their way of life.

Paul is given the most sustained speech, in which he tells of what happened, outside the kitchen, when he tried to make friends with his neighbour. When he had taken part in a peace march, his bus-driver neighbour had said a bomb should have been dropped on the marchers because they had delayed the buses:

And you should've seen the hate in his eyes, as if I'd murdered his child. Like an animal he looked. (p. 143)

This is introduced as an explanation of why Paul dreamed of a friend. But it raises wider issues: should all the kitchens, factories, offices and buses be taken away, and men left to discover themselves in their own time? As the interlude becomes an occasion for statements, the characters have only questions to supply. Wesker has found a dramatic vehicle for establishing false values more strongly than those he considers to be true.

All three parts of the play hold the kitchen up as a barbarity, an almost helpless inhuman world. Some men could take pride in their work if they had the time; some are capable of friendship if they found adequate response. The owner asks a rhetorical question when the ovens stop, but even he has no acceptable statement to make. If the Interlude spells out the message of the play too openly, at the close Wesker left all to his 'demonstration'. Like the end of *Roots*, the last moments encompass the whole stage and the whole *dramatis personae*; the effect is made even more firmly here, for there is no speech-making. The audience must look for their own answer.

*

Wesker's next play, *Chips with Everything* (1962), is again based on activity: the initial training period of conscripted recruits to the Royal Air Force. Again he knew this 'world' from first-hand experience, and he had kept a series of daily letters from his own training period. He has said that he became preoccupied, at this time, with 'the way in

173

which the rebel is absorbed in English Society', and so subject and theme 'came together'.*

This time he could dispense with an Interlude for, by alternating scenes on the parade ground or in the lecture hall with scenes in the recruits' hut, he could alternate between individual 'stories' and inept movements towards individual aspiration or action in their off-hours and the progressive moulding of the boys into a well-drilled squad of trained airmen in the hours of training. And this time, the inhuman activity is far more efficient: the ill-co-ordinated and motley collection of boys in the first scene, smirking or frightened or intent, as they learn to stand to attention, become what the Forces call a 'fine body of men', 'smart, alert, keen' (p. 71), and all identical in identical uniform, moving 'as one man' (p. 71). Because the world of the RAF is, in its own terms, almost wholly successful, the contrast with individual failure is all the stronger and more challenging. Because there are many alternating scenes, the individual dramas could be developed more fully.

Chips is a play that is in danger of being divided within itself. The story of Pip Thompson has beginning, middle and end, and it touches all the other characters so that it can seem, particularly in a reading, to carry the whole play. He is the son of a general and banker, and is in the ranks in order to avoid becoming an officer. At first, without condescending to hide his snob accent or his dislike of people who are unambitious, he interests and instructs his fellow-recruits. At a Christmas party he gets Andrew to recite a Burns ballad and the other boys to sing an '*old peasant revolt song . . . menacing the officers*' (p. 41). He organizes his fellow-recruits to steal coke for the stove in their hut, so demonstrating that they can achieve what they want only

* 'His Very Own and Golden City', op. cit., p. 195.

under orders. When Corporal Hill comments that 'You always need leaders', Pip gives scornful agreement:

Always, always, always! ... Each time you say 'always' the world takes two steps backwards and stops bothering. And so it should, my God, so it should –   (p. 51)

This is the end of the first Act, but in the second Pip decides to disobey orders in bayonet practice and Wesker is now ready for the conclusion to this particular story. A Pilot Officer, of his own age and background, copes with Pip's rebellion. First, he argues that the gesture has made no impression; Pip will be tolerated and ignored, and so he will, in time, become an officer. Then the Pilot Officer derides Pip's motives, mocking him for wishing to be a 'Messiah to the masses', to escape from where 'the competition was too great' (p. 63). His motive discovered – for his rebellion has in fact no loyalty outside his own need for self-esteem, as is shown in the next scene where he refuses to instruct the admiring Charles – his purpose exposed, he is ready to put on an officer's uniform and leave the ranks. This is effected in the last scene but one, and his first action is to persuade the Pilot Officer to tolerate the rebellion of Charles – and so to render it ineffective, like his own. Charles's rebellion, however, was less self-regarding, for he had defied an order so that he might protect Smiler, the recruit who has tried to escape.

However, Pip does not have the last scene to himself, and even as he becomes an officer he loses his individual interest. He reads out the postings of his former fellows, and as the audience learns that each has been disappointed in the kind of post he had desired and that Smiler has been put back three weeks to join another group, it realizes that Pip's language and voice is now, only, official, the men to him only numbers, ranks and surnames. The final scene shows the march past and the 'Present Arms' to the colours hoisted on a tall pole as the men face the audience. As the National Anthem is played the audience must watch the faceless, uniform figures. Some of the audience at the first performances in London stood, as is customary at the end of theatrical entertainments when 'The Queen' is played; this must have pleased Wesker, for his play had made them choose for themselves, whether to stand or not. But for any audience the slow and blatant sound of the Anthem during the immobile 'demonstration' will give opportunity for reflection and awaken far-reaching associations: how are they to view the 'fine body of men'? There is neither speech nor question at the end of this play.

Pip's story is only one among several. Smiler is given a long and rhythmically exciting solo-scene in which he tries to escape from the world that had branded him a slob and failure, for a physical incapacity he could not prevent or control. Charles has tried to learn, even at the cost of being ordered around by Pip. When Smiler needed attention, Charles took the servant's role from Pip and bathed his bleeding, swollen feet. Corporal Hill enjoys relaxing with the recruits, playing his mouth-organ, but at other times he is wholly committed to his job, bullying, threatening, wounding with sarcasm, encouraging as he thinks fit, all with equal spirit and resource. He announces the passing-out parade with pride and reassurance: 'You'll have the band, and it'll be marvellous' (p. 68). Andrew tries to help Pip when he is on his own after refusing the order. Ginger, Cannibal and Dickey have their dreams of what the RAF could offer; Wilfe is defiantly unimpressed. Even Dodger, eating sweets and thinking of girls or of storing and selling prams in the family business, is a distinctive individual who is seen responding to training.

The demonstration is not a simple one, for the success of

Corporal Hill and his masters has positive and obvious achievements: physically the men are indeed more 'smart, alert, keen'. Various scenes of training have prepared for this, and this progress has been contrasted by the inability of any of the recruits to establish a viable individual or corporate alternative to being led. The training has captured even the boys' enthusiasms and motivations. Hill begins by warning them that they are 'not at home', but that they have a new 'home' in the Training Establishment (pp. 17–18). When they are left on their own, their talk goes, variously, back to the real home, in Wilfe's lamenting song, Charlie's boasting, Pip's talk of his father, and Ginger's of the girl he will marry. But on the parade ground, Hill offers them drill that is done 'together', as if they 'were going somewhere' (p. 23). Hill's language implies a new life, and at the end of the scene he says:

We're going to be the happiest family in Christendom and we're going to move together, as one, as one solitary man.   (p. 24)

In the lecture room they are told to be strong, to support their officers by discipline, to be clean and to be physically 'like Greek gods' (pp. 26–7); here is an ideal of individual prowess offered by the service within a new 'family'. In Act Two the recruits are handed their rifles, and Hill is soon associating these weapons with their manhood:

The first thing is – not to be afraid of it . . . I know you think they're nice, boys. With one of them in your hand you feel different, don't you, you feel a man, a conquering bloody hero? You want to run home and show your girl, don't you? Well, they're not toys – you can kill a man wi' one o' them. Kill 'im! Your napkins are still wet – you don't really understand that word 'kill', do you?   (pp. 53–4)

The next stage is bayonet practice, and they are now asked to use all their hatred and to scream. One by one they act

177

like excited animals, but obeying orders. In the RAF's discipline there are clear substitutes for home, community, pride, aspiration, sexuality and quiet strength. At the passing-out parade, Corporal Hill goes further and offers them the seal of a higher, yet intimate, approval, and the illusion of superhuman achievement:

... you're men of the Queen, her own darlings. SLAM! SLAM! SLAM! Let her be proud. Lovely, that's lovely, that's poetry. No one'll be shot today, my boys. Forget the sweat, forget the cold, together in time. I want you to look beautiful. I want you to move as one man, as one ship, as one solid gliding ship. (p. 71)

The Wing Commander follows him, saying with a '*long broad, embracing smile*', that he is satisfied, that they're one of the 'best bunch I've had through my gates', that he is 'confident of the service' they will give. He concludes with a prayer: 'God speed you'. This is the cue for the saluting of colours with which the play ends. The RAF has spoken with all the good words the boys can understand. Through Wesker's careful, cunning and eloquent use of verbal imagery in this play, the RAF is shown to offer a complete alternative to the broken inoperative ideals of the world outside.

Pip's central story has its ending, and Wesker's attitude to it is clearly expressed. But the play opens up other problems about the dangers of discipline and the excitement and achievement of following one's leader; and, ultimately, still wider questions are implied about loyalty, war, obedience and government. By spectacle, action, words, contrasts, control of time and a final refusal to lead the audience into any one response, the play is disturbing and awakens thought on many of the more important issues of the world.

*

While the structure of *Chips* is clearly a development from that of *The Kitchen*, Wesker was also experimenting with new techniques in this play. The party scene allows a freedom of expression to a variety of responses so that it has the range of the Interlude in *The Kitchen* but not its obvious and mechanical articulation. The movement from scene to scene is often effected by taking short phrases from the dialogue, or the sound of marching feet, and using repetitions of these as a link that is free from particular time and place. So when Hill is bullying Smiler, his word 'remember' links with the following scene where the Wing Commander is dealing with Pip (p. 56). Similar repetitions of key phrases are found in the dialogue as well:

HILL: Well, don't you always need leaders?
PIP: Always, always!
HILL: Yes, always, always!
PIP: Always, always, always! Your great-great-grandfather said there'll always be horses, your great-grandfather said there'll always be slaves . . . (p. 51)

At the end of this final scene in Act One, as Ginger and Dodger look at the moon, Andrew repeats the final verse of the Burns ballad he had recited at the Christmas party.

Towards the end of the play, in Smiler's nightmarish soliloquy that represents his attempt to escape from the camp, general repetitions of bullying phrases lead into his more particular words; and these echo earlier scenes, and build their own echoes, in his cries to be left 'alone', to be taken 'home' and his apprehension of what 'they'll' do. Here the words are supported by the sound of a roaring motor-bike and a long following silence.

Words, sound and performance make up a complex theatrical reality in the solo-scene for Smiler, with only one man, an open stage and the illusion of a moon shining down

179

to create it. This is a change of style from the use of realistic details of properties and behaviour, and the three walls of the set in the plays of the trilogy. Scenically *Chips* is much freer than any of the earlier plays, the only specific requirements of the author being lighting changes and a few properties like beds for the hut, dummies for bayonet practice and a flagpole for the last salute. Physical performances now dominate the spectacle. In the last scene but one, the washing of Smiler's feet and the placing of him in bed are '*done lovingly and with a sort of ritual*' (p. 69), a silent 'demonstration' of the spontaneous communal response that is found temporarily in caring for the sick when it was nowhere achieved in response to positive aspirations. When Pip changes into officer's uniform and officer's routine in the middle of his fellow-recruits, Wesker has moved his play far from a representation of what could actually happen because he wants to demonstrate Pip's new conformity with economy and inescapable effect.

At this time in his career, Wesker was growing increasingly aware of the stage's opportunities for unmistakable, exciting and wide-ranging statement once a dramatist no longer sought a representation of 'real life'. In an interview for *Twentieth Century* in 1961, he said:

Recently . . . I had a fascinating experience in Rome, where we presented excerpts from all three plays of the Trilogy, playing them in chronological order of events: first, a couple of scenes from *Chicken Soup with Barley*, then to *I'm Talking about Jerusalem*, back to *Chicken Soup*, and so on. Of necessity, it was a small-budget affair. We couldn't carry any properties around with us, and had to make do with a few costumes, and the available tables, chairs and boxes. We had a backcloth, and John Dexter [the Director] organized the lighting. What fascinated me was what we discovered by playing these excerpts without the full paraphernalia of scenery and props. The plays not only survived, but all of us – cast, John Dexter and myself, to say nothing of the audience and critics – found the whole thing very exciting. Now, I am not sure what this means as a general principle, but as regards the plays, it suggests to me that they do not depend for their impact upon the setting and naturalistic use of props. The words were speaking for themselves . . .

[Now] I am working very much towards a reduction not only of scenery but of dialogue as well. I am becoming more conscious of style, and I bet the rest of my plays are no bloody good.*

Wesker's experience of his earlier plays in conventional productions seems to have influenced him in the same direction:

In my quiet moments I reassure myself by telling myself that a few people have really got what I am saying, but this is not enough to make me happy . . . There is a terrible truth, which is that people take what they want from a play. They are prepared to take it all, provided it is what they want. This is why I really haven't the time that John Whiting seems to have for *implication*. I'm tired of implication and subtlety. I hope that my alternative is not banality. I desperately want to be simple and direct.†

He has found that he was still far from writing plays for a wide audience that could establish values and be a tool for the better understanding of living.

There was little evidence that the artist had 'converted' his audiences in any appreciable degree, and so he turned to political action, suffering imprisonment for protests in connection with the Committee of 100. But, as a 'demonstration', sitting down outside the Ministry of Defence – a purely passive, almost defensive action – was not politically

* 'Art is not Enough', *Twentieth Century*, Vol. CLXIX (1961), 1008, pp. 191–2.
† ibid., p. 194.

positive enough; it did not have direct relevance to the values he sought to express.*

He spent much time organizing and raising money for Centre 42, but the fully active period of this art-producing body was hardly more than a year. The effort was only a gesture towards the kind of popular artistic life Wesker believed in. His response was to try to make his plays more direct, more simple, more strong. His position as a dramatist was clear: if *Chips with Everything* had fulfilled his purposes there would have been a revolution against the leaders of the land, or he would have been out of a job, ostracized by the society he wished to change.

*

The plays that follow *Chips with Everything* carry on its stylistic experiments and are, in different ways, inescapably effective. Wesker's mass audience is still not reached, and in critical favour he lags behind his early promise; but he, himself, has come to expect this. The task he now sees before him is to explore the potentials of theatre language.

Their Very Own and Golden City was first performed in Belgium in 1964, but it was not seen in London until 1965, by which time it had been extensively revised. Wesker has gone back to narrative, telling the story of an architect, Andrew Cobham, from his radical enthusiasms as an apprentice draughtsman in 1926 until he sits down in his old age to play bridge with a Tory Minister of Housing in 1990. But he juxtaposes the narrative sequence with flashbacks to a continuation of the first scene in which the young boy stands on his head in Durham Cathedral as an expression of pleasure and love, and discusses, sermonizes and makes promises about the future. Standing on his head is a 'demonstration' of thoughts and feelings that could turn the world upside down, and recurs occasionally in some of

* cf. A. Wesker, 'Art and Action', *Listener*, 10 May 1962, p. 807.

the narrative scenes. The play ends in the cathedral, but now as the young Andy moves among his friends, his affirmations are spoken by the old Sir Andrew. Wesker directs that he 'must deliver young Andy's lines wearily in contrast with the gaiety of the others'.

There is further experiment in setting, especially in Act Two, where one continuous scene, with twelve episodes, covers some forty years. Towards the end, '*A magnificent abstract set of a building site and its scaffolding*' is realized on the stage, with the '*howl of drilling, the whine of machines and the knock of hammers*'. Wesker has not been deterred from risking this spectacular climax by the thought that the dreams of a lifetime that have been shared by thousands of supporters can hardly be reproduced with sufficient 'magnificence' on the stage, or that an 'abstract' style might suggest an intellectual aridity or a merely theatrical stylization. In the same way, he accepts the need for actors to alternate between middle or old age and extreme youth within minutes or, alternatively, for two sets of actors, one young and the other older, to represent the two aspects of the same four characters. He is seeking theatrical effectiveness and striking images, and takes practical risks to do so.

Into the narrative and static frameworks he has placed many scenes of argument in his earliest style. Here, again, are set debates, arguments, statements and set reappraisals of purpose and achievements. Often they are now in large contexts: public meetings, the General Purposes Committee of the TUC, a formal banquet with a Master of Ceremonies and after-dinner speeches. In the search for directness and unmistakable impact, Wesker has mixed all his styles, covered a long time-scheme, moved between bed-sitting-rooms, public places, river-banks, a new city and Durham Cathedral. He has introduced numerous characters of different ages, backgrounds, influence and abilities. He places all on stage, despite ordinary scruples about convention and ease of working. Moreover, this play is as overwhelming in its theme as in its stylistic variety, wider even than that of *Chips*. It is specifically concerned with compromise in political, social, family and individual life. Wesker is being artistically inventive and bold on all fronts, but also greedy.

In *The Four Seasons*, written after the first version of *City*, there is a retreat from obvious abundance. This play is for two actors, man and woman, and has one set altered only in colour and detail. Its action covers one year and explores, only, the relationship between its two characters, Adam and Beatrice – no other character is mentioned by name. This experiment is in elaboration of dialogue and action according to the needs of character, situation and theme, but without regard to what might actually happen in ordinary time and in an ordinary room. His play surprised the critics who thought he had become overtly symbolistic. In view of this adverse response he explained:

if a curtain comes down denoting the passing of time [in a theatre], do you suddenly say, this is a symbolic play? You don't. The curtain coming down is a piece of theatre language. And this is what *Four Seasons* depends on. ... The whole of the [Winter] sequence consists in Beatrice sitting in a chair, and Adam talking to her. That is divided into three sections, and time passes over those three sections. Now, curtains don't come down, but lights change, and she stays there. And because I wanted to re-create the feeling of a woman who hasn't the energy to do anything, I actually *have* her doing nothing. I could have had her moving around and pottering, and she could have sort of exuded lethargy and ennui and despair. And it seems to me that the critics should have understood that I simply didn't want to go through that fussy business. So the lethargy was represented by her remaining in the chair, and Adam doing all the movement. One critic actually wondered whether they ever went to the lavatory.*

* 'His Very Own and Golden City', op. cit., pp: 200–201.

In short, he was taking his own kind of 'demonstration' further, using it for a more predominantly psychological theme than he had chosen before, and providing a more narrow and intense focus.

Some of the demonstrations, like those in *I'm Talking About Jerusalem*, seem to have no purpose beyond making clear the playwright's attitude. So Beatrice decorates Adam with bluebells at the beginning of *Spring*, and he dresses her in gold for *Summer*. Others are sustained by a spirit of game-playing or challenge. Some, like the episode where they embrace with bare breasts, are solemn ritualizations of what is quite normal and unconsidered in intimate private behaviour. When Adam makes an apple-streudel on stage for Beatrice, the performance is bound to remain precisely actual – or else the difficult recipe will fail – and here the demonstration is how activity, one for the other, changes their relationship: serving her, he becomes her master, giving precise orders; and then he gets caught up in his job so that she seems irrelevant.

Again, Wesker has made large practical demands and, for all its obvious theatricality, this play is hard to act. Without any verbal or physical preparation, Beatrice's silent immobility in *Winter* has to change to tears on page two. Moreover, the actress must avoid any impression of not moving because she is ill or lame. Stage directions instruct the performers to create what their words or actions do not necessarily imply: so he must show '*He can understand nothing*' (p. 143), and a page later both have to act as if '*They are really living in their own hells*'.

Towards the end, in the *Autumn* sequence, Wesker uses words to make large statements. Beatrice has not found the 'peace, majesty and great courage' that she had sought (p. 171). They both throw back confessions of guilt and disappointment to each other, knowing they will wound. By words they describe the rhythm and meaning of the play as a whole: each action has led to inaction and to comment and objection. When a statement or demonstration has been achieved, it is the dramatist and not the characters who, by his own invention or by the changes suggested by the four seasons, moves the characters on to new aspects of their relationship, new resources of their minds.

At the end, Adam and Beatrice part, and the room is as empty as at the beginning. While the two figures have remained the same, their words have changed from the banal – 'So many people have once considered me a rare woman' (p. 148) – to the fantastical ideal – 'I have a golden eagle for a lover' (p. 163) – to simple affirmatives and denials, and to tears and silence. Each element has its own kind of truth – in an interview, Wesker defended the 'eagle' image by saying 'people do say this out on the Heath',* and lovers do play with flowers – but they hold together only by the will and understanding of the dramatist and by the ability of the actors to give the accent of truth and the basic continuity of realistic portrayal which alone can support many of the episodes. Wesker again demands exceptional support from his interpreters and a willingness in his audience to follow wherever and however he leads. *The Four Seasons* is in some senses – in narrative, character, theme, spectacle – a small play, but all the time it is taking risks and seeking inescapable theatrical statement.

In *The Friends* (1970), Wesker returns more wholly to the style of the trilogy: argument, statement and domestic activity hold the stage. As Ronnie in the early plays bore an anagram of Wesker's own first name and showed close resemblances to his creator in experience and opinion, so this time there is Roland, bearing a second anagram, and

* 'Arnold Wesker: an interview by Giles Gordon', *Transatlantic Review*, 21 (1966), p. 19.

he often speaks like an older Ronnie. He too is concerned with 'delight', 'nobility' and 'majesty' (p. 15), but now these are in open conflict with distaste and self-defence.

How then has Wesker tried to 'be simple and direct', to force his audience to see what he wants them to see in his play? First, by restricting the play's scope, so that attention is not dissipated by narrative detail or larger issues not directly represented on the stage. There is no political demonstration off-stage. All the characters are engaged in the rise and fall of a chain of furnishing shops; all except Macey, the manager, are *between the ages of 35 and 38* (Wesker's own age group); all, except Simone, are from the same working-class background. The scene is one room, and the time less than twenty-four consecutive hours. Wesker also concentrates attention by having one character, Esther, die during the course of the first Act, and having her remain on stage all the second Act. This gives a crucial, immediate concern for all the characters. Moreover, she dies wanting to 'live', and at the end of the play the other 'Friends' place her in a chair, facing a portrait of Lenin, and Simone repeats three emphatic times, 'She wanted to live'. They all 'demonstrate' identification with her dying will by kissing her cheek *one by one* (p. 71), and then going quietly about their immediate business as if she were still alive.

Earlier, the disintegration of the Friends and their loss of purpose have been stated and argued in words, and also in more violent and less normal activity than Wesker has used before. There is a touch of melodrama, of which the characters are well aware, as if seeking for themselves the same kind of 'physical' reality as Wesker has sought as a dramatist. Roland cuts his back with a razor blade and rubs salt in; later he becomes catatonically dumb. Tessa smashes her guitar. Crispin cradles Roland and kisses him like an '*un-happy child*' (p. 58); earlier he had called Roland to him and they kissed on the lips, remaining '*clasped*' (p. 48). Manfred '*seems in a trance*' when he tells a 'dream' (p. 34). Simone is physically isolated from the others at the end, until she rallies them by speaking of their new situation and contriving the last tableau of Esther as queen.

The play stands or falls by this last 'demonstration' which, like that of *Roots*, has been carefully prepared. Only now the central figure is silent and unresponsive, and attention is focused on the remaining Friends and their strange yet outwardly simple reactions. To give 'meaning' to the demonstrations, Wesker has given Esther a speech in Act One:

I can't tell you how much I cherish everything. I know there's a lot that's obscene and ugly but it's never been too oppressive, I've always had the capacity not to be oppressed. . . . Someone is always rising up, taking wing, and behind him he pulls the rest of us; and I want to be there, for every movement, every sound.

(p. 32)

The others talk, often with difficulty or '*as though just discovering*' (p. 62), of the overwhelming need for loving or for strong intention, honesty, justice or the pursuit of happiness. In the closed circle of their activities, in their knowledge of each other, of success and of failure, Wesker takes them towards a final stand; and he makes a dramatic contrast by finishing in silence and stillness. The audience is forced to consider what holds them strangely there, around a seated, dead and temporarily beautiful woman who faces a portrait of the dead Lenin. Macey, the manager, is the only one to leave after he has kissed her. Wesker bets all on the audience finding an adequate response from earlier explicit moments.

The theatre language is now aggressively mute, as at the end of *Chips with Everything*, but the image of life in the whole action is much smaller in range than that of the earlier play. Wesker's second bet as a dramatist was that the audience could find interest and significance in his temperamental, insecure, clamorous, word-swapping, embracing, rejecting, and almost defeated *dramatis personae*, as they move and speak, marooned in their softly furnished living (and dying) room. There is a dichotomy between the exposure in the last silent theatrical statement and the withdrawal in the choice of setting and characters. Both are bold strokes, and together they suggest reappraisal and preparation.

6

JOHN ARDEN

Artificial Theatre

Serjeant Musgrave's Dance, *The Workhouse Donkey*
and *The Hero Rises Up*

When a character makes an entry in one of Pinter's plays, he
often stands silent, or moves at once to perform some
piece of business, like taking off a coat. Nearly always there
is some element of the unexpected so that the audience's
attention is alerted. In Osborne's plays new characters are
frequently on stage as the curtain rises, or are announced,
recognized and involved in the business on hand as soon as
possible; often they fulfil, or seem to fulfil, an expected role,
as the clients in *Inadmissible Evidence*, or Brother Bill and
Graham in *The Entertainer*. Osborne is concerned to sustain
the action, to effect a further exploration or heightening of a
situation. In Wesker's plays characters come and go with a
definite purpose limited by the immediate situation. Usually
they are expected or, like the Colonel in *I'm Talking About
Jerusalem*, they make themselves plain at once, so that the
other characters can be seen adapting, with individual
appropriateness, to the new arrival. All new entries are
calculated to throw the dramatic situation into a new light,
and time is taken to notice each significant change in the
involvement of the various characters. In Arden's plays,
however, entries are bold, explicit, efficient. The dramatist's
job seems to be that of bringing a new figure on stage,
labelled clearly and functioning directly. Each character

is there in his own right, speaking and acting, as well and as efficiently as he can, on behalf of some notion or idea as conceived by the author. The colours are primary, the action spring-loaded, and the result apparent at once. Each new entrant speaks for himself without much regard for how things happen in ordinary life.

In the second scene of *Serjeant Musgrave's Dance* (1959), the Mayor makes his entry. The office he holds provides his only name and all that the audience will know of him depends upon this function and the fact that he owns the colliery. He is preceded by the Constable who '*enters violently*' announcing, twice, 'His Worship the Mayor' and bringing the characters in the bar of the public house to silence (pp. 20–21). So the Mayor's entry is fully prepared for, but Arden also inserts a stage-direction insisting that he '*enters at speed, wearing his gold chain*' and requiring Musgrave to call his men to attention. The audience should recognize him instantaneously, and the contrast between his formal chain and informal speed of entry should awaken expectation. Then his speech tells all:

Mrs Hitchcock, I'm seeking the soldiers. Ah, here they are! Well, I'm the Mayor of this town, I own the colliery, I'm a worried man. So I come seeking you when I could send for you, what do you think of that? Let's have a look at you. . . . Ah. Haha . . . Clear the snug a minute, missus. I want a private word with the Parson. Serjeant, be ready outside when I send for you.

(p. 21)

The Mayor could hardly avoid seeing the soldiers who are standing to attention to greet him, but nevertheless he makes this purpose explicit. Then his recognition of their presence becomes verbally explicit too: 'Ah, here they are!' His next task is to identify himself, which he does in a series of three short phrases, ending with 'I'm a worried man'.

Instead of indicating his 'worry' by anxious rhythms, hesitations or absent-mindedness, or by allowing his informal speed and his delay in seeing the soldiers to speak for themselves, Arden has him announce verbally his inner thoughts. The character must make his concern absolutely clear, even if it is not very credible that a man in his position would so wear his mind upon his sleeve. The Mayor even makes a specific verbal point about his informality, asking the soldiers – and the audience – to notice how precipitant he is. Then he announces that he is having 'a look' at them, summing them up. All is clearly stated verbally, as well as visually; and the play can then move on through consultation.

The rhythms of the Mayor's speech are rapid like his movements, but forceful. Arden does not write: 'I'm seeking the soldiers, Mrs Hitchcock', but uses the address first to alert attention, and also to leave 'soldiers' emphatically at the end of the line. 'Ah, here they are!' is staccato, and after a brief contrast – perhaps a rest – with 'Well', the threefold self-announcement runs clearly with its repeated *I*'s to emphasize its form. The 'worried man' is not so forceful in rhythm as the other two, but it is short and so the series neither flags nor draws all to a single point. A longer, more elaborate sentence follows, but the rhythm is soon shortened again by 'what do you think of that?'. The following pause is enlivened by 'Ah. Haha', which has quickening rhythm (and, indeed, little else to contribute). Then the Mayor's orders have, like the earlier announcement, three phrases, this time growing in length without losing force. All is emphatic, one element at a time. Even the Mayor's taking thought and a kind of awkwardness have been briskly established.

The entry is artificially exciting: nothing understated or merely suggested by subtextual tensions; all is vigorous and explicit. No one deflects attention; a contradiction in behaviour is verbally pin-pointed. Taken on their own, each word and each phrase is simple. Physical performance is alive, like the speech. We could say that Laban's 'pressing' and 'punching' are the characteristic forms of language and movement.* A lot is accomplished in a short time. Moreover, this entry is characteristic of Arden's theatre language, weight and movement giving dynamic energy. The fascination of his plays lies chiefly in what is going on, not in careful debate or sustained argument, not in a progressive revelation of inward tensions, purposes or despair, not in verisimilitude of setting or behaviour, not in a display of temperament or sensitivity.

*

Arden is a primitive among dramatists. At first this may have been a defence against the rival successes of television. He recognized that other playwrights, such as Wesker, worked on the assumption that:

new plays should be naturalistic reflections of life familiar to their audiences, and that the important contemporary issues that they wish to handle are best presented against such a background.

But Arden considered this kind of drama was more suited to 'the drawing-room fireside auditorium' of television, and judged that:

The essential artificiality of the public stage will become apparent again. . . . People must want to come to the theatre *because* of the artificiality, not despite it. . . . I am pleading for the revival of the Poetic Drama, no less.†

Neither Fry nor Eliot could provide an appropriate example

* See page 58, above.
† 'The Reps and New Plays: a writer's viewpoint', *New Theatre Magazine*, Vol. I, no. 2 (1960), pp. 23–6.

of poetic drama for Arden, nor was he prepared to leave performers or directors to create the necessary theatricality. He recognized Brecht as the kind of theatre-poet that he looked for – in his verse passages for *The Caucasian Chalk Circle* and in his use of folk tales, folk language, songs and abundant stage action. But, nearer home, Arden argued that the 'bedrock of English poetry' lay in the ballad:

In the ballads the colours are primary. Black is for death, and for the coalmines. Red is for murder, and for the soldier's coat the collier puts on to escape from his black. Blue is for the sky and for the sea that parts true love. Green fields are speckled with bright flowers. The seasons are clearly defined. White winter, green spring, golden summer, red autumn. The poets see their people at moments of alarming crisis, comic or tragic. The action goes as in Japanese films – from sitting down everyone suddenly springs into furious running, with no faltering intermediate steps.

What does this mean in terms of the theatre?

To start with – costumes, movements, verbal patterns, music, must all be strong, and hard at the edges. If verse is used in the dialogue, it must be nakedly verse as opposed to the surrounding prose, and must never be allowed to droop into casual flaccidities. This is the Brechtian technique, more or less.*

Like ballad singers, Arden did not wish to argue, but to offer a fable, full of climactic activity and clear statement, and let the audience draw its own conclusions.

But Arden could not be a true primitive, for he chose this style self-consciously, for intellectually perceived reasons. Behind his simple, strong and active figures lies a concern for general problems of contemporary society: pacifism, public welfare, health service, management, public images and personal values, political expediency, work, intellectualism, protest and so forth. In writing a play, Arden is concerned to illustrate attitudes and explore a problem.

* 'Telling a True Tale', *Encore*, Vol. VII, no. 3 (1960), pp. 24–5.

Serjeant Musgrave's Dance started in his mind 'with the last act':

When I wrote it, I was roughly aware of what the climax was to be – the soldiers staging a public meeting, apparently a recruiting meeting, which would turn into a protest. In order to make this credible, it was necessary to lay out a number of scenes in which the soldiers *showed themselves for what they were*, and at the same time all the people in the town revealed enough of their personality to *illustrate their attitude towards war*.*

Theme and basic action also came before individual character:

Take the character of Musgrave. I decided what he had to say, and why he had to say it, and roughly what he was going to do about it, before I worked out the character. The character came to fit the actions.†

Arden has set his play strongly and clearly to work in order to follow his thoughts: he writes plays, he once said, because he likes to 'see them acted',‡ to see what he thinks and feels.

In *Musgrave's Dance*, the dialogue repeatedly gives cues or signposts to the thought behind the play. For a simple example, when the Serjeant is sending his men to reconnoitre the town, he does so briskly and sharply, so that the stage empties rapidly and purposefully:

East; south; west; I'll go north; I'm told it suits my nature. Then meet at the churchyard rail and tell me what you've seen. Let's make it sharp.

    [*They go out.*] (p. 27)

The reference to his 'nature' is by no means necessary to his

* 'Building the Play: an interview with John Arden', *Encore*, Vol. VIII, 4 (1961), p.24; my italics.
  † ibid., p. 31.
  ‡ ibid., p. 22.

orders; it is Arden, the dramatist, being explicit about a small decision in order to make a general point about his character. It slows down the order, but that can be enlivened again by the last dismissive sentence.

At all times the characters of this play are liable to fill in the immediate business with accounts of the past or of future consequences. The Mayor after his first entry discusses the next step with the Parson; but at the same time he tells the audience some facts that must be perfectly familiar to this stage audience:

I think we'll use 'em, Parson. Temporary expedient, but it'll do. The price of coal has fell, I've had to cut me wages, I've had to turn men off. They say they'll strike, so I close me gates. We can't live like that for ever. There's two ways to solve this colliery – (p. 22)

Here, again, is an expression of doubt along with a decision, a threefold sentence to describe the situation, followed, this time, by three separate sentences, the third leading into what is, at last, a response to the present situation. There is rhythmic vigour in this exposition, and it is that alone which prevents a lag in active dramatic interest.

Sometimes one character is made to act as stooge to another so that Arden can provide an exposition of some point of view or of past events in order to complete the play's statement. So in Act Two, Musgrave calls Annie, the barmaid, to him:

MUSGRAVE [*calling* ANNIE]: Lassie.

ANNIE: Hello.

MUSGRAVE: These are my men. They're here with their work to do. You will not distract them.

ANNIE: I won't?

MUSGRAVE: No. Because *they* know, whether you know it or not, that there's work is for women and there's work is for men: and let the two get mixed, you've anarchy. (p. 51)

He tells her directly to leave the men alone, but she is made to question this, rather than laughing it off or pretending to be obedient. So it is clear that Arden wishes Musgrave to make a general point more important for the ideas behind the play than the consistency of the character he is talking to. A challenging antithesis raises general considerations about women and men, and then Arden introduces the intellectually important concept of 'anarchy', which Annie can hardly be expected to understand. She promptly questions the word and Musgrave has got his platform:

Look, lassie, anarchy: now, we're soldiers. Our work isn't easy, no and it's not soft: it's got a strong name – duty. And it's drawn out straight and black for us, a clear plan. But if you come to us with what you call your life or love – *I'd* call it your indulgence – and you scribble all over that plan, you make it crooked, dirty, idle, untidy, *bad* – there's anarchy. I'm a religious man. I know words, and I know deeds, and I know how to be strong. So do these men. You will not stand between them and their strength! Go on now: take yourself off.   (p. 51)

Significant words are again placed forcefully at ends of phrases, and 'duty' is given an isolated position: in 'I know words . . .' the three-fold sentence recurs. While telling the audience all that Annie can't easily understand, Musgrave continues to explain and to label the situation with short and potent verbal tags.

Arden also gives explicit general meaning to his characters' speeches by using certain words repeatedly in different contexts, especially references to primary colours and to simple opposites such as light and dark, cold and hot. So Musgrave's description of duty, 'drawn out straight and black' gains part of its strength by echoes from other earlier speeches, not all by him. Talk about the weather, army

197

life and a game of cards start preparing for these later echoes in the very first scene of all:

Brr, oha cold winter, snow, dark . . . cold night . . . The black spades carry the day. Jack, King and Ace. *We* throw the red Queen over . . . our Black Jack Musgrave . . . an old red rag stretched over four pair o' bones . . . You know what they used to call 'em in them days – soldiers, I mean? . . . Bloodred roses, that was it . . . you bloodred bloody roses, you! Ooh, brr, bitter and bleak. (pp. 9–14)

The setting of the snow-covered colliery town and the red tunics of the soldiers present visually the same colours and contrasts as the verbal drama. One of the Serjeant's men draws attention to this specifically:

We're on the run, in red uniforms, in a black and white coal-field; and it's cold. . . . (p. 29)

But the colours are not always used simply. Musgrave does not see the 'word' that he wants to bring to people as black and straight, like himself and his duty, but 'white' and 'shining'; and the town is 'a hot coal . . . despite it's freezing':

choose your minute and blow: and whoosh, she's flamed your roof off! They're trembling already into the strikers' riots. Well, their riots and our war are the same one corruption. (p. 36)

The repeated references to colour alert attention as well as indicating connections and giving precise meaning.

For certain statements, Arden changes from prose to a verse-form of short lines and clear rhymes. So when Annie is asked by Mrs Hitchcock – who knows well enough – to tell 'what a soldier's good for', she speaks in general terms:

> Because we know he'll soon be dead
> We strap our arms round the scarlet red
> Then send him weeping over the sea. . . .
>
> (pp. 17–18)

For Musgrave himself, Arden uses first a private prayer and then a nightmarish talking in his sleep. Both these soliloquies have greater freedom and directness in the use of verbal images than any piece of dialogue could easily be given:

Fire, fire! Fire, fire, London's burning, London's burning! . . . Burning. Burning. One minute from now, and you carry out your orders – get *that* one! . . . I'm on duty, woman. I'm timing the end of the world. (p. 64)

Musgrave wishes to bring the town to judgement by revealing the skeleton of Billy Hicks, a young soldier senselessly killed in an ambush and the cause of a subsequent outrage. For this moment of clearest statement, when Musgrave reveals his 'burning word' which is also his 'dance', Arden uses very short-lined verse:

> Up he goes and no one knows
> How to bring him downwards
> Dead man's feet
> Over the street
> Riding the roofs
> And crying down your chimneys
> Up he goes and no one knows
> Who it was that rose him
> But white and red
> He waves his head
> He sits on your back
> And you'll never never lose him
> Up he goes and no one knows
> How to bring him downwards. (pp. 84–5)

The message of the repeated line is comparatively simple and the red and white colours of Billy's tunic and bones are eloquent through echoes of earlier speeches; but the whole 'burning word' is not at all simple. There are references to a haunting and a burden, implications of guilt, and a direct address to the people – who for this scene are largely the theatre audience – that brings the message home to 'you'. Arden is seeking not only clarity but also the memorable word, the word that can grow in the mind of the hearer. He prepares special attention and requires special delivery for such words, using artificial means and not the strict imitation of ordinary speech or the impression of a man discovering truth for himself: the climax is a put-up job, an artificial statement.

Arden's choice of setting and dramatic structure is calculated to keep attention alert. Instead of setting the action in a single room, or moving it between two contrasted scenes, or varying it according to strict narrative requirements, Arden chooses scenes that provide a series of different views and different confrontations. A canal bank, a pub and a churchyard make up the first Act. At first the soldiers are on the move, carrying heavy baggage, and the sardonic bargee, Joe Bludgeon, is the only person they encounter. Once in the pub, a series of meetings are arranged, presided over by Mrs Hitchcock, but with the attendant Annie dominating the scene on two occasions, each time on account of her private knowledge. Then at sunset, in the churchyard, the soldiers are alone for argument, passion, and then agreement, with the colliers menacingly around. The Act concludes with Musgrave's prayer watched silently by Bludgeon who parodies his attitude, smirks and breathes a last 'Amen'. The story has been told and the audience knows or senses what each character 'stands for' but, more than this, it has also seen the soldiers in varied surroundings, the last under isolated and strained conditions. Stage business is varied to the same ends. At first the soldiers were seated with one on watch and the others playing cards, and at the end they march out 'briskly' in the near darkness under Attercliffe's orders. They do not wait for Musgrave, leaving him alone, unaware of the mocking Bludgeon. This movement on stage is calculated, for Musgrave then '*walks downstage, crosses his hands on his chest and stands to pray*' (p. 37): now, for the first time, he faces the audience, as close to them as possible; and the audience must watch closely in the half-light.

In his prayer Musgrave speaks of the 'Word' he must bring to the town, and also of his 'Dance', a 'deed' more 'terrible' than any word. There are indeed several incidents that are dance-like in the play, moments when the narrative is held back to display meaningful and sustained activity. Act Two opens with noisy conviviality in the pub that includes dancing, music and '*beating time*' (p. 38), a corporate scene of bravado and high spirits but with Musgrave sitting alone, silent and still. Later, with a roll on the drum, the Serjeant makes an announcement, but only to say that the serious meeting is yet to come. The party breaks up and is followed by a 'Fred Karno' (p. 52) sequence in the streets at night. The colliers play at being soldiers in a mechanical kind of dance and once or twice they achieve a brief unanimity. This episode is not necessary for the narrative, but enables Arden to show in action that men, even those with a grievance, can become robots, controlled by routine and proud of it. For the third and last scene of the Act, Arden introduces a different kind of setting that represents a large brass bedstead for Musgrave inside the pub and, at the same time, the stables where the men go to sleep in the loose boxes, to be visited by Annie and by sudden violence. Musgrave has his nightmare; Sparky, the rebellious soldier, is killed; Walsh, the serious collier, tries to steal the guns; the Constable, Parson and Mayor all arrive in haste, and Bludgeon is there to assist. But the Act ends with a dance-parade, for Musgrave takes command

by beating the drum, handing out flags and colours, and
calling for patriotic fervour:

BARGEE: Rosebuds of Old England!
MAYOR: Loyal hearts and true!
PARSON: The Lord mighty in battle!
MUSGRAVE: GOD SAVE THE QUEEN!
   [*General noise, bustle and confusion.*]

The fears, doubts, comforts and alarms of the night, are
resolved into a general unreflecting parade of enthusiasm.
It is a 'dance' of acceptance, mindlessness, effort; all
characters are transformed in what seems like unison. But,
just before this, Musgrave has heard that the snow is
melting and the Dragoons are coming to the town; in a
moment he has made his decision to call a meeting for
early the next morning and so, within the general scene and
while he shouts the last and loudest, he carries forward
his purpose. He is a puppet-master as well as performer.

For Musgrave's climactic 'Dance', in Act Three, Scene
One, all the characters face the audience, acting as if they
are the 'platform' of a public meeting. They are '*properly
dressed*', but there '*is no crowd*' so the '*speeches are delivered
straight out to the audience*'. Arden directs that the responses
that are made from off-stage should be '*rather unrealistic – as
it were, token-noises only*' (p. 76); in this way they will not
deflect from the main 'reality' which must be between
audience and stage. Now Billy Hicks's skeleton is hung up in
full view; Musgrave's cat is out of the bag and Arden's
last, full-scale and dramatic dance-display is ready:

MUSGRAVE *begins to dance, waving his rifle, his face contorted with
demoniac fury . . . as he dances, [he] sings, with mounting emphasis.*

(p. 84)

No response is possible, but he holds his audience, on stage
and in the auditorium, at gun-point, so that he can slowly

'explain'. Arden has provided both bomb-shell and lesson: he wants his audience both agape and reasonable; he wants Musgrave both efficient and mad, as he confronts his audience with the horror of war and himself with the difficulty of doing or saying anything that will alter the situation. At length Musgrave '*sits down and broods*', and '*There is a pause*' (p. 90); his hand is played out, and the drama moves forward without his volition. Annie enters to cradle her dead lover; Walsh, and then Attercliffe back out; Sparky's death that was hushed up in Act Two is now disclosed; Hurst tries to fire on the crowd, and is killed by the Dragoons who arrive at just the right time. Musgrave and Attercliffe surrender, and then Arden is ready for yet another visual and physical display. The other characters join in *their* dance, with free beer, relief and forgetfulness: only Annie sits cradling Billy's skeleton and Mrs Hitchcock watches from a window. In action as well as verbal statement, in 'dances' and 'words' on a brightly lit and 'open' stage, Arden's purpose has been displayed fully.

But the Serjeant's protest and the people's relief in the Dragoons' arrival are not the end of the play. A final quiet scene in prison brings back a sustained focus upon Musgrave and his one remaining soldier. Mrs Hitchcock brings a drink, and she and Attercliffe do most of the talking. He speaks and sings of the withered rose of his love and his soldier's life, and of the greengrocer who with his gift of an apple stole his love. So the verbal symbolism receives its last quiet statement, the green apple being acknowledged as having a seed within it that the soldiers' red deaths are most unlikely to emulate: who will even remember them? Only when Mrs Hitchcock says she hopes Musgrave's dance will be remembered does the Serjeant drink, after which he is silent. He is finished, as the play is as well when Attercliffe has sung his song and posed a question:

They're going to hang us up a length higher nor most appletrees grow, Serjeant. D'you reckon we can start an orchard?

Arden has added the prison scene, not only to bring attention back to his principal character and complete an unhurried exposition of his theme, but also to ensure that, after the major confrontation of Musgrave's Dance, the audience is left finally with a definite question. Musgrave dominates this scene not by words or actions in which the audience can follow him with sympathy, but by his silence. He is a challenge to understanding, rather than the means to it.

The rhythms and changing involvements of this last scene illustrate the same overall dramatic purpose. The interchanges of recrimination, justification, regret and refusal bring much of the 'pressing' and 'punching' that are present also in the exposition:

MRS HITCHCOCK: It's time you learnt your life, you big proud serjeant. Listen: last evening you told all about this anarchy and where it came from – like, scribble all over with life or love, and that makes anarchy. Right?

MUSGRAVE: Go on.

MRS HITCHCOCK: Then *use* your Logic – if you can. Look at it this road; here we are, and we'd got life and love. Then *you* came in and you did your scribbling where nobody asked you. Aye, it's arsy-versey to what you said, but it's still an anarchy, isn't it? And it's all your work. (p. 102)

Musgrave's 'Go on' has little energy, being neither sustained nor sudden, yet it is direct and firm; it is contained, disclosing nothing. Then Attercliffe joins the attack, bringing both terminal and threefold emphasis:

To end it by its own rules: no bloody good. She's right, you're wrong. You can't cure the pox by further whoring. Sparky died of those damned rules. And so did the other one.

It is now that Musgrave's speech becomes broken. State-ment and punching emphasis yield to a helpless noise and then the falling, 'dabbing' rhythm of acknowledged defeat:

MUSGRAVE: That's not the truth. [*He looks at them both in appeal, but they nod.*] That's not the truth. God was with me . . . God . . . [*He makes a strange animal noise of despair, a sort of sob that is choked off suddenly, before it can develop into a full howl.*] – and all they dancing – all of them – there.

He has only the one word 'No' to say further, but Atter-cliffe picks up the rhythms, '*melancholy but quiet*' (p. 103). His song sustains interest, giving a 'floating',* thoughtful expression to the themes of the play in almost general terms. Its gentle and flexible rhythms allow the audience to join in his thoughts, and gives time for them to register. Arden has now achieved appropriate attention for his concluding question.

*

Arden's theatrical language is so definite, strong and per-sistent in statement that there has been some confusion about his exploratory and questioning purpose. Audiences expect him to take sides. In an Introductory Note on *Live Like Pigs* (1958) Arden records that:

On the one hand, I was accused by the Left of attacking the Welfare State: on the other, the play was *hailed* as a defence of anarchy and amorality. So perhaps I had better declare myself. I approve outright neither of the Sawneys nor of the Jacksons. Both groups uphold standards of conduct that are incompatible, but which are both valid in their correct context.

The clarity of every statement is the cause of these difficul-ties of interpretation and of the peculiar excitement of Arden's plays. In the *Guardian* on 24 October 1959, the critic,

* See, again, Laban's terminology, page 58 above.

Philip Hope-Wallace, responded to the first performance of *Serjeant Musgrave's Dance* in a manner that is close to Arden's expectations. The play is 'long and challenging' he wrote:

Even now, at curtain-fall, some of its import escapes me, but for the best part of three hours it has worked on my curiosity and often put that ill-definable theatrical spell on my imagination. I think it is something short of a great play. But wild horses wouldn't have dragged me from my seat before the end.

In a comment, two years later, Arden defined his engagement in writing:

All the time I write I find I am writing, partly indeed to express what I know, feel, and see, but even more to test the truth of my knowledge, feelings and vision. I did not fully understand my own feelings about pacifism until I wrote *Serjeant Musgrave*: nor about old age until I wrote *The Happy Haven*. Even yet, both plays seem to leave much unresolved about the questions they raise. I see myself as a practitioner of an art which is both Public and Exploratory . . .*

In 1966, he was still more convinced that his task was *not* to convince:

I always resent plays in which the audience is brought in by the author to take one side of the argument. I feel that the extremely involved problems that we are up against today – war, sex, or whatever – are so complicated that you can't just divide them up into black and white. It is the job of the playwright to demonstrate the complexity, to try to elucidate it by the clarity of his demonstration. But to go further and start deciding for his audience I think is rather presumptuous. If I was able to give the solution to *Serjeant Musgrave's Dance* I would be the Prime Minister. And I am not.†

* 'Building the Play: an interview with John Arden', op. cit., p. 41.
† 'Who's for a Revolution' (an interview with John Arden by Walter Wager), *Tulane Drama Review*, Vol. IX, no. 2 (1966), p. 46.

Arden has convictions about how his characters should be-
have and the consequences of their actions, but not about the
problems raised by his plays in their widest manifestations.

There are two obvious dangers in this attitude to playwriting; first the characters are likely to be simplified by an
author who condescends towards them as mere 'illustrations' of his theme, and, secondly, the playwright may
alienate his audiences by sitting on a fence, raising strong
issues and declaring himself neutral. A third consequence of
Arden's strategy is that he may not be as open-minded as
an explorer should be, and he may advocate certain answers in spite of himself. Is *Serjeant Musgrave* putting a warm
heart, virility and an open or inactive mind above all other
qualities? Arguably, Mrs Hitchcock and Annie have
Arden's least critical and least complicated attention in the
play. They seem to know what to do at all times, and they
can be still and unruffled. A play in performance can be
indecisive only with the greatest difficulty: someone must
have the last word. The centre of the stage is held by one or
more characters, or else it makes its own point – that there
is no centre to the composition.

Arden seems aware of the difficulty of appearing neutral
or disengaged in dramatic conflicts. In *Live Like Pigs*, most
of the scenes are introduced by ballads sung out of dramatic
context, the first of them raising the widest social implications and identifying clearly with the underdogs:

> O England was a free country
> So free beyond a doubt
> That if you had no food to eat
> You were free to go without.

> But if you want your freedom kept
> You need to fight and strive
> Or else they'll come and catch you, Jack,
> And bind you up alive . . .

In such general terms, the tune and judgement remain the same when introducing the last scene, where violence has broken out. But the ballads give a point of view, not an allegiance in the dramatic confrontation: the violence has broken out on both sides. The last statement of the play is the sound of the ambulance bell, as the authority decried in the ballad steps in to salve some pain.

In *The Happy Haven* (1960), the opposing sides are the Doctor, with his nurses and orderlies, and the five inmates of the home for old people. Both present themselves directly to the audience in lecture-like soliloquies, but the old folk win by hoisting the research doctor on his own experiment, and so turning him into a baby again. Arden here seems to be on the side of the underdogs, but their victory does not touch the major problems raised by the play: how can old and helpless people have a just or happy life? What should be the relationship between medicine and compassion, research and service? Can frightened, isolated people ever become anything but what they are? It does not help the audience towards a response to these problems to have a conceited and foolish doctor discomforted; it merely makes one basic stance clear, and offers some fictitious grounds for gratification at the end of the play.

Both *The Workhouse Donkey* (1963) and *Armstrong's Last Goodnight* (1964) have one character used as a presenter for the action. Dr Blomax in the first of these plays is a southerner working among a town of native northerners; Lindsay in the second, is a poet, intellectual and diplomat among warriors and men of power. But neither character remains outside the action, and neither is able to control events effectively when they themselves are fully embroiled. Arden has used them for contrast and clarity; they represent the author's ability to stand outside the major issues of the action, not his view upon them. They suggest perhaps that

Arden is committed only to an attempt to understand: at least they represent the possibility of a committed point of view.

The various choices that Arden has made of setting, theme and character almost everywhere imply committal: *Left-Handed Liberty* (1965) and *Armstrong* are political-historical plays, *Workhouse Donkey* is full of speech-makers and politicians, *Musgrave* centres on a public meeting. The old-folk in *Happy Haven* are natural non-agitators, but their characterizations are sharpened by the use of masks and direct address to the audience, and the situation compels them to fight for their lives – their lives as they finally choose that they should be. The Sawneys and Jacksons, the neighbours of *Live Like Pigs*, both wish to be left alone, and the writing of this play is less given to statement and challenging emphasis than any of the others; but, when their ways of life impinge upon each other through originally unexamined differences, they both become committed, to fight at least. In the final confrontation Rachel goes further and achieves a passionate denunciation as full of punch and precision as any speech in *Serjeant Musgrave*.

By the end of all the plays one further step of committal has also been made by the dramatist: the climactic confrontation is attended by the 'public', or at least by outsiders to the main action. In *Serjeant Musgrave* and *The Workhouse Donkey* the theatre audience is made to feel incorporated into the drama, by a gun and speeches pointed directly at them, and by entry through the aisles and banging on the doors of the auditorium. In *Live Like Pigs*, a whole neighbourhood and the forces of law and order come into play. In *Armstrong*, the hero is tricked, Lindsay stands aside and the King becomes decisive for the first time, and the stage is filled with his soldiers; for the very last short scene, Lindsay speaks of future men and women.

At the end of the plays, too, Arden's characters are most committed, displaying themselves in action and words with greatest clarity. At this point the audience is not invited to identify with any hero, or to take sides without further thought. Individually they stand, each for himself, explicitly making the claim that Arden intended. The Note to *Live Like Pigs* shows that the Jacksons were not even regarded as 'typical' of a particular kind of family. They were created as they are in order to give a sharp statement:

> They are the people I have chosen for the play, because they illustrate my theme in a fairly extreme form.   (p. 95)

*

The Workhouse Donkey shows the variety and energy of Arden's dramatic invention, his clarity, and his refusal to take sides too openly. 'I had considerable difficulty in preparing *The Workhouse Donkey* for the stage,' the author's Preface to the printed version explains: 'My chosen subject-matter proved both labyrinthine and intractable.' Arden represents himself as being forced to choose, where he would have preferred to leave choice to his audience:

> I would have been happy had it been possible for *The Workhouse Donkey* to have lasted, say, six or seven or thirteen hours (excluding intervals), and for the audience to come and go throughout the performance, assisted perhaps by a printed synopsis of the play from which they could deduce those scenes or episodes which would interest them particularly, and those which they could afford to miss.

This sounds like Bertolt Brecht's pursuit of an 'epic smoke-theatre' where the audience smokes, talks and relaxes, where each member leans back and 'thinks his own thoughts'.*

* cf. J. Willett, *The Theatre of Bertolt Brecht* (Methuen, 1967 edn), pp. 145–6; B. Brecht, *The Messingkauf Dialogues*, trans. J. Willett (Methuen, 1965), p. 19, etc.

But *The Workhouse Donkey*, as produced and printed, is a three-hour, three-act play, complete with progressive exposition, narrative excitement, climaxes of action, display and emotion, and an ending that brings all elements together in a final pay-off. It was prepared for an audience that is *not* permitted to smoke or move about; and Arden's hand is shown in the organization of the play if not by the clearer means of argument or debate.

Much life is shown in little space. Rather than relaxing the audience, Arden has alerted it. The plot is crowded with incident and 'character'. The large cast is divided into numerous groups: Labour politicians, and Conservative, the Police, and the electorate who are further sub-divided into working and professional classes, hang-abouts and entertainers. There are nineteen scenes in twelve distinct locations, one of which is transformed between its first and second appearance. By all these means, the action is kept on the move, and Arden uses surprise and simultaneous action to give it a further explosive quality. In the first scene the central interest is the arrival of Colonel Feng, the new Chief Constable, and laying of the foundation stone of a new Police Headquarters; but while Feng and Boocock, the Mayor, inspect the Guard of Honour to the sound of a Brass Band, Alderman Charlie Butterthwaite, nine times Lord Mayor of the town, talks with the stone-masons. With the political issues made dominant, Dr Blomax then introduces his daughter, Wellesley, to the audience while Butterthwaite talks aside with the Labour Councillors. At the beginning of Act Two, the stage is not crowded as Superintendent Wiper calls on the Conservative leader, Sir Harold Sweetman, late at night, but Lady Sweetman's presence is established before they speak on stage, and Maurice, their son, meets Wiper as he is leaving: so political and private issues are awoken at the same time. The last

scene of this Act is the discovery of a burglary at the Town
Hall, and Arden introduces journalists taking flash-light
photographs of eight specified dramatic confrontations in
the single situation; and, at the same time, Leftwich the
nightwatchman is to be seen stealing '*at least one banknote*'
for himself (p. 104).

In *Serjeant Musgrave's Dance*, 'crooked Joe Bludgeon',
the bargee, was used to instigate diversionary incidents and,
indeed, to control the plot, rather like a Vice called 'Mis-
chief' in a medieval play; he is an unaligned, amoral
instigator of complications and, where necessary, short-cuts.
In this play, the plot is far more diverse and yet the action
springs from the clearly aligned characters, all of whom
seem capable of initiating new interests and surprises.
Blomax announces that he has married Gloria, the Man-
ageress of the Copacabana night-club, having left the stage
earlier with the apparent intention of arranging an abortion
for her child fathered by Superintendent Wiper. Feng
proposes matrimony to Wellesley Blomax when she has
been associated only with Maurice Sweetman, and he has
voiced no personal interest or needs until just before their
casual meeting. Butterthwaite is suddenly revealed as
owing Blomax £500, and Leftwich discovers Butterthwaite's
theft of just that sum from the Town Hall when he has
just been said to be watching television. Lady Sweetman
and Mrs Boocock are suddenly revealed, in separate scenes,
as the powers and decision-makers behind their respective
husbands. The night-club becomes the new Art Gallery
after only one brief and very vague allusion to the possibility.
The general impression is full and complicated, each figure
dynamic and potentially independent.

In *The Happy Haven*, nurses and hospital orderlies were
given specific and rather mechanical business to build up an
impression of Dr Copperthwaite's precise, irresistible and

insensitive power. At the close this machine is replaced by four distinguished Visitors, who sip tea and chatter, and, when the old folk have their revenge, they stand open-mouthed and gasping. The old people's last action before leaving the stage with their victim is to release the Visitors who run away crying, 'Help! Help! Help! . . .' This use of a small, almost anonymous and silent chorus to establish setting, character and theme, and to show the fall-out of the major event of the plot, is much elaborated for *The Work-house Donkey*. Its chorus has several guises: policemen on parade and duty; an applauding crowd of electors; Councillors of two parties; guests at a Sweetman cocktail party; dancers and hostesses at the night-club; journalists, hurrying from one side to another; and lastly the regulars at the Victoria and Albert pub and a band of 'the lowest types in town, layabouts, tearaways, every man of 'em half-seas over' (p. 125). Some of the chorus actions are in strict unison, as those of the police on parade or the Councillors in procession; sometimes speech accompanies the routines, as when journalists ask questions and make notes on their pads. At the night-club the action is dispersed, with solo turns and individual encounters, but each incident, supported by music and dancing, is part of a general effect of party-making, titillation and relaxation. Here Butter-thwaite, his cronies and young Sweetman are drawn into the party, so that they tend to be submerged in the general scene. But there are also two break-downs in this episode, the first as a loud electric bell signals twelve o'clock when the police are expected to make a raid. More sedate dancing to 'The Blue Danube' follows, but as Sergeant Lumber enters in plain clothes even this merriment '*fades away*' (p. 66) and the party is over. At the end of the scene only Butterthwaite is singing and '*laughing grossly*' (p. 69). In the last scene, there are Sweetman's guests and policemen on stage, and a third group of the chorus, now changed into the drunken rabble led by Butterthwaite, break in at the doors of the auditorium and threaten to take over the stage and building. The attackers are controlled and all, except one '*little*' demonstrator, are kept out of the theatre (p. 127). The police are once more, and more openly, in command, but when Butterthwaite is '*removed*' singing of his own exploits, the song is taken up by a crowd outside and '*concludes (if time allows) with a fortissimo reprise of the first stanza*':

> Out he goes the poor old donkey
> Out he goes in rain and snow,
> For to make the house place whiter
> Who will be the next to go?   (pp. 130–31)

With one scapegoat removed in evident humiliation and triumph, Arden uses the chorus in yet another way: all the characters of the play, except Feng, who is also banished from the town by his own resignation, now act '*as chorus*'. Freed from their individual concerns, they all stand on stage, speaking together as if totally assured and with no apparent dissent:

> No one's going to *dare* to interfere.

After this defiance they conclude the play, with a longer joint speech commenting on the play and addressing themselves directly to the theatre audience:

> We smell as we think decent
> If we tell you we've cleaned our armpits
> You'd best believe we've cleaned 'em recent. (p. 133)

The chorus has supported the major climaxes, speeded the exposition and created a sense of place and occasion; but beyond this, it takes over the play at last, counter-stating all the varied and energetic individual stakes in the dramatic action with a demonstration of Arden's view of accepted, normal, defiant hypocrisy in public life.

The energy of individual characters is made clearest and most dominating in a series of soliloquies and set speeches of self-presentation. These are mostly in verse, but some in prose and others in song. At the beginning most are given by Dr Blomax, who combines a statement of his own interests with an introduction of people and themes. Feng, Boocock and Butterthwaite all first hold the stage in public speeches. Sweetman and Feng break from prose to verse to express their motivations. Blomax and Butterthwaite are the first to sing, in support of a 'processional entrance' for the latter at the head of the Labour Councillors (p. 30). Wellesley asks young Sweetman to 'describe' her, and he does so in verse. Whether it is Butterthwaite singing in praise of himself or Maurice Sweetman describing an image of his beloved, the vocabulary changes with the form of utterance: the politician demurs from being a Bonaparte, bowing 'to the public voice' (p. 30), Maurice sees his true love enter with 'Golden and dusty' feet:

> Her hair was tied in a high tight ribbon
> As sleek as a pool of trout
> And her earlobes like the Connemara Marble
> Moved quietly up and about.   (p. 39)

The politician is general, grandiose and posing; the suitor lyrical, mythical and gently absurd. Blomax can vary the style still further: nursery-rhyme for Feng:

> . . . he cared for nobody, no, not he,
> And nobody cared for him!   (p. 44)

or hackneyed and plush advertisement-copy, laced with business jargon and ballad simplicity, for Gloria:

JOHN ARDEN

Big Gloria is a gorgeous girl
And keeps many more employed
Whose gorgeous curves for gorgeous money
Are frequently enjoyed . . . (p. 45)

For a song about himself, he is emphatic, proverbial and childishly repetitive:

If it ever gets too hot
I can pull out my hand
I can pull out my hand
I can pull out my hand . . . (p. 51)

Boocock sees himself heroic and comic:

He sets up a strong staircase
For to stride up in his pride:
And reaches nowt but rheumatics . . . (p. 54)

Sweetman does not sing, but gives a careful catalogue of his achievements and frustrations, concluding with an expectation of satisfaction that has almost melodramatic emphasis. Feng starts with a New Testament quotation, scrupulously modified to suit himself, but breaks into verse for survey, question, doubt and paradoxes about his profession: he pursues the right word, offers conclusions and contradictions, and finishes tersely confident only in himself:

I have no hope and therefore walk alone:
Only alone can I know I am right. (p. 78)

The dialogue breaks into soliloquy in various ways, each appropriate to the speaker and each reaching further and more precisely into the grounds of their motivations. Nothing important to the action is avoided; subtextual implications are never cloaked or merely suggested. Each solo speech shows individual potential and awakens the audience to listen in a new way.

216

This element in Arden's presentation of character ensures that the audience is drawn closely to each of the major
characters in turn, not to sympathize with them so much as
to listen with attention undeflected, to see and to understand how they work. Even Superintendent Wiper has his
brief self-revelation as the consuming 'big fat Alfred'
(p. 83). The motives that are displayed in solos or duologues
are often shabby and usually limited by self-interest. Even
Wellesley, who cares for people and trees and has no
political axe of her own, pitches her hopes no higher than
the opportunity to choose for herself, 'unprejudiced, when I
want' (p. 88). She marries a youth she knows she can manage, and her own admiring father calls her a 'snooty little
bitch' (p. 90). Feng, the upholder of law, trusts only himself, and disappoints himself; he finishes by walking out
and promising to whitewash Wiper.

The abundant dramatic action of *The Workhouse Donkey*,
its choice of character and style of presentation seem
calculated towards political and moral satire. Self-interest,
hypocrisy and the habit of acceptance are seen on all sides,
through the various mutations of cocktail-party smoothness,
boozy and jocular argument, public applause, routine
formalities, subservience, denigration and trickery. Even
the character-names – Boocock, Hopefast, Hardnut, Sweetman, Wellington, Lumber, Gloria, and so on – suggest that
each portrait is intended, in Arden's own words about the
earlier Jacksons, to 'illustrate a theme in extreme form'.
There is neither character nor enterprise that the audience
is clearly invited to latch on to throughout the play, as an
obvious centre of sympathy or hope for solution. The plan
for a new Art Gallery is part of a corrupt political programme and is put into effect to cover up a financial and
moral wangle. The upright Chief Constable is without
human sympathies and dangerously innocent in a world of

political intrigue. The medical practitioner is talented but
also corrupt. Gloria cares more for her job than for her
child or lover, and changes into a discreet superintendent
of champagne glasses.

We could imagine John Arden speaking in the words of
Jonson's Asper in *Everyman Out of His Humour*, and seeking
to set up

> a mirror,
> As large as is the stage whereon we act,
> Where they shall see the time's deformity
> Anatomized in every nerve and sinew,
> With constant courage and contempt of fear.

In Jonson's comedies, especially *Volpone* and *The Alchemist*,
is found the same abundant action and corruption. But the
comparison is not complete, for Arden's characters are less
expert in their vices. His corrupt policeman is not like
Jonson's corrupt advocate who speaks convincingly as a
responsible, learned, compassionate and impassioned moral-
ist. Arden's retired policeman Leftwich has some good sense,
but his larceny is not hidden, like Abel Drugger's greed, by
scrupulous concern for quality and industry. Sweetman
worships gold, but does not have the ardour or the personal resource of Jonson's Volpone, or the vision of his
Mammon. Arden's creatures are smaller, more transparent
and far less ingenious. Nor are they created with Jonson's
sharp ruthlessness and indignation: this dramatist has
taken no 'pride, or lust, to be bitter'; the child of his Muse
is not born 'with all his teeth', but seems to grin even as he
punches.*

Arden's zest and good humour have echoes of Brecht's
insistence on '*spass*', or fun. His transparent and pungent
characterization, his use of song, proverb and catch-

* Compare Jonson's Epistle to *Volpone*.

phrase, his episodic structure and simple, cartoon-like staging, are also reminiscent of Brecht, especially of the author of *The Threepenny Opera* and *The Caucasian Chalk Circle*. But Brecht is more soberly dialectic than Arden in *The Workhouse Donkey*. The twin tales of *The Chalk Circle* are set within a frame story of earnest debate among members of a commune about development of natural resources; and *The Threepenny Opera* presents 'a sort of summary of what the spectator in the theatre wishes to see of life' as well as the opposing picture of what he does not want to see.*

Brecht's *Mother Courage* illustrates more sharply the distinction between the two playwrights, for in this play the pain of war, in personal and social terms, is directly and precisely rendered on stage, whereas in *Serjeant Musgrave* the war is in the past; and there is no compensating picture of peace. Political engagement, religious consolation and military discipline and comradeship are all demonstrated in *Mother Courage* in sober, simple style, without the farcical or melodramatic elaboration of Arden's plays, where a 'Fred Karno' sequence or parodistic heightening are seldom out of key. Arden's are crazier plays, as if Azdak from *The Chalk Circle* were to go unchallenged by Grusha or by the 'Expert of the Federal Reconstruction Commission'.

Aristophanes, in use of chorus and dance, topicality, caricature, abundant action and political and moral theme, also offers comparison with Arden. But the Greek comedian does not choose a petty town for his setting, or make the action depend on merely local concerns. His dramatic structure is based without concealment on large themes, and if a little man does try to fly on a mission to ask for peace, he meets the gods themselves and not other little men, dressed in various but limited authority. At the end of the Greek comedies the stage fills with celebration, often

* See Brecht's Notes *Plays*, Vol. I (1960), p. 178.

around such a figure as Royalty, Reconciliation or Harvest Home.

Jonson, Brecht and Aristophanes clearly offer a double view. While Jonson scourges the vices of mankind he is also intent to raise echoes of true values; he will even punish his Fox with 'mortifying' precision, breaking all the rules of comedy, in order to make clear that he writes in order to satisfy the 'principal end of poesie, to inform men in the best reasons of living'.* Aristophanes does not imitate ordinary human actions, but transposes them into fantastic worlds, showing them in strange guises and manifesting both conflicts and joyful idealistic celebrations. Brecht often contrasts two evils without a clear evocation of relevant good, but there is always an invitation to sober consideration that the audience cannot evade.

Where, then, is the double view in *The Workhouse Donkey*? Is it, against all best example, merely a gay exposure, a ribald and earnest parade of trickery and self-interest dressed in the merest rags of respectability? *Serjeant Musgrave's Dance* has the women and the defeated Attercliffe to speak against Musgrave, Dragoons, politicians and colliers; and it ends with a question, to mark Arden's own exploration. But does not *The Workhouse Donkey* present characters Arden has sized up all too clearly, characters he both despises and plays with? The end of the play is defiance, not question, assertive rhythm not hesitating.

I think Arden's play is most innovating in its theatre language in that these questions can be asked about it. He places the audience in such a position that they ask, 'Is that all?' While their sober political and moral judgement would readily condemn all the characters, their response to the play includes pleasure and some hint of wishing to see life returning other rewards than the hypocrisy clasped in

* *Volpone*, Epistle.

self-defence by the assembled cast at the end of the play. This is effected chiefly, if not wholly, through the workhouse donkey himself, the conceited, stupid, nefarious Butter-thwaite, and by the euphoria of protest that continues undefeated outside the new Art Gallery.

The action of the play, for all its labyrinthine complications, has one moment towards the end of Act Two that is crucial, and precipitates the denouement of the final scenes. Dr Blomax asks Charlie Butterthwaite for repayment of £500 owed to him. The debt has been incurred through betting on horses and, if publicized, would bring scandal on the Labour Party of which he is the effective leader. Unbeknown to Charlie, however, Blomax is asking for the money in order to discredit him and so protect Gloria, his new wife, and Wellesley, his daughter, but he has *explained*, and subsequently sworn, that he needs it because he is being blackmailed for unprofessional conduct. Charlie doubts and questions this, but when Blomax reminds him of services rendered, he does not hesitate:

It has never been said that Charlie Butterthwaite was the man to watch his mates fall under. (p. 99)

The moment is held by song: 'Gratitude', he sings, is the 'king-post of his roof-tree':

> It holds the tiles above his house-place
> The smoke-hole for his fire
> It overhangs his weighty table
> And the bed of his desire!

To raise the necessary money he suggests robbing the Town Hall, and he is not joking, as Blomax assumes. From this point on he becomes progressively more reckless. As he plans, or rather precipitates, the theft, he sings of his birth in the Workhouse, as an unwanted donkey who found in fact he was a 'naked human being!' (p. 102). Having robbed the safe, he plans to give himself a blow on the head to make it look as if his key to the safe has been stolen. The surplus money – there is £1,000 available – he scatters about the stage, singing as he goes. This childish, feckless action makes fun of all deliberation and responsibility. Blomax protests that his need is not so urgent, but he is unheeded and at the end does as he is told.

From this point the style of presentation changes too, for now Charlie has all the songs and most of the solos – a few of these going to Blomax who reverts to his presenter's role as at the beginning of the play. The only other verse of any sort is given to Feng and the final chorus, and if this were not enough to ensure Charlie's dominance, his songs and solos in Act Three are all on a crowded stage, the last as the solitary vocal protest while the other characters side gratefully, and for the most part inconspicuously, with the obviously corrupt police.

In the third Act, after doubts and delays, Charlie gives all his Post Office savings away to men in the bar and to layabouts. Boocock, the Mayor, is prepared to believe him innocent, but Charlie is defeated and knows it. Suddenly he has found that he is exposed and free, and he hastens to be back as he began, penniless and derided. He provides drink for his equals and brings them to the feast, prepared by Sweetman and attended by all the other characters in the play. Almost alone he forces an entry, sweeps some plates off the buffet and sits cross-legged on the table eating iced cake and drinking champagne. He sings comparing himself to Lazarus demanding food at Dives's door. He crowns himself with a ring of flowers and sets a tablecloth around his shoulders as a gown. He borrows the words of Jehovah to express his pride and scorn, but he knows, as his supporters do not, that he offers no promised land; 'the only place you're going is into t'black maria'. He is a scapegoat, not a saviour or redeemer; and all traces of his existence will be covered up, 'Till none can tell what beast was here' (p. 130).

Arden has offset the parade of corruption and hypocrisy with a drunken rabble led by a king who in defeat and loss has discovered recklessness, truth and comradeship. The play ends after a climactic eruption of noise, drunkenness, disorder, generosity, corruption and ease – all 'old essential attributes of Dionysus' as Arden claims in a Preface to the printed text. The god's other attributes – lasciviousness, nudity and fertility – had already been displayed at the Copacabana Club early in the play; here Alderman Butterthwaite had half enjoyed himself, and everyone else had discredited or disclaimed the carnival spirit.

Much depends on performance at the end. If Charlie shows a sense of seriousness, peace and excitement within the mockery and donkey-play, so may the audience; his rhetorical words and command of attention, if not of all events, will help him achieve this. Or conceivably it would be better in performance, because more challenging to understanding, if Charlie seemed oblivious of his new role, acting as if dazed and puny, or high and mad, so that the judgement implicit in his words seems to come without his cognizance. Somewhere in the whirring words and crazy, mocking actions, the audience must find their own balance: the unprecedented moment in the drama calls for a new alignment. Arden is relying here on the theatre's ability to surprise and overwhelm, and at the same time to raise an expectation of satisfaction which an audience can seldom manage to resist.

But, of course, having set up this contrast within the play and sprung this shift of attention, Arden has shown his hand. None of the characters is a critical voice or author's mouthpiece, none is obvious hero or sympathetic centre, but Arden has made his judgement on the world he has created: the political and moral issues 'illustrated' by the assembled cast are to be contrasted and compared with qualities of carnival, protest and recklessness, and with the self-knowledge that comes from defeat and rejection. No positive political programme is submitted and Arden does not follow his last-minute 'hero' beyond the moment of protest and clarification. The question that is not posed directly, but which is implied in the theatrical experience as a whole – 'Is the audience satisfied?' – remains for further consideration: what hope can Charlie suggest?

*

John Arden writes journalism and gives interviews quite freely, and he has often taken occasion to say that he does not know what alternative there is to political and moral corruption.*

Even the question at the end of *Serjeant Musgrave's Dance* is more about private life than about political practice or decisions. It is not surprising therefore that Arden does not oppose political and moral ideals against the examples of corruption in *The Workhouse Donkey*, as might Aristophanes, Jonson or, perhaps, Brecht. He opposes them with a personal, Dionysiac outburst that leaves the rest of the characters unaffected and uncomprehending. In a discussion of Ben Jonson, Professor L. C. Knights is assured that

the satire presupposes certain general attitudes in the audience, and that it builds on something that was already there,†

but Arden, in *The Workhouse Donkey*, is assured only that he can hold political and moral practice up to ridicule and scorn, and then present a theatrical demonstration of

* See, for example, above, pages 205–6.
† *Drama and Society in the Age of Jonson* (1937), pp. 188–9.

qualities that one character discovers from within his earlier, more conforming, yet always irreverent, *persona*. Early in the play Charlie Butterthwaite alludes to his early career as protector of human rights, but his involvement in this role has become obscured by the more than nine years that he had exercised political power. He regains his messianic activity by defending a corrupt professional man and calling people to his side who have never 'clocked in' with the dutiful workers.

We have seen that Arden described many of the qualities of Charlie's outburst – noise, disorder, drunkenness, generosity, corruption and ease – as 'the old essential attributes of Dionysus'. He went on to claim that they are essentially theatrical:

The Comic Theatre was formed expressly to celebrate them: and whenever they have been forgotten our art has betrayed itself and our generally accessible and agreeable god has hidden his face. (p. 9)

The conclusion of this play, by showing a personal change in an exciting and excited moment over against an established world of political activity and personal fixity, is presenting one theatrical reality over against another, moving from caricature to enjoyment and awakened recognition, displaying some of the most potent resources of theatre. The last moments of a performance should be both irresistible and unreflective; a state of being should be released on stage that will not be wholly predictable, either for actor or for audience. Arden is attempting to give 'what we laughably call "vital theatre"' a chance to 'live up to its name' (p. 8).

A straightforward programme for a dramatist might well be based on such a strategy but, having let the Dionysiac theatre speak for itself, Arden seems less confident, not more.

JOHN ARDEN

His problem has two main aspects: what is the nature of
the theatrical experience that he has raised, and where can
such a full theatrical experience be created in our present-
day theatres and with our various theatre companies? He
has experimented widely, with professional and amateur
companies, and with classes of children. He has acted in his
own plays, taught at a university, accepted a commission
to write on a specific subject, collaborated with his wife in
playwriting and production, and joined a team brought
together to create an (abortive) American musical. He has
written a play that is all stage-directions and, having written
a full text for a short play, chose to have it performed with a
class of girl guides improvising nearly all their own words –
and preferred that version to his own.* He rates professional
finish and acceptability less important for performance of
his plays than a virtually unlimited commitment by everyone concerned in the production. Considering plays at
the National Theatre, the Aldwych and the Citizens' in
Glasgow, Arden wrote that:

It is becoming more and more clear to me that it is impossible
for workers in the British theatre ever to finish their job properly
. . . once [a play] has passed into the hands of a company, the
pressures of time and money will combine to ensure that it will
be presented in a manner so slapdash and unconsidered, that if
it were a ship to be put to sea or a building to be lived in, a
prosecution for dangerous negligence would inevitably follow.†

If he must choose between slick professionalism and committed amateurism, Arden will choose the latter; and I
suspect that this is because his dramatic purpose requires
climactic incidents where what is revealed must be explorat-

* cf. 'Who's for a Revolution' (an interview with Simon Trussler)'
op. cit., p. 51.
† *Guardian*, 16 May 1964.

ory and honest before all else. Arden wishes to use the theatre to create or release a response that cannot be predicted, to discover what is involved in certain human activity:

we must plug the idea of a *theatre* as a place where interesting things happen without regard to what the things specifically *are*, before we can indulge ourselves with internecine disputes about subject-matter, styles of presentation, or philosophies.*

For the writer, as for other workers in the theatre, good work involves subject matter that he 'personally' understands and feels, and also 'passionate affirmation'.† But beyond this there is little certainty if the theatre is fully used:

there is nothing the dramatist can do but find a modest furrow and dig in it as hard as he can and as truthfully as he is permitted to do. If he doesn't get pushed out of it by his 'friends' and colleagues, or pulled out of it by the police, he might just manage to delve deep enough to find something like a bit of bedrock. I haven't done so, yet.‡

*

The Hero Rises Up (1969) offers the clearest example of Arden's pursuit of drama almost for its own sake, as a surrogate for conscious, considered intellection, as a means of discovery in its own terms not as a stimulus for debate or platform for verbal affirmation. This play, in which his wife, Margaretta D'Arcy, collaborated, tells the well-known story of Nelson. A 'Necromantic Prologue' in burlesque academic style foretells the familiar events and warns that the audience must make what it can of the hero who will be displayed:

* 'Poetry and Theatre', *The Times Literary Supplement*, 6 August 1964, p. 705.
† ibid.
‡ 'Matters of Public Interest', *Guardian*, 5 July 1968.

The technique I shall employ for this necromantic experiment does not involve catch-penny invocations and incantations: which are nowadays completely discredited. No: all I need is this simple electrostatic apparatus – here – combined with your absolute concentration and co-operation. When Lord Nelson and his woman are summoned before us, I want you all to observe them, what they do, and what they say: and to learn from it such lessons for your future as you may. *That* is the part of the proceedings in which I have no competence to guide you. If you are wise, you will benefit: if you are foolish, you will not . . .

(p. 15)

Titles are provided for each scene on slide-projections or placards and these again foretell events and direct attention to issues that will shortly be self-evident. Examples are: YOU CAN'T ARGUE WITH A DEAD MAN; THE HERO'S TRIUMPHANT RETURN; or, with prodigious irony, THE HERO'S HAPPY HOME. The story is well-known, the characters speak clearly for themselves, the action is presented in clear colours and simple confrontations, and often has the extra energy of parody and farce. The scenes are a series of cartoons, instantly recognizable, using certain phrases and actions repeatedly, like shorthand and familiar clues. Often the stage is held by a single character making his motivation and purpose clear in a solo song or a speech in very short-lined verse. In the first Act, Nelson is given song, dance and posture to make a political and personal decision clear:

[*He whips out his sword and commences a fantastic dance, whirling the blade around him in the air. He sings.*]
> The King of Naples is a King
> And he wears a golden crown . . .

When song and dance are finished, a '*great swoop*'

[*takes him across to the* KING, *before whom he falls dramatically on one knee, the sword raised in salute.*] (p. 25)

Agreement is shown by characters following each other around the stage in a circle, disagreement by one character 'coming forward' to manifest his own point of view as if no one else were on stage. Drums beat and sudden action fills the stage to take the drama from consultation to combat.

The action moves from Naples, to under the sea, to London and on to the country, to Copenhagen, Trafalgar and Nelson's passage to an eternity of fame. The play moves with artificial speed and variety, and the dramatist's task has been to present each element in the story as sharply as possible, not to establish a real-seeming atmosphere, nor build up expectation or mystery. When Nelson and Lady Nelson quarrel irrevocably over Emma Hamilton they do so at a London party after wild dancing, laughter and applause:

LADY NELSON: Horatio: I am resolved –
NELSON: This is entirely ridiculous –
LADY NELSON: If you will not give her up, then –
NELSON: You have no dignity, Lady Nelson –
LADY NELSON: Then you will have to give up me.   (p. 60)

A stage-direction underlines the effective contrast: '*This exchange has fallen into a pool of embarrassed general silence.*' And other contrasts ensure a critical response: Nelson, drunken and supported by Emma, speaks of dignity; Lady Nelson is 'resolved' that Nelson must make the break, his decision is hers. The Prince steps in to propose a toast and a new scene is announced: REBIRTH THROUGH THE FLAMES. Arden has effected his purpose, making apparent the basic ironies and leaving the audience to think what they can, sympathizing with none of the four persons individually involved in the short dramatic moment, nor agreeing simply with the caption.

229

The party scene develops further to encompass more general considerations. The Prince speaks for 'sound morality' and calls on Nelson for support. In effect a spotlight now shines on Nelson as he answers, with only a moment's doubt: 'Morality, Your Royal Highness . . . My own father is a clergyman . . .' The reference to the Crown, the Church and his father is quite sufficient for the Prince: 'Exactly so: and you have proven it, my lord, to the last drop of your blood.' Heroism, however mistaken, confirms values, however mistaken too, and the action moves on towards the burning of immoral and degenerate books from the shelves of the host's library. As this second celebration is conducted with gusto, Emma prompts Nelson to reply to Lady Nelson and, in complete contrast, Emma's husband raises his single voice against the book-burning: 'Any man that can burn books must be an absolute madman.' Where should the audience look, and to what action should they give their attention? Arden has made sure that in this artificially brisk dramatization there is an artificial complication of contrasts and ironies. The audience cannot feed on any single response. The scene ends with Emma announcing her pregnancy, Lady Nelson remembering her husband's wounds and illness, and Nisbet, her son, concluding matters with a prat-fall of ineffectual solemnity:

[NISBET *makes an effort at sobriety and leads his mother away, tripping over his own feet.*] (p. 67)

A soliloquy for Nelson after he learns that he is a father shows how this theatrical style can present a developing understanding, resolution, apprehensiveness, guilt, acceptance, fear and, finally, a hurrying reassurance in habitual lies and acceptance:

[*He tears open the letter, and reads it wildly to himself.*]
By this time she has a child.
By this time she has a daughter.
By this time *I* have a daughter.
Born with a false name
In a false and secret corner
And *I* must fly my flag once more
Wide agape on the open water . . .
Horatia Nelson Thompson
That is the lie by which we must call her:
She has a liar for a father
And a liar for a mother –
What lies will lie before her
As she walks into a world
Where all true men are defeated
By the falsehood of treacherous murder
And false men are accepted
With all the credit of the conqueror?
But I must write a letter to my Angel,
I can find neither pen nor pencil:
'O my dearest dearest Emma –!'
[*He starts feverishly to write . . .*]   (p. 69)

Unlike the 'white word' of Musgrave's dance, this is not premeditated, nor is it a single blow at a sitting target. Nelson is at the moment of speaking confronting his past and future, and his various responsibilities. His thought moves from 'she' to 'I', to 'we', and from 'liar' to 'Angel', from finding names to looking for pen or pencil, from a 'secret corner' to the 'open water'. Single lines and phrases hold and challenge attention, and the whole invites the audience to judge. The ambiguity does not arise from subtextual suggestion but from textual contrasts, each element clearly expressed: for example, how can Nelson be both 'true' man and 'false', and how warm are the blinding endearments with which he finishes?

After the first performance of *The Workhouse Donkey*, Arden had testified to dislike:

> Some Critics said:
> This Arden baffles us and makes us mad:
> His play's uncouth, confused, lax, muddled, bad.*

Still more critics complained after *The Hero Rises Up*, not only of the playwriting but also of the production for which Arden and Margaretta D'Arcy were likewise responsible. In a Preface, the authors explained their main objectives:

> We meant to write a play which need not be *done properly*. That is to say: we wanted to produce it ourselves, so that it would present the audience with an experience akin to that of running up in a crowded wet street on Saturday night against a drunken red-nosed man with a hump on his back dancing in a puddle, his arms around a pair of bright-eyed laughing girls, his mouth full of inexplicable loud noises. If you do see such a sight, what do you do? Nine times out of ten you push past among the wet mackintoshes and the umbrellas, muttering to yourself something about 'likely to get run over, ridiculous old fool – but why were those girls *laughing*?' and that's all. But you don't at once forget him: and although you know nothing about him and never will know anything about him, he has become some sort of *circumstance* in your life. You can't sit down and analyse him, because you haven't got the needful data: you can't ask him for his 'symbolism' – if he has any, you yourself will have provided it: and you can't go back and 're-evaluate' him, because the police will have moved him on. But there he was: and you saw him. (pp. 5–6)

Such an intention is hugely ambitious. Theatrical excitement has to become a 'circumstance' in the life of the audience. The Ardens italicize 'circumstance', but 'life' is perhaps the more significant word. They want their play

* Author's Preface, p. 10.

to engage attention as an exceptional, baffling and irremovable experience. At all times it must look accidental˙ *and* exceptional, and yet be accepted as real: a threefold objective that demands technical and imaginative agility, and 'passionate affirmation', from every member of the cast, as well as the authors. The production must be highly artificial to match the writing and truthfully explorative to bring a sense of unpredictable reality. Only so will the audience be assured and able to take freely from the play whatever they can see.

Its theme is comparatively simple: a hero whom 'we' needed, and who 'did what we required'. But what the play does is to explore the constituents and consequences of this story, and so to display it for the audience to experience. Irony, contrast, pungency, simplicity, noise, movement, unlikeliness, disproportion and theatrical artifice are all put to work, continuously and variously. Ideally the audience will be immersed in the production, and need to make an effort for survival.

By making their theatre language more artificial, the authors have given it bright, strong colours, furious movement, naked clarity in each aspect. They believe that, despite the difficulties of performance, this is the way to make the play memorable. They have rejected a hero presented so that he gains ever more sympathetic and subtle attention, the debate or conflict that is staged in terms recognizable in everyday life, the group of characters turned this way and that to reveal progressively the nature of their commitment to themselves and each other. Artificially they have tried to create carnival, extension of normal behaviour and, from the audience, an alerted attention to large issues. They trust the theatre to bring truth in realization, and the audience to find truth in understanding. These are large expectations to have of their necessary collaborators, and both have often failed them.

The Ardens find themselves in a dilemma, for to ask less of production or response would be to undermine the basic strategy of their playwriting. Faced by a world that no one can fully understand, they hope to capture in the artificiality of theatre something of the complexity and perplexity that they see around and within themselves. They wish to display involvement, rather than offer comment or guide, or means of perception. They refuse to take a slow pace, to leave out or under-emphasize discordant elements, or to use less confusing and constant contrasts, because they believe that this would be false to what is required in life and false to what the theatre should be able to achieve. They do simplify each and every moment, cutting out half-lights, subtextual suggestion, secondary characters, minor issues and complications, but this is only in order to make the whole more 'baffling.' They have recognized the theatre as a surrogate for living, and they work restlessly to make it so. They question the assumption that theatre, like politics, is an art of the practicable, because they believe that practice in this world and age is almost always at fault.

7

The Dramatist's Theatre

The latest plays by all four dramatists that we have considered strain the resources of theatre. At the beginning of their careers each writer recognized a comparatively simple purpose. Harold Pinter alerts attention so that the audience becomes more aware and more questioning. He can present each element of theatrical experience – speech, presence, gesture, sound, grouping, movement, rhythm and progression – with such precision that the audience becomes attentive and perceptive. But as he does this, the demands upon his actors for honesty in performance and the ability to relate element to element become ever more taxing. Pinter's imagination in his later plays encompasses a wider range of behaviour and social reality than before, but the means whereby the 'relaxed' and inwardly realized dramatic illusion is created have never asked for so much hidden work from the actors in their task of creation and elimination. Moreover, the audience is left without the comparatively easy excitements of *The Room* or *The Birthday Party*, where the unexpected is expressed in entries and exits, actual violence and physical transformations. Pinter has discovered drama in the smooth and ordinary surface of life. His plays reveal violence, helplessness and momentary joys of sensation and thought in forceful confrontations and with almost titanic measure, but always the everyday scale and confusions of life are expressed as well. By becoming engrossed in the minutiae of theatre language, Pinter has increased the range of his perceptions, and has insisted on actors, designers, directors and audiences sharing a similar, demanding (and rewarding) journey towards finesse.

John Osborne started by setting his characters to fight themselves and each other, and gave them arias, songs and close combat in which to make magnificent 'fusses' or simple, deep-touched stands. Actors could stretch themselves in these roles, and audiences were confident that, in one turn after another, the performance would be alive with energy and invention. Words were used resoundingly and pathetically, and physical performances were clear and varied. But, for *Inadmissible Evidence*, one actor is kept on stage throughout the long play, and part of this character's dilemma is his almost total lack of new resources when belief in his social and personal roles fail him. In later plays, the scale of performance is greatly reduced, the action being restricted to exchange of news or opinion, very few entrances and exits, a number of drinks and a series of consultations about past, future or possible activity. Verbally and physically, the actors' tasks are still demanding and, since the obvious excitements are removed or lessened, they must hold attention more by the quality of performance and a pervasive sense of an undesired and unavoidable unreality. Osborne has not chosen 'show-biz' characters in order to evade the presentation of ordinary human confrontations, but to represent the small, sharp edge of the continuing yet intermittent sense of disbelief that he experiences in and around himself. Either he is forcing theatre language to change with his own mind, or possibly the theatre is drawing him on to a sharper recognition of the bases of his life. Both ways, the going is more difficult, despite Osborne's undiminished zest.

Arnold Wesker, who starts by using the theatre to represent life and as a platform for argument and assertion, becomes increasingly concerned to make the theatre 'demonstrate' the values in human involvement in a form more bare, bold and inescapable than life. Argument is still an element in the later plays, but more and more the demonstration relies on a particular and highly charged moment in which the actors have to hold attention. In *The Four Seasons*, Wesker's purposes would founder completely if his actress were incapable of giving precise and varying 'meaning' to twenty minutes of silence. In *Their Very Own and Golden City*, the leading actor must stand on his head to express joy and a basic seriousness. Speeches have become more operatic without losing a continuous echo of ordinary speech.

John Arden's later plays include a whole-day's Carnival for the students of New York University in which he himself took part, and in which the audience were enlisted in opposing sides of a War Game. One of his own long speeches announced that he had created the dramatic event as part of his job as a secret agent, to provide 'Washington watchdogs with a firm list of suspect students'.* In later, fully scripted plays, the strength, variety, freedom and commitment that he demands from his actors have increasingly led him to be dissatisfied with professional theatre-makers. He now works chiefly on his own, in collaboration with his wife and with casts of his own choice and under his own direction.

*

Besides increasing their demands upon their interpreters, each dramatist has moved towards increasingly idiosyncratic forms of drama. From the first they have felt free to experiment whenever they saw the need. Ordinary rules about exposition have been flouted, especially by Pinter and, in *The Kitchen*, by Wesker. Time and place have been free to change, so that Archie Rice moves from home to

* 'John Arden's NY War', *Flourish*, Vol. 9 (1967), pp. 1, 8, 9 and 16.

nightmare or Pinter uses a blackout to change the characters' alignment artificially. Narrative is often a small element, and character is sometimes defined by the play's action as much as by a fully imagined background, physique or temperament. Style changes from imitation of ordinary behaviour to soliloquy, oration, dance, proverb, song, interrogation, ritual, physical activity or sustained silent tableau. These dramatists all know that the theatre can be free from the constraints of what used to be called a well-made play. On occasion they feel no need to reproduce an illusion of life, or even to give life-likeness of detail.

They were fortunate in that Samuel Beckett's *Waiting for Godot*, first performed in English in London in 1955, had made all these claims in one evening's entertainment. Words and actions were here controlled by a new dramatist who was already a practised and confident writer. Echoes of long-accepted religious and philosophic thought and an exciting ambiguity in the use of language both caught attention. Words and actions were often very funny. But more than this, the whole play was sustained by a steady, clear-eyed appreciation of the nature of human consciousness, so that it carried conviction by unity of thought and feeling, as well as by the confidence of its artifice. No young dramatist could have commanded his audience as Beckett did, nor taken their expectation so far in one stride.

The setting of *Waiting for Godot* is fantastic: a road, or a bog, with a single tree, and the audience recognizable, from time to time, out in front. The moon rises at the end of each Act, promptly on cue. The two main characters, Estragon and Vladimir, meet and separate, unaware of time or place, and giving only a sketchy impression of lonely and persecuted life outside the confines of the play. Pozzo and Lucky are joined together as master and servant; when first seen, they are due to part, but they return still more dependent on each other, the one in self-willed slavery and the other through incapacity. The ordinary business of living is scarcely represented, save in hunger, pain, fear, apprehension and occasional, short-lasting happiness or satisfaction.

Other dramatists could show the way towards fantasy, especially Ionesco, whose *Lesson* was first seen in English in the same year as *Godot*. His plays are 'realized dreams': their source is:

not submission to some predetermined action, but the exteriorization of a psychic dynamism, a projection onto the stage of internal conflict, of the universe that lies within: . . . it is in the deepest part of myself, of my anguish and my dreams, it is in my solitude that I have the best chance of rediscovering the universal, the common ground.*

His characters may have several noses, may fly into the air, turn into rhinoceroses or unconcernedly pick poisoned mushrooms in the drawing-room. Ordinary actions, like the serving of coffee or taking a pupil through a lesson, may become exaggerated through repetition or through unreasonable or climactic emphasis, so that the ordinary becomes fantastic, comic or terrifying.

In some measure, the four younger English dramatists have followed Beckett and Ionesco towards fantasy as a means of giving dream-like intensity and range, but none has been so surrealistic as Ionesco or attempted the same kind of timelessness and generality as Beckett. Pinter is the most fantastic of the four, but he has never cut free from all representations of ordinary living.

In *Waiting for Godot* another important claim was made on the audience's perception. Even as the play is being given,

* 'Foreword', *Plays*, Vol. I, trans. D. Watson (Calder & Boyers, 1958), pp. viii–ix.

there are reminders that the characters are truly actors in a theatre. So theatrical performance becomes, in itself, an image of human activity. Often this is presented by implication alone: Estragon and Vladimir engage in cross-talk reminiscent of music-hall comedians or circus clowns; they do a trick with three hats; Pozzo 'explains the twilight', and expects attention and then appreciation. But there is more specific treatment as well: Lucky is called upon to entertain by dancing or thinking, and Estragon and Vladimir talk about their theatre audience. After the audience's interest has been caught by Pozzo and Lucky, the two tramps spell out the theatrical image:

VLADIMIR: Charming evening we're having.
ESTRAGON: Unforgettable.
VLADIMIR: And it's not over.
ESTRAGON: Apparently not.
VLADIMIR: It's only the beginning.
ESTRAGON: It's awful.
VLADIMIR: It's worse than being at the theatre.
ESTRAGON: The circus.
VLADIMIR: The music-hall.
ESTRAGON: The circus.   (1st edn, p. 34)

The reference to the circus is illuminating. Pozzo is the ring-master with his whip, who flogs the weakest, dependent clown. Estragon and Vladimir appear as the superior or dignified clown and 'He who gets slapped'. Estragon says Lucky 'played the fool', and in the French version Pozzo calls him a 'knouk' which is defined as a kind of 'bouffon' kept for entertainment. Even the Boy may be the boy who customarily interrupts the clowns' act with a message from the landlord of the tavern 'around the corner'. At the close of the play, when the tramps end another day with another resolve to commit suicide, they effect, apparently by accident, a further routine clown's trick of trousers falling down;

immediately after this piece of traditional comedy, they make their final gesture by not moving from the stage as both verbally agree to do so. The characters' 'performances' are seen as habitual attempts to exist, without too much consciousness or too much pain. The characters put on an act, for themselves as for others; they are amused, when they let themselves 'go' and think of nothing but the immediately available entertainment.

The effect of this element in Beckett's writing is harder to discern in the four younger dramatists. But both Osborne and Pinter introduce music-hall routines, sometimes with the characters' consciousness of theatrical impersonation. Each of them, on occasion, directs a character to 'take the stage' and to put over a performance, a claim for attention or an attempt to impersonate some other character, stronger, more successful, or more assured than he himself can expect to be. Osborne's characters are commonly caught between belief and disbelief. Arden's main characters are all speech-makers, and have the unbounded vitality of theatrical illusion. In later plays he sets the action moving with the speed, variety and colour that have more connection with carnival than with life. Wesker is the least ostensibly theatrical, but the Interlude of *The Kitchen*, the party of *Chips with Everything* and the public meetings of *Their Very Own and Golden City* are like plays-within-plays. In these episodes the characters speak for their 'dreams', not their realities or, in the later plays, for their attempted compromises and not their true failures. All four dramatists seem committed to the theatre partly because of its ability to present an illusionary element that they find in life, to define pretence and disbelief, and to show the effort needed to sustain commitment in private or in public.

In his language, Beckett also showed the way ahead. Pinter's debt is the most obvious, though indirect: he has said that he admires Beckett's work 'so much that something of its texture might appear in my own'.* The 'texture' springs from Beckett's sense of verbal ambiguity – so in *Endgame*, a painter is said to be an 'en*graver*', being 'ap*pall*ed' and seeing only 'ashes' in all the 'rising corn'† – but even more from his awareness of subtextual meanings and misunderstandings. The ambiguities allow words or phrases to stand out from the rest of the dialogue to awaken impressions in the audience's minds which may well be supposed absent from the speakers'. In a letter, Beckett spoke of the ability of the words in *Endgame* to 'claw' at the mind.‡ At rehearsals of a revival of *Waiting for Godot* in 1964, he is reported to have said:

This is a play full of implications, and every important statement may be taken at three or four levels. But the actor has only to find the dominant one; because he does so does not mean the other levels will be lost. All that matters is the laugh and the tear.§

But the comic and the pathetic are not always easy to identify on first reading, for Beckett's sense of subtextual implications enables him to mask involvement, so that what is truly comic may be expressed pathetically, and vice versa.

In his study of *Proust* (1931), Beckett described an artist's use of dialogue and reaction in terms that are applicable to his own plays:

He was incapable of recording surface. . . . The copiable he does not see. He searches for a relation, a common factor, substrata. *Thus he is less interested in what is said than in the way in which it is said* . . .

* 'Harold Pinter Replies', *New Theatre Magazine*, Vol. II, no. 2 (1961), p. 9.
† *Endgame* (Faber, 1958), p. 32.
‡ Letter to Alan Schneider, *Village Voice*, March 1958.
§ Report by Kenneth Pearson, *Sunday Times*, 20 December 1964.

The verbal oblique must be restored to the upright: thus 'you are charming' equals 'it gives me pleasure to embrace you'.*

There are substrata in actions as well as words, and what is heard and seen depends on the hearer and onlooker at least as much as on the doer. Beckett recounts how Proust's narrator hears his grandmother's voice on the telephone and, because it is not accompanied by her physical presence to which he is accustomed, he hears the voice 'for the first time, in all its purity and reality', so that he does not recognize it at first. He rushes to Paris and surprises his grandmother reading a book: 'the notion of what he should see has not had time to interfere its prism between the eye and its object', and now he sees a 'mad old woman', not the face 'mercifully composed' by his own 'solicitude of habitual memory'.†

Beckett also notes the moment when Odette says to Swann, her husband, that Forcheville, her lover, 'is going to Egypt at Pentecost'. Because of Swann's feelings of 'doleful resignation', it is as if he hears other words; he effectively translates the remark into 'I, Odette, am going with Forcheville to Egypt at Pentecost'. For this hearer, the future of the speaker seems already present, and his suffering is acute: he has infected the speaker with his own mobility of thought. Beckett takes more examples to show that:

When it is a case of human intercourse, we are faced by the problem of an object, whose mobility is not merely a function of the subject's, but independent and personal: two separate and imminent dynamisms related by no system of synchronization.‡

In Beckett's plays the characters change for each other,

* *Proust* (Grove Press, 1931), pp. 63–4.
† ibid., pp. 14–15.
‡ ibid., pp. 5–7.

and so do objects, the past and the effects of words. Mostly
the characters speak ordinary words that neither represent
them accurately nor carry definition; when they seem to
agree, they may severally be thinking of different objects
or resolving on opposed actions; when they seem to differ
they may well be of the same mind. But occasionally their
perception is sharpened by a word that, as if by chance,
breaks through habitual responses. Almost any passage in
Godot might be quoted as example:

VLADIMIR: How they've changed!
ESTRAGON: Who?
VLADIMIR: Those two.
ESTRAGON: That's the idea, let's make a little conversation.
VLADIMIR: Haven't they?
ESTRAGON: What?
VLADIMIR: Changed.
ESTRAGON: Very likely. They all change. Only we can't.
VLADIMIR: Likely! It's certain. Didn't you see them?
ESTRAGON: I suppose I did. But I don't know them.
VLADIMIR: Yes you do know them.
ESTRAGON: No I don't know them.
VLADIMIR: We know them, I tell you. You forget everything.
   [*Pause. To himself.*] Unless they're not the same . . .
ESTRAGON: Why didn't they recognize us, then?
VLADIMIR: That means nothing. I too pretended not to recog-
   nize them. And then nobody ever recognizes us.
ESTRAGON: Forget it. What we need – Ow! [*Vladimir does not
   react.*] Ow!
VLADIMIR [*to himself*]: Unless they're not the same . . .
ESTRAGON: Didi! It's the other foot! [*He goes hobbling towards the
   mound.*]
VLADIMIR: Unless they're not the same . . .   (pp. 48–9)

Vladimir starts by trying to understand, but Estragon
joins him to pass the time. Vladimir talks of Pozzo and
Lucky, but Estragon thinks of others and of himself.

Vladimir agrees, but is beginning to doubt his own eyes. Estragon begins to speak of their needs, but becomes conscious of his own pain. He makes a direct appeal to Vladimir, but Vladimir does not hear.

Here is drama that is independent of unambiguous statement or sustained eloquence, that shows the results of feelings obliquely, that moves from dialogue to solo-speech at any moment, that has talk to hide silence, and silence as eloquent as talk. Language is laughable and pathetic, necessary and inessential. Within the freedom of such a style, other dramatists could find encouragement for expressing their own sense of subtextual energies, the hide-and-seek of personal relationships, and the changing motivations and forms of expressiveness.

But the greatest step that Beckett made in *Waiting for Godot* was still more basic: to write a play that did not tell the audience what it was about. Who is Godot, why do the characters persist in acting as they do, what could they do, or what might they do, to change their predicament and ameliorate their suffering, or is this even possible? There are many clues, often at variance with each other: is the tree the tree of life or a symbol of renewal; is it a willow, reminiscent of forlorn lovers and of Judas, or is it a 'shrub' or 'bush', or is it reminiscent of the 'Tree' on which Christ died, to which Vladimir explicitly refers? When Estragon 'does the tree', he stands as if crucified on one foot with arms spread out, and he asks, 'Do you think God sees me?': closing his eyes as he is instructed he '*staggers worse*', stops and cries '*at the top of his voice*': 'God have pity on me! . . . On me! On me! Pity! On me!' (pp. 76–7). Elsewhere a barefooted Estragon explicitly compares himself to Christ: but the similarity is faint and momentary. He is also selfish, suicidal, cruel, spiteful, stupid, deceitful, ungrateful. Besides other characters are also, momentarily,

Christ-figures. Lucky is the suffering servant, or fool, who is being taken to the fair to be sold: in the French version this destination is named, specifically: '*Saint-Sauveur*'. Even Pozzo, returning blind, is held up by Vladimir and Estragon whom he takes to be highwaymen – the sufferer between two thieves. Godot, who never appears, may seem more meaningful, especially to English audiences who hear echoes of 'God' in his very name. He keeps sheep and goats, sends messengers to say he will appear, and probably has a white beard. Vladimir believes that Godot can both save and punish. But he cannot be identified with the Christian God: he shows no sign that, like Lucky's hypothetical 'personal God', he 'loves us dearly'. Vladimir, who seems most assured of Godot's existence, speaks of him consulting his family, agents and books before taking a decision, as if this were 'the normal thing'; besides, Vladimir has other gods, the 'Saviour' who forgives, for some unknown reason, from the cross, the 'cruel fate' which consigns men among a 'foul brood', and, perhaps, the 'reinforcements' of other men which put an end to waiting for Godot.

Waiting for Godot is mainly about a state of being, that cannot be defined except by the play, but which seems to relate from time to time to many notions about what life is and might be. In performance, the audience is stimulated to question and remember, to laugh and pity, and slowly a 'common factor', a relation, develops in their responses, gaining strength from the 'substrata' of the interplay. Beckett has shown that theatrical illusion can communicate, by its hidden structure, the unifying and creative vision of its author, which never speaks directly. He has encouraged other dramatists to use the theatre for expressing what they sense rather than what they say in words. The danger is incoherence, if the writer's responses are not based in experience, and settled in manner of working. The opportunity is that of by-passing limitations and barriers of language, of presenting a whole reaction to life, instinctive and subconscious as well as conscious and explicit.

*

No other dramatist has followed Beckett all the way, but few, if any, can remain unaffected by his achievements. He has restored the theatre as a necessary art, a form which allows a specifically twentieth-century consciousness to be explored and presented. No other art form has both the mobility and the physical reality of the theatre as Beckett used it. No other could so nakedly and consistently show man, involved with himself and with others in time, operating in all his faculties or with suspended consciousness.

The younger dramatists have not shown Beckett's rigour, being unwilling to limit theatrical means to so few and so unaccommodated human figures. But, while employing a closer imitation of ordinary life and greater variety of incident and character, those who have worked in the theatre for ten years or more have all proved to be pioneers and experimenters, using the medium with increasing boldness and for more specifically theatrical effect. Unfortunately this has made their work progressively more specialized, more difficult for audiences as well as performers. Sometimes dramatists seem obsessed by their technical means.

In keeping with this development among writers, it is significant that the 1960s saw a large increase in what can be termed 'pure' theatre. Professional directors have used devices of actor-training to build up entertainments through rehearsals. Actors improvise on given themes, and so develop a settled production that represents a specifically theatrical response to topical issues. The published text of the Royal Shakespeare Company's *US* (1968) is a record of one example of this kind:

The Book of US is intended as a record of the attempt to distil a theatre performance for London out of the immense flood of information about Vietnam and the thoughts and feelings of a group of actors, writers, directors, designers, musicians preparing a year ahead and rehearsing over fifteen weeks.

(Editorial Foreword)

Companies of actors, as that at the Victoria Theatre, Stoke-on-Trent, study newspaper reports, political speeches and other documents and, under the guidance of a director and perhaps an author, they choose speeches, incidents and confrontations that can be presented in theatrical re-creation, often in a variety of styles. A sequence of these episodes makes up a 'Documentary Drama', exploring the bare bones of past events by the expedient of making them 'work' theatrically.

Classical texts are, likewise, ransacked for material to improvise upon, for dramatic situations that can be exploited without regard for the author's original dramatic strategy or the implications of the play as a whole. *The Marowitz Hamlet* (Allen Lane The Penguin Press, 1968), subtitled 'a collage version of Shakespeare's play by Charles Marowitz', shows how a reliance on the techniques of theatre craft, especially those of actor-training and of direction, can lead to mere sensationalism, rather than finesse or strength or genuine discovery. Stage-directions give a taste of the quality of presentation:

Hamlet moves downstage into a spot of his own. Fortinbras, standing strongly behind him, slowly fades out.

Cut into new scene.

Sound-Montage: All lines are chanted and overlap.

The main figure moves into a prepared world of light, and a contrasting figure, with a purely physical representation

248

of strength, is artificially reduced to nothing. One scene can sharply contrast with another, the sense of shock depending as much upon the speed of change as on the originality or power of representation. Words can be forced into chant and inaudibility. Transpositions of time, place and dialogue are freely introduced in this version of Hamlet; characters speak out their roles, or sing, whenever the director decrees. All characters can be on stage at once, without any purpose being expressed by their entry and without serving any necessity of narrative. After death, they revive and laugh. This collage of 'worked up' elements from *Hamlet* is a collection of a theatre director's armoury of art and artifice. Toys, games, rhythmic co-ordination, music-hall routines, fondling and brash sexuality, imitations of silent films, hysterical laughter and wordless responses from the whole cast, all are present and are used to provide sensational drama without the traditional aid of narrative or immediately meaningful structure. An old-fashioned trial scene is engineered to wind up proceedings.

The truth is that in 'creating drama' through improvisation or rehearsal, or by the exploitation of self-advertising techniques of presentation, there is little chance for second thoughts, or for the actors or directors to discover responses beyond those that are familiar to them. Often the natural insecurity of rehearsals will make them accept the immediately effective, rather than the penetrating or careful. And the pressures of a public performance to come, the first night when a show must be provided, cause the theatrical explorers to grasp what comes quickly and to work on that, rather than to seek for further alternatives, the unlikely or the difficult. Only in a theatre like the Berliner Ensemble, where Brecht could plan a response to Shakespeare's *Coriolanus* for four years and where actors are used to slow, searching, critical, creative and unified rehearsals, can the exploration of the theatre's reality be undertaken in rehearsal without loss of quality.

Given highly original and patient actors, a director with uninhibiting authority and an author able to work freely with other people's material, a theatrical response to character, ideas, themes, situations may well be deeply considered and wholly, not cheaply, theatrical. But failing these almost impossible conditions, the alternative is for the dramatist to rehearse his play in the freedom of his own imagination, unconfined by pressures of time and open to many adaptations. If the theatre is indeed an art form that draws forth potent images, a single artist's imagination provides sufficient field; and if that artist is gifted in the use of words he may pass on his text as the first stage in the creation of a production alive to the talents and imaginations of all concerned. In rehearsal it will develop and change, and in reproduction it will alter again; but if the dramatist has set out the words and actions with sufficient clarity it will not easily slip back into the easily observed and casually created.

*

But the playwright's theatre, given talent, success and originality, is also open to the dangers of technical over-sophistication. Arden and Wesker each try hard to be folk dramatists, but their work grows in difficulty. One might argue that the characters, language and activity of *The Hero Rises Up* are all instantly comprehensible, and that its theatrical trickery is open and blatant. But this is not enough to escape the charge of over-theatricality, of presenting something that is ostentatiously a technical triumph in its high-powered abundance. Its audience requires a sophisticated theatrical taste if, as the author wishes, the caricature figures are going to raise a response as if they were 'some sort of circumstance' in actual life.

The increasing theatrical specialization of the author may well leave his audience behind: this is a recurrent danger. Moreover, his financial success and the exploitation of his abilities by impresarios and publicists will separate him far enough from his public without this further hazard. The best safeguard in these dangers might be a continuous involvement with play production, and hence, directly, with an audience. An active role in a permanent theatre company does seem to have been a significant influence in the case of Shakespeare, Molière and Brecht, to name the obvious examples.

Plays must be theatrical if they are to exploit the potentials of the art form, and it is inevitable that a sustained career will complicate and refine technique. But if a study of theatre language has one general implication for a dramatist it is the need to find some defence against the dangers of success: isolation, and too easy an acceptance of 'pure theatre'. The best achievements of the last twenty years have shown that, when a sense of theatre is combined with an active, imaginative and full involvement in living, a playwright can speak with power, subtlety and life-reflecting attraction.

Bibliography

The plays that are most fully studied in this book are quoted from the following editions. Unless otherwise noted, the latest revised edition is preferred to a first edition.

JOHN ARDEN

Serjeant Musgrave's Dance, Methuen, 1960.
Live Like Pigs in *New English Dramatists 3*, Penguin, 1961.
The Happy Haven, in collaboration with Margaretta D'Arcy in *New English Dramatists 4*, Penguin, 1962.
The Workhouse Donkey, Methuen, 1964.
Armstrong's Last Goodnight, Methuen, 1965.
The Hero Rises Up, by John Arden and Margaretta D'Arcy, Methuen, 1969.

SAMUEL BECKETT

Waiting for Godot, Faber, 1955; revised edition 1965.

JOHN OSBORNE

Look Back in Anger, Faber, 1956.
The Entertainer, Faber, 1957.
Luther, Faber, 1960
Inadmissible Evidence, Faber, 1964.
Time Present and *Hotel in Amsterdam*, Faber, 1968.

HAROLD PINTER

The Birthday Party and other plays, Methuen, 1960; includes *The Room* and *The Dumb Waiter* (the latter is also in *New English Dramatists 3*, Penguin, 1961).
The Caretaker, Methuen 1960; revised edition 1962.
A Slight Ache and other plays, Methuen, 1961; includes *A Night Out*, *The Dwarfs* and revue sketches; the first stage version of *The Dwarfs* is in the 1966 reprint, the second in that of 1968.

252

The Collection and *The Lover*, Methuen, 1963.

The Homecoming, Methuen, 1965.

The Tea Party and other plays, Methuen, 1967; includes *The Basement* and *Night School*.

Landscape and *Silence*, Methuen, 1969; includes *Night*.

ARNOLD WESKER

Chicken Soup with Barley, Roots, I'm Talking About Jerusalem: The Wesker Trilogy, Cape, 1960 (and Penguin, 1964).

The Kitchen (first version) in *New English Dramatists 2*, Penguin, 1960; revised edition in *Penguin Plays 2*, Penguin, 1964 (and Cape, 1961).

Chips with Everything, Cape, 1962; also in *New English Dramatists 7*, Penguin, 1963 (and Cape, 1962).

Their Very Own and Golden City in *New English Dramatists 10*, Penguin, 1967 (and Cape, 1966).

The Four Seasons in *New English Dramatists 9*, Penguin, 1966 (and Cape, 1966).

The Friends, Cape, 1970.

Index